THE DANCE
HAS MANY FACES

Martha Graham, "rebel and giant" of the modern dance. Photograph by Walter
Strate Studio.

The English ballet star Margot Fonteyn as a "child of light" in the Liszt-Ashton *Dante Sonata* ballet. *Photograph by Black Star. Courtesy of Dance Magazine.*

THE DANCE

HAS MANY FACES

Edited by Walter Sorell

THE WORLD PUBLISHING COMPANY

CLEVELAND AND NEW YORK

Published by The World Publishing Company

FIRST EDITION

ABS 1051

Design and Typography by Jos. Trautwein

ACKNOWLEDGMENTS

THIS IS A BOOK of many contributions, and my heartiest thanks go to each of my contributors because they alone made this book possible.

It is not an anthology in the usual sense of a collection of essays which the editor has found in other books or in magazines. The outline of the book with the topics it contains was preconceived, and it was the editor's task to find the performing dancer and dance expert able to write on a specific aspect of the art.

Like any producer or director of a play who faces the task of casting, I spent days and nights of anguish. But while they deal with actors who are willing, nay eager, to act, I was dealing with dancers who shy away from writing, a medium of artistic expression for which they are neither trained nor have the inner calling. Knowing the dancers well (and loving them despite all their idiosyncrasies, the "lone wolves" as well as those "cocoon-enveloped" and "I-am-different-from-you" personalities), I realized at the very outset that the final choice in the casting of these essays would be a compromise result of all my desires and endeavors, of my hopes and plans and those many imponderabilities over which we are not the master.

All this is mentioned to make stronger the expression of my appreciation for the achieved results of my collaborators, whose unconsciously drawn self-portraits the reader may be able to study between these covers; it is said to add weight to my feelings of gratitude for their cooperation.

To many more, both in the States and in England, I give deep-felt thanks for their stimulating encouragement and counsel; and special acknowledgment of their kindness to cooperate is expressed to *Dance Magazine* which preprinted José Limon's essay and part of Iva Kitchell's article; to the *Dance Observer* which preprinted a curtailed version of Jean Erdman's contribution; to Boosey and Hawkes, Inc., for permission to use an example from the score of Stravinsky's *Apollon Musagètes*.

THE EDITOR

To

MARIA, the great friend

CONTENTS

THE DANCE HAS MANY FACES

ILLUSTRATIONS

A NOTE

"IN THE BEGINNING was the dance . . ." I look up from the type-writer and recline. I glance at the finished manuscript: *The Dance Has Many Faces*. Then my eyes meander over the roofs of New York until they are arrested by walls of majestic simplicity. The Rockefeller Building. My eyes contract, and the image before them, blurred in the heavy haze of a hot day, begins to move. It moves in a slow rhythm, hardly noticeable, it comes closer and then recedes farther and farther . . .

Years melt away. I am quite young. I am still so small that I must fold my coat and sit on it to get a better view of the stage. My eyes burn with the fever of enthusiasm. I still remember how the prince arrives to liberate the princess; how he fights the dragon and kills it; and how he takes her into his arms and carries her to his castle. It is a miracle of colors and movements.

"Marionettes," says my elder sister, sophisticated and imitating the grownups. She grasps my hand to get me safely across the street. "Puppets," she adds as though this word would be explanation enough and do away with the whole problem.

"But didn't you see how brave he was when he drew his sword —when he ran through the fire—"

"He didn't do a thing, he is made of wood and cloth. Mr. Teschner moved him on strings. Couldn't you see—"

I lie in bed, with my eyes tightly shut to make believe I sleep. I continue to weave the story of the prince and his princess, to dream my own world of images, of graceful movement and adventurous action. Strings, how ridiculous! Shall I wake her and show her how the puppets move, so self-evident, organically as if animated by God—how beautiful, with such precision—and the flickering trembling tongues of fire behind which the dragon hides—didn't they devour material, space, were they not out to plunge the whole world into a magic of burning red?—what a wonderful dance of horrifying imagery—

It was my first experience with movement. Richard Teschner was a great painter who had never lost the imagination locked in a child's brain. His puppets had the bizarre reality of a child's dream vision. Everything on his little stage was alive, and it was alive because it moved, moved with graceful lightness and a buoyant joy in movement.

If my sister was right, and she undoubtedly was, then Mr. Teschner's fingers which set the many puppets in motion performed a masterpiece of coordinated movement. His fingers danced the princess' grace, the hero's braveness, the slow-moving viciousness of the dragon and the many entrechats and pirouettes of the fire's flames.

Years later, the stimuli to the world of imagery in me was pushed closer to human experience. I still remember the enchantment I felt at seeing a balloon rise into the sky and at seeing the little girl look after it, gradually rising on her toes with the disappearing balloon; her slender legs, her entire body growing upwards, her arm stretched out, pointing at the infinitesimal dot that once was her balloon with enraptured expression in her eyes.

Maybe I do not quite remember it any more and only imagine I do because of Peter Altenberg, the last of the Viennese romanticists, who sung in his prose of the little girls in the gardens, of their beautiful movements, their natural grace and the dream of a great wonderful world which Peter thought he saw in their eyes. I grew up in this city of a long forgotten gaiety and imbibed Peter's enthusiasm for the innocent charm, the beauty of line, the harmony of movement. I drank in his words in those years most susceptible to the flight of imagination and most ready for the acceptance of worship. It is long since that Peter died, unknown in these lands of realism and almost forgotten where he was born as a prince of exuberance. His words had kindled a flame in me that burns on and on in my soul . . .

I could lie on meadows for hours and watch the clouds go by, like dancers of a celestial ballet, changing their rhythm with the tempo of the wind and their figures as if they were costumes, melting into oneness and separating again for a solo turn. I liked to sit close to a brook and follow the music of its movement and the dance of its many ripples; I liked to stop at a corn field to get the feel of the endless waves.

Then I saw Grete Wiesenthal dance a waltz. The swinging and sweeping body and her billowing skirt were like the surge of the ocean, the falling and rising of an all-embracing movement, no longer directed and controlled by the will of one person. I still associate the experience of her waltz with the sparkling play of the gigantic fountain on the Schwarzenberg Square in Vienna which was lit up at the Kaiser's birthday and then glittered in all colors ranging from red to violet.

The years grew. I was no longer sent to bed at ten and was old enough to be taken to Paris. It was my first trip into the world and the first and last time I saw Isadora dance. There is little I retained from it in my mind. Perhaps, her figure crossing the stage, her arms lifted . . . But there was the same freedom of movement, the same unfolding of strength and grace in rhythm and line as I recalled from the movements of the little girls in the Viennese gardens when they watched their balloons vanish.

After the performance, at supper, someone of our company brought Isadora Duncan to our table. Everyone seemed to adore her. It was wonderful to look at her. Some people can be so close to you and others remain so aloof! She was both.

"How is America?" she asked the man who had brought her to our table. And a strange tremble, full of memories, full of sadness and longing, lit her mouth.

It was wonderful to see her sit down and get up and the way she held her head. Or does my memory trick me again and exaggerate an incident that had an every-day quality? I no longer know.

The years move faster. Through inflation and the dawn of destruction. The pictures become clearer, the remembrance of the things I have seen have the shape of yesterday. Ruth St. Denis, Mary Wigman, Kurt Jooss, Trudi Schoop, Harold Kreutzberg and Gertrud Kraus, they all are with me and alive, my vision can rebuild their movements, my mind can rebuild their ideas.

I open my eyes. The manuscript lies before me. *The Dance Has Many Faces.* Many have tried to sketch their contours, but in spite of the variety of so many faces, there is unity. The fanatic belief in their art binds them together. The diversity of their opinions is balanced by the stability of their work. Their temperaments, however divergent they may be, their minds, on whatever level they may function, are only directed toward one goal: to serve the dance.

As the dance is born with man, it will exist as long as man exists. As it exists in life and nature everywhere in thousands of disguises, it will even survive man and stand at the cradle of what may come after him. Since nothing stands still but is in eternal flow whose rhythm is the universal pulsebeat of movement, the dance will be when the world will no longer be and another world will take its place. For nothing can cease to exist without being replaced. This is the essence of the all-embracing rhythm of an unknown celestial power which we have feared and worshipped under many a name and which may destroy us when man will come close to re-create scientifically its "invisibility" and to discover its great secret . . .

w.s.

New York, 1951

SOURCES OF THE DANCE

*... Dancing as an art, we may be sure,
cannot die out, but will always be undergoing a rebirth. Not merely as
an art, but also as a social custom, it perpetually emerges afresh from
the soul of the people ...* —HAVELOCK ELLIS

LA MERI

The Ethnological Dance Arts

THE TERM "ethnological dance" is one which has sprung
up within the last decade and is applied, loosely, to all
the racial and ethnic dance forms of all the peoples of
the world. The title is a cumbersome one, as I should know
very well since I have worked in its shadow for many years.
"Ethnological dancers" specializing in one style only, are called
"Spanish dancers" or "Hindu dancers" or, at most, "Oriental
dancers"; but my own talent has lain not in the further perfection of a single form but in breadth of interpretation of the
bodies, techniques, psychologies and souls of the many peoples
of East and West alike. This type of study engenders a great
tolerance which is often mistaken for lack of dedication; while
technical ease and a deep, personal love for the peoples represented give to the uninitiated the impression that the dancer is
"tossing it off." This is a grave error brought about by the Western habit of thinking. We have come to consider the word
"technique" as applicable only to the movements which are so
showy as to approach acrobacy: leaps, turns, extensions, etc. The
term actually applies also to the arms, hands, head and expres-

3

sions in any type of dance, and it is an error to applaud the technique of a ballarino if his legs are good but his arms bad. The *aficionado* of the Spanish dance seldom employs the word "technique." It is too all-embracing to be used casually. He says that Argentina's castanets are without equal; that Pastora Imperio's *brazeo* (arm-carriage) is divine. And he is fully aware that technique is useless unless it is put at the service of emotionalism. In the oriental dance the whole focus of attention changes. The technical vehicle of the emotionalism is the *upper body* culminating in the hands and face. The lower body is the accompaniment to the melody of the upper body. But rare indeed is the Western critic (or audience) who can re-focus his attention to properly watch the Eastern dance. And the *punkhita* (trembling) hand like the Spanish castanets does not *look* difficult, and so its mastery evokes no applause, either manual or printed, such as accompanies the execution of the thirty-two pirouettes. And let me parenthesis here and now that the great ballarinas are *not* deluded by ease of execution into believing that the exotic techniques are easy!

Strictly speaking, the ethnological dance does not include the folk dance, the former being an art dance and the latter a communal dance. But I believe it is safe to say that all ethnological dance arts spring from communal dance.

Hindu Natya, which is the most complete dance science alive today, sprung from communal worship. The *hasta-mudras* (hand poses) which form the basis of the Hindu dance originated as a ritual in the chanting of the Rig-Vedic hymns. At first only the priests used these mudras—much as the Catholic priest or Jewish rabbi uses ritualistic gestures. The high priest alone was aware of the esoteric meanings, but the exoteric meaning was one which illustrated the words of the hymns. A later development was the devadasi—the temple dancer, whose function was not unlike that of the occidental choir singer, save that the former "danced" with her hands instead of singing, or while singing. During the glory of the Vijayanagara Empire, the kings—great patrons of the temple arts—raised the art of the devadasi to a far greater perfection, and paved the way for its eventual branching into secularization. It was at this time that the nrtta (pure dance) developed, adding as interlude to the nrttya (pantomimic) passages, both steps and mudras which had no function beyond that of mere decoration. It is said in South India that since the fall of the Vijayanagara Empire, Bharata Natyam has deteriorated; but to those of us fortunate enough to have seen it performed, it remains a great and perfect dance science. Still used in the temples where it was born, today it also knows the concert stage.

The story of Bharata Natyam—its slow growth over the centuries with roots in the very heart of the Hindu religion and every branch, flower and fruit the loving work of the people of the land—is the typical story of all the true ethnological dance arts.

The indigenous Japanese dance is a refinement of the indigenous folk dance, and to these forms have been added the arts of China and India when the techniques of these two great countries had already evolved from communal to art forms.

The delicate theater dance of Java is a combination of the imported Hindu technique superimposed on the purely Javanese ancestor-worship rituals.

Bali's dance art is still a communal affair, her greatest artists being simple members of a community where all dance. And in Ceylon the devil dancers are mostly farmers who have inherited from their fathers the right to perform ritualistic dances whose technique is definitely South Indian.

The Burmese dance drama was imported from Siam during the years of Burma's dominance over that country. But the true Burmese dance, that of the "posture girls" which precedes the dramas, is a combination of the communal Pwe and the ritualistic dances to the thirty-seven "nats"—the gods of pre-Buddhistic days.

Nearer to their communal origines are the choreographies of

the Occident. The Spanish dance, whose great antiquity cannot be questioned, has many facets in its folk expression. From the north come the dances whose roots lie in the dark earth of ancient fertility rites. From the central Mesa come dances which have passed rapidly from the fields through the court to the theater. From the south come dances of the *sudras* of India (flamencos), of the Moors and of the soil. From the east come dances of pyrrhic origin, and Egypt and Phoenicia likewise have left their mark on the choreographies of Iberia. But it is within the last century that this eclectic dance has been combined into an art form which can take its place beside the theater art of Java or Japan. For dance dramas have been written, choreographed and executed in the pure idiom of the Spanish dance, and today tradition is being crystallized.

The Polynesian dances are still communal at home. It is with their transplantation abroad that they are becoming "theater." And now, indeed, is the crucial moment of unfolding for this naive and beautiful idiom. It is in need of a great native artist who will move it out of the cabarets and into the concert halls: to do for it what Argentina did for the Spanish dance.

There is often a great danger in the passage from a folk expression to an art form. Emasculation may lie between. The Scotch dances were born as the emotional expression of a bold and warlike peoples. Not many years ago I saw them done by the Gordon Highlanders. It was the most thoroughly exciting performance I have ever witnessed. But what of the passage of this dance towards the academization of artistry? One sees girls of twelve, hung with the medals of past awards, executing reel, fling and sword dance in virginal ballet slippers—*battement*, trained toes beating slim calves with careful precision. But is this the Scotch dance? God forbid! For the breath of life has gone out of it and it has forgotten why it was born.

One day in my Spanish class I suddenly realized that at the

earnest badgering of certain of my pupils, I had been for some months teaching *steps* with painful precision; and that all these steps had not led to the execution of a single copla of the Sevillanas! I tried in an impassioned speech to my gaping students to explain my feelings, my violated principles—and I sailed out of the classroom registering the vow that I *never again* would teach, via the route of precise technique, a dance whose very essence lies in its emotional fathering.

For the ethnologic dance is not a product of the mind but of the emotions. Style is its essence, but technique, as we are all too prone to understand it, is of purely relative importance. Neither Argentina nor Argentinita ever executed a double vuelta-quebrada; and, if they did or did not, it would have had no bearing on their value as artists. Technique—bodily control—must be mastered *only* because the body must not stand in the way of the soul's expression.

It is my opinion that all ethnologic dance arts are the slow processing of the communal dance. I do not believe that a dance art can be expressive of a certain people unless it is the product of a cross section of that people. The ballet is not an ethnologic dance because it is the result of the work of Italy, France, Spain and Russia. As such it cannot represent fully any one of the four. By the same reasoning the American modern dance is the product of individuals, and not of the American people. We cannot hurry the production of art as we do the assembly line. I do not doubt that with the passing of the years, nay, of the centuries, the American moderns will have made their contribution to our country's dance. But we cannot afford to disregard the jitterbug, whose expression is an exact parallel of the flamenco. Both gitano and "rug-cutter" beat the floor in ecstatic counter-rhythms to satisfy an inner emotional urge, little aware of the effect on those who watch him. One hundred years ago the average cultured Spaniard felt toward the flamenco dance much as many cultured Americans feel toward jive, et al. But today flamenco is a recognized and beloved art both at home and abroad, and has been fused with the Andalusian dance to produce the neo-classic dance art of Spain. Here lies a lesson which we cannot afford to disregard. For it has always been, and will always be the emotional experience of the *folk* of the race which is the backbone of the country's ethnologic art.

The teaching of ethnologic dance, if properly done, requires a good deal more from teacher and pupils alike than might be supposed. In India the *guru* (teacher) is said to have far more influence than have the parents on the growth and formation of the pupil's character. For the study of the dances of the East entails not only the mastery of physical techniques, but of spiritual and psychological growth. Without a knowledge and understanding of the culture, the religion, the folkways which give birth to the art, it is impossible to perform that art. This is equally true of the dance of Spain, Polynesia and other Occidental lands. If *guru* and pupil are natives, backgrounds and social habits are relatively identical and there is no need to begin by building a bridge of understanding. If the *guru* is native and pupil foreign, then the latter must have a great knowledge, a great instinct, or both, to ferret out and analyze the essential bodily, spiritual and psychological differences between his own culture and that of his teacher. If both *guru* and pupil are foreign to the art with which they work, then the *guru* must carefully and *individually* resolve a system of disclosing to the pupil, step by step, the thousand subtle differences in the emanation and physical reactions of the native and the foreigner. If the pupil is young, open-minded and brings to his study a great love, a great desire and an unquestioning respect, the way is possible. But the pitfalls are many and to the *guru* each pupil presents a different psychological problem.

The physical techniques vary from race to race and from

country to country. They are conditioned by the clothes worn, the ground walked on, the manner of sitting and bowing and worshipping, the physical characteristics of the people. The base of ethnological characterization is the backbone. Without a control of the spine-line so perfect that it has become instinctive, it is impossible to interpret the dances of Japan or of Spain. I have named these as examples because the spine-line of the two differs so widely. The most sensuous part of the Japanese feminine body is the back of the neck, but the Spanish woman lifts her breasts proudly upward.

The spine-line is just the beginning. Each part of the body has a different characteristic from country to country. Toes turn in in Japan, forward in Burma, out in Java. Feminine thighs cling, masculine spread in nearly all forms of ethnic dance, since there is a deeply felt consciousness of sex in all ethnological forms. (For this reason psychotherapeutists claim these forms to be healthier psychologically than ballet or modern.) In Java feminine upper arms cling to the body, masculine lift outward; and in Spain upper arms arch upward. Hands—which in all humanity are so revealing—show widely differing traits from country to country; and all over the East, the manual technique is the keynote of choreography. The carriage of the head is a part of the spine-line, but characteristic neck movements show throughout the Orient. And what of the face? Here we have the subtlest technique of all, for emotional expression must ripple like an undercurrent beneath the masklike face of Siam or China; and a lamp must be lit behind the fabulously complicated muscular *mukhaja* (face technique) of India.

Few indeed are the foreigners capable of judging the ethnological dance beyond the point of an instinctive aesthetic reaction to a great beauty. And because in many forms of ethnic dance the art carries the artist, the strangeness and strength of the art itself is believed to be the strength of the artist.

Inversely, once the strangeness has worn off, the watcher (or

critic) reaches that no man's land between instinctive reaction
and knowledgeable judgment and is quite incapable of seeing
the inner qualities of the individual artist. By inner qualities I
mean the good points—such as expressive hands, controlled toes,
sincere emotionalism—which might be momentarily overshad-
owed by such drawbacks as youth, inexpertness, or even momentary difficulties such as a bad stage or poorly played music. The
knife cuts two ways. A watcher, accustomed all his life to ballet,
applauds vigorously the "technique" of a young ethnological
dancer although that dancer *locks* his knees, which in this field is a
technical error as grave as loose knees in ballet. But we are accustomed to certain lines and we loudly condemn all others. We
have not yet learned (with the Javanese) that the cultured person is possessed of humility and lowers his eyes; that only the
vulgar go through life with round, staring eyes and open mouth.

The ethnological dance is the product of the necessity for
pure emotional expression. Even the casual observer will con-
cede this point to the Spanish dance. Purely emotional from
egotistic castanets to sadistic heels and sexually aware in every
line and movement of both masculine and feminine body, it
has no reason to exist at all without the driving strength of
emotional pressure behind it. But the Javanese dance is not less
the product of the necessity for emotional expression. Here again
we must not think the emotional level of all people is identical
with our own. We, like the Spaniard, must "spit it out," "get
it off the chest." But the Easterner must rise above, must seek
Brahmananda. And can you watch the Javanese dance without
feeling a strange, new calm envelop you? This is a choreography
with an unequaled power, for it carries a quasi-hypnotism in which
watcher and dancer seem to leave themselves behind, and lift
their astral bodies to move in some suspended place between
heaven and earth. But we are afraid of this hypnotism, and we
squeeze our eyes shut like frightened children and whine, "I don't
like it! It isn't exciting!" It *is* exciting; but exciting on a far

higher plane. But our fear has made us intolerant and unfriendly, not only toward exotic dancers but toward each other. Indeed, the unfriendliness and intolerance of the individual dancers toward each other is a heavy deterrent in the development of America's dance. The strange, snobbish scorn for those who "are not as I am" is an evil factor in the dance world, already struggling under the too-heavy burden of the technical unions and the managerial trusts.

12

The experience of beauty is pure, self-manifested, compounded equally of joy and consciousness, free from admixture of any other perception, the very twin brother of mystical experience, and the very life of it is supersensuous wonder . . . It is enjoyed by those who are competent thereto, in identity, just as the form of God is itself the joy with which it is recognized.

—VISVANATHA

————

RUTH ST. DENIS

Religious Manifestations in the Dance

I SEE myself standing on a hill behind our old farm house in New Jersey, lifting my arms in an unconscious gesture of oneness towards the round silvery glory of the moon. At the same time I'm listening to the whisper of a faint breeze as it gently sways the tips of the tall pines. I begin to move. It is my first dance urge to relate myself to cosmic rhythm. With a motion of complete joy, as a free being in a world of infinite depth and beauty, I surrender myself to the unseen pulsation of the Universe.

This mood is natural, for I am about sixteen and just beginning to experience the unfolding of my emotional life. Ideas regarding new forms of worship are not to come to me for many years, but I am growing sensitive to the positive and negative forces communicated to me by the stellar pageantry above my head and the warm earth beneath my feet. The first lyric questions of life and love are rising in my spirit, and for one brief moment I experience a glorious fusion of my threefold self—physical, emotional and spiritual. These are translated later into what might be termed the technical, aesthetic and creative. But at this moment of ecstasy there was no separation. I was an exultant unity.

I believe that my whole creative life stemmed from this magic hour under the stars on that hilltop. It was then that my religious consciousness emerged to flower years afterward into definite forms of religious dancing in which there is no sense of division between spirit and flesh, religion and art. It is this same unity that inspires and governs my every vision for the votary dance of the future.

As I see it, the deepest lack of Western cultures is any true workable system for teaching a process of integration between soul and body. Obviously, no effort has been made by the church as a whole, probably because of its long fostered conflict between the Goodness of the Soul and the supposed Badness of the Body. I yield to no one in my admiration for the character of St. Paul, but I have ever profoundly disagreed with his attitude of spirit versus the life of the senses. His doctrines, spread over the Western world, have led to such a contempt for the body and its functions that we have a divided and disintegrating consciousness regarding our total personalities.

The great mission of the dancer is to contribute to the betterment of mankind. I have written elsewhere, "the highest function of the dance is to ennoble man's concept of himself." This cannot be accomplished until the creative artist, whatever his field, becomes aware of himself as a citizen of the world and of his responsibility to lead instead of follow, to unfold instead of repeat and to bring self-realization to its highest point of expression. Some illumined seer has proclaimed that the artist of today is the prophet of tomorrow. But in order to attain the fullest self-realization through the dance we must understand that the arts—not just dancing but all of them—are never a religion in themselves, never objects of worship, but are the symbol and language for communicating spiritual truths.

During the early beginnings of the Rhythmic Choir and the modest choreographies relating to the dancing of hymns and selected passages from the Psalms, we used only what might be described as free lyric movements. I had previously used certain semi-Greek and running rhythms for considerable work along the lines of music visualization. As we applied this freedom of movement—freedom in the sense of having no specific technique such as ballet or even modern—we discovered that the spirit of joy or grief, ecstasy or anguish which we put out through these movements gave them their significance. I used lyric movements, partly because they were sufficient for us at that time and partly because I had no other form which seemed more to my hand to express spiritual states. At the back of my mind, however, I knew the time would come when a more definite and appropriate language of movement would be evolved.

It was in New York City—66 Fifth Avenue, to be specific—that I first saw La Meri. She was giving a lecture and demonstration in the Museum of Costume Arts, and she opened up to me a whole world of expression through her scholarly and beautiful exhibition of the symbolic hand gestures of Hindu dance culture. A few weeks later she was established at the same address in the studio directly below me. This was a rather famous building that housed a French cinema on the main floor and some noted dancers upstairs, including Martha Graham who had made this her stronghold for years. La Meri was on the fourth floor, if I remember correctly, and I was on the fifth. There it was that she began the activity which has developed into her internationally known Ethnologic School and Theater.

Above her I was occupied with my little Temple services which had as their dominant feature a Rhythmic Choir. This Choir met every Monday evening to practice and to rehearse for the Thursday evening service. One night, right in the middle of attempting to visualize some particular Psalm, I suddenly had a brain wave. I left the group sitting on the floor where we had been discussing the possible form for the Psalm, and dashed downstairs. To my delight I found Meri at the end of her class. I begged her to come up to my studio, convinced as I was that she had a great contribution to make to my Temple work. I knew that the moment has come for us to study her *hasta-mudras* in order to utilize, in a more translated manner, this universal speech of the hands. The Choir followed her gestures and explanations in open-mouthed wonder as she revealed to them what she had to me, a marvelous new means of expression.

Alas, I fear that we have not been very scholarly or faithful to the vision she gave us that night, but we are still stumbling along. As a group we profited aesthetically by her teachings, while I personally have been refreshed and released by my attempts to translate the rich sonorous phrases of the Psalms into a kind of *hasta-mudra* for the West. I also have done a number of my own poems in this way. But what is most important, my students have been trained in a new medium for interpreting the Lord's Prayer, the Doxology and many of the sublime Psalms. I still feel that we are mere beginners. But whatever we have accomplished, or may accomplish in the future, we place to the credit of La Meri for her aesthetic and spiritual fusion of East and West.

As we continue our specialized application of the *mudras*, I find there are, roughly, two phases of adaptation. One needs but a free and beautifully lyrical movement of the whole body, with the hands used only in a decorative and expressive manner. The other definitely requires the specific language of the *hasta-mudras*.

It is not my intention, nor was it Meri's when she gave us our initial inspiration, to limit our hand language to the Hindu. There are the Egyptian symbolic gestures, created of course by the priesthood for communicating Egyptian theology to the people. For centuries the Mass, our great Christian ritual, has had its authorized system of symbolic gestures which are well understood by the priesthood of the Catholic Church, but little known by the Protestants and other sects. It is our aim to use the *hasta-mudras* as a stimulus to exhaustive research in the language of the hand rather than to impose their specialized forms upon our culture. I am working upon a series of Psalms done both as plastic and as space-covering routines using a variety of hand gestures.

"The Cathedral of the Future" is my way of designating ideal conditions under which to explore the limitless possibilities of religious dance. Its construction must employ the entire range of modern architecture, scientific lighting and the use of materials characteristic of the age. Yet it should retain the dignity and functional adequacy of the magnificent religious structures of the past. I could go on endlessly describing details of such a cathedral but will limit myself to the few factors necessary for the greater expressiveness of celebrants and congregation.

First, it must be a "seeing" cathedral and not a mere "listening" one. The altar should be a wholly mobile place where the developing human spirit, making use of the total octave of arts, can reveal its changing and expanding consciousness. Objectively the altar should be a large circular area with a beautifully curved background capable of being lighted in a variety of effects. It must be harmoniously integrated into an auditorium assuring perfect visibility from every angle. Here in our studio-chapel we experimented one evening with what we called a "Litany of Arts." When this Litany brings into active focus all of the arts it will be the keynote of the Cathedral of the Future. Dance and drama, painting and sculpture, poetry and oratory, music and fine craftsmanship should enrich the consciousness of the celebrants, educate and inspire the congregation. Besides providing an avenue

of self-expression for the minister and his officiating priests, the
Cathedral of the Future must impel its communicants to spontaneous participation.

It is my entirely modest vision for this cathedral that its activities should more than rival contemporary offerings of stage and
screen or their equivalent. Through a new pattern of audience-
participation and the soul-satisfying dramas concerned with man
himself rather than the constant comings and goings of his objective world, this dynamic center of wisdom and beauty should
surpass in sheer attracting power any theater or other secular exposition of the arts. To state it briefly, I want to see the House
of God the most fascinating and perfect creative center ever conceived, the flower of civilization.

To be sure the cathedrals of Europe fulfilled this ideal in
many respects. But now, by virtue of our mechanical genius, we
can quickly be transported from any given spot to somewhere
else. Competing with the church there are theaters of various
types, sports claiming national interest, men's and women's clubs
of every description and a thousand other diversions to which
our systems of rapid transit can take us. The result is that the
unity of man is hourly disintegrated, because he *takes from without* instead of *giving from within*. The prime function of the
Cathedral of the Future will be to promote his integration on a
high level.

I wish to make it clear that I consider the great popular
churches of today, with their allowed-for rumba dance halls, their
ping-pong and bingo games, their social discussion groups where
any current topic utterly unrelated to man's spiritual self-realization can occupy the excited oratory of their youth, as glaring
examples of the church being invaded by the world instead of
conquering it. Such activities may be a means of holding young
people to membership, but they are among the disintegrating
forces and bear no relationship to my ideal cathedral.

I do not expect to see this dream—miracles aside—brought

into manifestation in my time. But I do hope that some of our youth will be inspired to work on it from day to day and year to year so that a hundred or more years hence, leaning from the golden bar of heaven, I can be pleased and proud that seeds now being scattered have germinated and ultimately come to fruition.

DORIS HUMPHREY

Dance Drama

DANCE DRAMA began at the moment when the first man bridged the separated "I" and "you" with "tell." It began when the savage, bursting with the experience of his "I am," invented the first movements for telling a memory. Eons of movement and sound had existed before him in the animal kingdom, some of them as rhythmic and highly organized as a ballet. He himself had inherited all these movements and had developed many more in the process of becoming a man. But there came a day when a different feeling possessed him. The new element was the need to explain the emotional self, not just to feel it but to tell it to another. It must have come as a memory of experience, the difficult kill or the dangerous foray, after which the conscious "I" returned with a new desire, to communicate. There were, as yet, no words, so he described his adventures with movement and perhaps with sounds of the voice too. How could this have been a dance drama? Because it was rhythmic, it told a story, the body movements were dramatic, not realistic, and because it had an objective, an audience. That it was rhythmic, and not just pantomimic, seems beyond question. Our man, being close to nature, was bound up in her rhythmic structure, and besides, how could he have described running or walking

20

without falling into a pattern? Constrained to stay within telling distance, these movements would fall into a beat, and as this is a pleasurable sensation, no doubt it was prolonged, especially if claps or sounds of appreciation came from the "you."

So it seems clear that dance dramas were the earliest conscious communications of men, antedating words, music, and all the other arts. This point would not be important, except that it emphasizes dance movement combined with dramatic feeling as fundamental in our culture, and that the age-old springs are in emotion, rhythm, and communication. Let all dancers and dramatists forget this at their peril! Deep in the bodies of men lie the memories of these things. Every man responds to rhythm, knows the feel of the killer and lover, and from these the primitive acts of running, leaping, striking, defending, grasping, tearing, relaxing, caressing, shouting; and his body remembers how to crawl with fear, burn with anger, ache with fatigue, kindle with power and success. Without these memories, even those which are moribund from over-civilization, there would be no dance drama today, or indeed any drama, for the rousing of action-memory in the onlooker, by whatever means, is the sole key to good theater. The most ancient and most direct appeal to the dramatic sense is through the art of the dance, the special inheritor of body experience, the container of every movement man has ever made.

The long ages passed; the simple dance of the savage became an elaborate ritual which was bound up with every thought and feeling in the life of the community. By 4000 B.C. many dance dramas in Egypt and other ancient lands took days to perform and exceeded in length and fervor anything of the sort that has followed. In every part of the world where men settled, they communicated with their gods through dance and related the stories of their race to each other with dance, music and poetry.

The height of the development seems to have been reached in the early Greek tragedy, with its chorus of singers and dancers. Slowly, however, the dancers lost their place of importance, not only in Greek tragedy but throughout the ensuing forms of culture. People continued to dance, nothing could stop so fundamental an urge, but no longer with the same high purpose, and the story is one of an unhappy decline throughout Europe. After the fall of Greece and Rome, the great darkness which engulfed the affairs of men extended likewise to the dance, and it was many centuries before any notable resurgence took place. When it did come, it was a re-doing of a pagan memory, for the Christian church frowned on the body with its life instinct for dramatic movement and would not countenance the dance.

Long after the gods had vanished and the new religion was well-established, people, at a loss for dramatic subject matter arising from their own lives, turned back to mythology and the glories of Greece with a nostalgic enthusiasm. This was the Renaissance which surged throughout Europe, permeating all cultural thought. Especially in the dance there was a great eruption of gods, goddesses, satyrs, fauns, nymphs, all set in the most elaborate dramatic form with massive production and orchestral score. Even the social life followed the pattern. Kings and Princes entertained with the help of the Bacchae and Eurydice, with Phaedra and Hippolytus. This era seemed poverty-stricken for original art stemming from the times, and illustrates, at least in the dance field, a yearning to be a part of a believed ritual expressed in action. An account of a social event of the times seems quaint and picturesque to us, yet how much of imagination and buoyancy is in it compared to the drabness of our own social affairs. The following ballet was performed at the marriage of Galeazzo Visconti, Duke of Milan, in 1489:

> The guests were led into the banquet hall where the table was bare. At the same time disguised figures entered the room through another door; Jason and the Argonauts appeared in war attire, did homage to the newly weds, and spread the Golden Fleece as a covering over the table. Then Mercury appeared; he

had stolen the fatted calf from Apollo and everybody danced around the Golden Calf. To the sounds of the horns, Diana and her nymphs brought in Actaeon, transformed into a stag, and congratulated him on his good fortune in being eaten by Isabella, the ducal bride. Orpheus carried in the birds which he had caught when, charmed by his song, they had come too near. Theseus and Atalanta hunted the Calydonian boar in a wild dance, and proffered their captive in a triumphant round. Iris in her chariot brought the peacocks, Tritons served the fish, and Hebe with the Arcadian shepherds, Vertumna and Pomona, nectar and dessert. After the meal, Orpheus appeared with Hymen and the gods of love. Connubial Faith, brought in by the Graces, presented herself to the Duchess, but was interrupted by Semiramis, Helen, Phaedra, Medea, and Cleopatra, singing the charms of unfaithfulness. Connubial Faith ordered them out and the goddesses of love threw themselves with torches upon the Queens. Whereupon Lucretia, Penelope, Thomyris, Judith, Portia and Sulpicia laid out at the feet of the Duchess the palms which they had earned by a life of chastity, and, rather unexpectedly, Bacchus, Silenus and the satyrs appeared to conclude the ballet with a lively dance.

Very shortly after this period the dance drama was to enter another decline, as the great dramatists, composers and poets began to take over the drama and the stage. Also there was the Church. The two together combined to overwhelm the dance drama for several hundred years and to reduce it to a pretty interlude in an opera, or a ballroom scene in a play. Partly, too, this was due to the durability of the play-script and the musical score; the word and the musical sign could be transferred, sent on a journey intact, studied, criticized, while the dance suffered from its evanescence. When the curtain came down the play-script was still in the hands of the prompter, while the dance was locked in the bodies of the dancers. The Church, too, chose the dance as a special target of condemnation. This was logical, given the premise that the spirit could reach divine grace only by purification of the vile and degenerate body. Therefore anything which tended to glorify the body must be banned, and theologians strove mightily to uproot and cast out that evil thing, the dance. A vivid description of this attitude is afforded by a Puritan, one Phillip Stebbes in his *Anatomie of Abuses*, written in 1538. It recounts, not the iniquities of the stage, which was a favorite subject, but something in his mind much worse, a celebration in which he detects the stench of paganism.

> Against May, Whitsonday, or other time, all the young men and maides, older men and wives, run gadding over night to the woods, groves, hils and mountains, where they spend all the night in pleasant pastimes; and in the morning they return, bringing with them birch and branches of trees, to deck their assemblies withall. And no mervaile, for there is a great Lord present amongst them, as superintendent and Lord over their pastimes and sportes, namely Sathan, prince of hel. But the chiefest jewel they bring from thence is their May-Pole (this stinking ydol, rather) which is covered all over with floures and hearbs. And then fall they to daunce about it, like as the heathen people did at the dedication of the ydols, whereof this is a perfect pattern, or rather, the thing itself.

This May-Day celebration was a relic of a prehistoric fertility rite, originally a communication to the tree spirit. Mr. Stebbes was right about the origin, it was pagan, but he did not know that the religious significance was lost, and he could not know the innocent urge of people to make merry together in the dance. Civilized people do not believe in tree spirits any more, yet the May-Pole dance survives the Puritans and all other vicissitudes and is performed to this day all over Europe and North America, one of the few remaining communal dance dramas.

One outstanding exception to the exclusion of the dance by the Church existed a little later than Puritan days and deserves mention. The followers of the Shaker faith, or more properly the Society of True Believers, led by Mother Ann Lee, emigrated to the United States from England in the early nineteenth century. After establishing colonies here, they invented a ritual of which dance was a welcome and important part. Their ceremonies also aimed at purifying the body, in common with general Christian principles, but they came to the unique conclusion that this could be done better with the dance than without it, a conception which has yet to be adopted generally with any conspicuous success. The Shaker ritual met all definitions for great dance drama. It had a lofty purpose, it was dramatic, communicative and rhythmic, and in addition was truly communal, engaging every man, woman and child in the colony.

There was one more blow in store for the dance, and this came from the attitude of the educators, who in setting up a formula in the Middle Ages for the intellectual training of men (women were not educated), considered the dance neither necessary nor nice. In this they took their lead from ecclesiastic opinion and made certain that the educated man should look upon dancing as a frivolity of kings, a crude pastime of the peasants, or as a questionable entertainment in the theater, usually surrounded by sin. After several hundred years there came a reluctant admission from some that young ladies might have a limited education, and this might include dancing which seemed to be an aid to grace, a quality much admired in the female, even by educators. Romanticism had come in, the female was looked upon as an ethereal creature of grace and beauty, and the emasculated dance, which enhanced these values, was for women and not men. This is the very attitude which prevails today. Although dancing is established as a part of education for women in the United States and elsewhere, ninety-eight per cent of the males are taught only to shuffle around a ballroom with their feet. Every sizable woman's college has a department of dance in these days, but directors of men's colleges still think in medieval terms in regard to dance training.

By the nineteenth century the dance and dance drama had

fallen on evil days indeed. Except for some technical advances in the theater it was far inferior to music, poetry and drama, had lost its dignity, had no cultural purpose except to amuse. The immense impact of opinion, both religious and secular, seemed to be about to smother the original art. The collective attitude was that dance was an inferior activity, at best an amusement, at worst a sin. There were, however, a few artists and philosophers whose lone voices cried out against this loss to culture, whose tongues told where the true values lay. There were not many, and they were widely separated, one of the most eloquent being Jean Georges Noverre who wrote in the middle of the seventeenth century:

> Ballets . . . ought to unite the various parts of the drama, most of the subjects, adapted to the dancer, are devoid of sense, equally unmeaning and unconnected. Dancing . . . ennobled by the expression of sentiment, and under the direction of a man of true genius will, in time, obtain the praises which the enlightened world bestows on poetry and painting, and become entitled to the rewards with which the latter are daily honored.

It was not until the twentieth century that Noverre's prophecy even began to be realized.

Just as the dance was about to expire with a giggle in its tinsel dress, a marvelous flow of dance genius came in such an abundant stream that this tattered and beaten sister of the arts came to life with the glow and vigor of a young Diana. The opening years of the twentieth century saw the Russian Ballet startle the world with its matchless dramas, dancers and choreographers. In quick succession there appeared Isadora Duncan, Ruth St. Denis, Mary Wigman, to mention only the peaks of genius, and finally the modern American dancers, Martha Graham, Hanya Holm, Charles Weidman and others.

Now in the middle of the century, some progress has been made to restore the dance drama to a significant place in our culture, but probably it will be long, if ever, before we match again the great period of the dance drama, the apogee, when each man, woman and child took part in great dramatic festivals with heart, soul and body. Even the savage, so contemptuously regarded as uncivilized, knew a greater, because more deeply felt, dance theater than we are ever likely to know. The modern theater, movie house, gymnasium and studio are only partial substitutes for these former great experiences, but they are the best we have for restoring some of our lost oneness, and even this is perceived as yet by only a few.

The contention of these few is that dance, and dance drama, persistently robust after thousands of years of snubbing by asceticism, scholasticism and puritanism, can make profound revelations of that which is significant in the relations of human beings, can restore the dignity of the body, which prurience and hypocrisy have damaged, can recall the lost joys of people moving together rhythmically for high purposes, can immeasurably improve the education of the young, can, to a much larger extent than it does, restore vitality to the theater, can contribute a moral stimulus to the furtherance of more courageous, coordinated and cultured behavior.

THE MECHANICS OF DANCING

> The great artist is he who in his individual emotions and experiences reflects the emotions and experiences of all mankind, and so by sympathy and knowledge penetrates more deeply into the hearts and lives of his fellowmen . . . So art may be defined in its result as the adequate translation of emotional experience into some external form. It is the expression of the feeling within by means of line, or color, or sound, or movement so that others may share the feeling. —MARGARET H'DOUBLER

GEORGE BALANCHINE

Marginal Notes on the Dance

TECHNIQUE is the method or the details of procedure essential to expertness of execution in any art, says Webster. When people, even professionals, speak of dancers as good or bad technicians, they usually refer to their speed or force or physical strength. Technique of the dancer consists of the combined elements of acquired muscle strength and their complete control and coordination. Basically, it is not a question of being able to move according to one's own will, but to move where and how the dancer may be directed.

Only well-trained muscles can execute soft and controlled movements, or any arbitrary movements they are asked to perform. I remember having once watched a strong bird picking up a few thin threads. I was greatly impressed by its arrested muscle strength and the graceful ease with which its entire body moved

towards the little thread on the ground, how its entire system seemed concentrated on that one spot. I felt that its beak could have torn my arm to pieces, so much power was in it; but now it moved with surprising lightness in the direction of its object, with perfect control and coordination.

As in every other art, there are degrees of mastership. Most dancers think they have achieved the peak of their technique when they feel comfortable in the execution of their movements. It is too often, however, a state of "not wishing to be disturbed." They are using the same phrases over and over again and gradually begin to lose the power to progress. But there is another stage of comfort in which the dancer has acquired so much ability that he has no longer to think of his technique, it has become second nature to him. As any good instrumentalist—and no musician can fool his audience as easily as can a dancer—must be aware of precisely this artistic level as a steppingstone to perfection, so must a dancer, in order to be "great," realize that this stage of comfort is the foundation of his potentialities.

Technical perfection must be no more than a means to a desired end: the perfect artistic accomplishment.

I have gradually learned that movements and gestures, like tones in music and shades in painting, have certain family relations and, as groups, have their own laws. The more conscious an artist is, the more he comes to understand these laws and to respond to them. I have tried to develop my choreography inside the framework that such relations suggest.

To achieve unity one must avoid separating elements similar in blood and essence. In spite of the fact that movements may have different names, they may nevertheless belong with each other because of their inner relationship. Only one's artistic feeling and experience can decide on their similarity.

I have often likened head, trunk and arms to a painting suspended in the air. Looking at a painting, we first observe the architecture of its design and the shading of its colors; in most cases, it is the subject matter that strikes us last, also least. We are little interested in who the people are in Rembrandt's *Night Guard*, for instance, or what they are doing. It is the structure of the painting, the almost mysterious distribution of light and shade, the singularity of the half-dark that holds us spellbound, not the subject itself nor the portrayed men; it is Rembrandt's genius behind it.

One is born to be a great dancer. No teacher can work miracles, nor will years of training make a good dancer of an untalented pupil. One may be able to acquire a certain technical facility, but no one can ever "acquire an exceptional talent." I have never prided myself on having an unusually gifted pupil. A Pavlova is no one's pupil but God's.

The ballet is theater, and theater is the magic of a world of illusions. As long as the sweat of classwork is evident on the stage, illusion is defeated. Acrobats can defy gravity and conquer the air. If they aim to create a feeling of illusion, it is of a different nature from that of the dancer. Their intention is to prove complete mastery of their own body; to challenge themselves and the imagination of their audience; and to perform with "ease" in the face of danger. The dancer too must show his mastery of muscular coordination. But he does not stress "ease" in relation to the encountered danger. His presentation is an aesthetic manifestation. The element of danger is, in his case, non-existent, or reduced to a minimum. The acrobat's precision is mainly derived from the necessity of concentration on the element of danger. It lends his presentation the breath-taking quality it usually has. To muster the same concentration, the dancer must imagine that every movement he does is performed on a rope without a net.

In the dance, any leap must have its justification within the framework of the dance composition, otherwise it is pointless. It must produce the illusion of having grown out of the music and the preceding step, in other words it must be motivated. It should never be a piece of showmanship only to prove the dancer's muscular strength and technical skill. This is the acrobat's domain. Of course the dancer must convey the impression that gravity can be overcome by simply lifting himself up and floating through the air. However, since his is not an act but the creation of artistry, his stress cannot be on how to go up into the air, but how to produce the illusion of suspension in the air and how to come down. Landing on the ground again must be both artistically perfect and logical as a prelude or link to the very next step.

We move in spherical ways. Everything that is part of the universe seems to be round. Angular movements, to me, only exist to point out roundness. To speak of angular in a derogatory way is like calling music dissonant. After all, dissonance makes us aware of consonance; so do angular movements make us aware of pleasing roundness. We cannot have the cool shadow without light.

I even see a certain softness and roundness in the straight lines and angular forms of a cubistic painting. We must beware of expressing personal limitations, because all this is a matter of conditioning. When you hear music overamplified for some time, it loses the quality of loudness for your ears.

The same holds good for grace, certainly the most misused noun applied to the dance. No ungraceful movement per se exists, because the most "ungraceful" position can be performed most gracefully. Grace in movement is the final result of one's technical achievement; it is the ability to produce a maximum of dance action with a minimum of effort; it is a climax of consistency and the utter control of balance.

Nor do I approve of the epithet "ugly" in reference to any creation of art. (Only pseudo-art, amateurish creations, can be called ugly.) Mozart was being reproached for having used "wrong" notes in his *C Major Quartet* which one of his noble patrons tore to pieces because of its radical dissonances. What

was termed "ugly" more than one hundred and fifty years ago is
delighting our senses today. This only proves that absolute truth
in art does not exist and that we are being conditioned to accept
it unconditionally.

I am so often told that my choreographic creations are "abstract." Does abstract mean that there is no story, no literary
image, at best a general idea which remains untranslated in terms
of reality? Does it mean the presentation of sound and movement,
of unrelated conceptions and symbols in a disembodied state?

I said on another occasion * that no piece of music, no dance
can in itself be abstract. You hear a physical sound, humanly
organized, performed by people, or you see moving before you
dancers of flesh and blood in a living relation to each other. What
you hear and see is completely real. But the after-image that remains with the observer may have for him the quality of an
abstraction. Music, through the force of its invention, leaves strong
after-images. I myself think of Stravinsky's *Apollon*, for instance,
as white music, in places as white-on-white as in the passage from
the pas d'action appearing on page 37.

For me whiteness is something positive (it has in itself an
essence) and is, at the same time, abstract. Such a quality exerts
great power over me when I am creating a dance; it is the music's
final communication and fixes the pitch that determines my own
invention.

Some choreographers seem to be so uncertain of their own
medium that not only do they seek the ballet that "has a story"
but they also have the story told in words. To me these are no
longer ballets, they are choreographic plays. Any amplification
necessary must come from the music which may, at times, make
use of a chorus. Much can be said in movement that cannot be

---

* "The Dance Element in Stravinsky's Music," *Dance Index*, Vol. VI,
Nos. 10, 11, 12, 1947.

expressed by words. Movement must be self-explanatory. If it
isn't, it has failed.

The dance has its own means of telling a story and need not
invade the field of the drama or the cinema. The quality of the
movement and the choreographic idea decide whether the story
is understandable. In most cases, the criterion of success or failure lies in the choice of the subject matter.

Music is often adjectived as being too abstract. This is a
vague and dangerous use of words and as unclear to me as when
my ballets are described that way. Neither a symphony nor a fugue
nor a sonata ever strikes me as being abstract. It is very real to me,
very concrete, though "storyless." But storyless is not abstract.
Two dancers on the stage are enough material for a story; for
me, they are already a story in themselves.

I approach a group of dancers on the stage like a sculptor who breathes life into his material, who gives it form and expression. I can feel them like clay in my hands. The minute I see them, I become excited and stimulated to move them. I do not feel I have to prepare myself. All I know is the music with which I am at least as intimately acquainted as a conductor of a symphony with his score. Of course, the contours of an outline, though sometimes only vaguely, exist in my mind—certain visualizations from listening to the score.

I am therefore greatly dependent on the rehearsal time at my disposal. When Tchaikovsky was once asked how he was able to compose whenever he had to, he is said to have answered: "My Muse comes to me when I tell her to come." Paraphrasing this answer of his, I often say that my Muse must come to me on "union" time.

My imagination is guided by the human material, by the dancers' personalities. I see the basic elements of the dance in its aesthetic manifestations, that is, in the beauty of movement, in the unfolding of rhythmical patterns, and not in their possible meaning or interpretation; I am less interested in the portrait of any real character than in the choreographic idea behind the dance action. Thus the importance of the story itself becomes reduced to being the frame for the picture I want to paint.

In the "storyless" ballet, the question of the costumes and sets gains importance. The stage designer has little to go by if he cannot derive his inspiration from the musical score, as the choreographer does. Then he must be present at the rehearsals and have the choreography furnish him with sufficient ideas. The "storyless" ballet is a great challenge to the designer's imagination, since he lacks any literary stimulation. On the other hand, there are the costumes and sets which can underline and help— with their composition of color and form—to make the visualization of music plastic and dramatic.

The designer must always be aware that the image he produces is part of the total effect with the only aim to create the necessary atmosphere for the dance composition with his sets and to stimulate the spectator's fantasy with his costume designs. This circumscribes his task. His contribution is by no means an accessory, but it must never be dominant. The sets must be in harmony with the idea of the dance composition and they can undoubtedly lead to new choreographic ideas. The costumes must not only fit the dancer, but also—what seems even more important—the dance action, that is, the idea and the movements which express it.

Whether a ballet has a story or not, the controlling image for me comes from the music. Stravinsky's music had the most decisive effect on my work and has always made itself felt in the direction of control and amplification.

My first real collaboration with Stravinsky began in 1928 when I worked on *Apollon*. I consider this the turning point of my life. This score, with its discipline and restraint, with its sustained oneness of tone and feeling, was a great revelation to me. It was then that I began to realize that to create means, first of all, to eliminate. Not a single fragment of any choreographic score should ever be replaceable by any other fragment; each piece must be unique in itself, the "inevitable" movement. I began to see how I could clarify by limiting and by reducing what seemed previously to have multiple possibilities.

Although my work has been greatly linked to Stravinsky's music for the last twenty years, I do not feel that one specific style of music lends itself better to the projection of sound into visible movement than another. But it may be difficult to fulfill certain composers' personal inspirations.

What I mainly expect from the composer whose work I am to visualize is a steady and reassuring pulse which holds the work together and which one should feel even in the rests. A pause, an interruption, must never be an empty space between indicated sounds. It cannot be just nothing, since life goes on within each silence. It must, in fact, act as a carrying agent from the last sound to the next one. The secret for an adequate rendering of the musical score into visualization lies in the dynamic use of silence and in the utmost consciousness of time.

The composer is able to give more life to a bar, more vitality and rhythmical substance than a choreographer, or a dancer for that matter. The musician deals with time and sound in a highly scientific way, his medium of creation lends itself to a strictly definable method, to organization and translation of a formula into artistry.

It is far more complicated for the dancer to recite a formula. The choreographer will never be able to achieve such precision in the expression of movement as the composer through sound effect. Not that we do not know what we are doing. Our technique certainly has method, but it is far more interpretive than subject to mathematical rules. Whenever I feel I have found the "inevitable" movement, I can never be as sure as in music that it might not need some clarification after all.

In my choreographic creations I have always been dependent on music. I feel a choreographer can't invent rhythms, he only reflects them in movement. The body is his sole medium and, unaided, the body will improvise for a short breath. But the organizing of rhythm on a grand scale is a sustained process. It is a function of the musical mind. Planning rhythm is like planning a house, it needs a structural operation.

Music written for theater, that is, to accompany danced or sung action, has certain limitations not shared by other music. While in one sense music is the most important initial feature of dance, inasmuch as it serves as root-rhythmic base, it cannot exceed a certain point of importance without competing with the action for which it is composed. Theater-music is intended to order and emphasize the activity in spectacle. It is music with a "program"; it indicates and describes for the ear what the eye sees. Its description is frequently far from literal. There is visual as well as aural counterpoint ...
—LINCOLN KIRSTEIN

MORTON GOULD

Music and the Dance

Today, the dance medium, ballet and modern, as well as the theater generally, afford exciting potentialities for the composer, a direct performing outlet and a ready-made audience. There are also the added possibilities of successful concert extracts and recordings. This has been a very potent activity on the part of our contemporary European colleagues and some of their most widely performed compositions are derived from ballet. Stravinsky is the most obvious example. It is only in comparatively recent years that our own symphonic composers have taken to ballet and theater as a consistent form of creative activity.

It is impossible to discuss here all the different styles and

41

approaches, but I will attempt to speak of some personal observations on the various factors involved.

Good ballet music is good theater music. The combination of stage and physical movement must be implemented by choreographic and musical design. The composer has a dual responsibility. He must mold the form and architecture of his music to the balletic design and, at the same time, keep the musical patterns logical in themselves.

Considering that very often the choreography is dictated by physical and mechanical necessities, this can turn out to be a vexing problem and difficult to solve musically. There are comparatively few ballet scores that can be played in their entirety as concert pieces. For the most part, you will see listed for musical performances excerpts from or "Ballet Suites" extracted from the complete work.

By mechanical and functional requirements are meant such situations as getting a group off the stage so that the next section and group may come on, padding through action and music for a change of set, or lighting effects, stage action that might be important to carry or connect a story line.

The question of how self-sufficient ballet music can be in terms of following purely musical directions, rather than specific choreographic requirements, is hard to answer satisfactorily. It mainly depends on the kind of composer and the kind of choreographer involved, on their individual approach, craftsmanship and flexibility. Some choreographers allow composers a free hand and fit balletic patterns to the music. Others have positive ideas about what they want, and this involves a close sympathetic cooperation between the composer and choreographer. The ideal combination is a choreographer who is almost a composer and the other way round. But even this has its pitfalls, because a choreographer of this sensitivity is apt to try to think musically for the composer and if the composer has a positive style—plus his usual ego—there is an immediate friction and confusion on both sides.

A good premise for the composer, when writing music for ballet, is to realize that the first objective is an effective theater piece and that only the understanding cooperation between choreographer and composer—and whatever other elements may be necessary—is the way to achieve this. The composer must be reconciled to adjusting and to considering factors of which he would not have to think were he just writing an abstract piece of music.

As an example, let us take the simple idea of a pas de deux. The idea and mood is settled on and the composer is inspired to create sixty bars of music which convey, from his point of view, the mood and form. The choreographer, however, may find that this is not long enough for his purposes and needs, let us say, forty more bars. He also might decide, rather than keep the same mood throughout the movement, to point up different places, or he might want a big climax and a period of silence before continuing. This makes it necessary for the composer to re-evaluate the whole concept musically. Now his problem is to fit the balletic deviations and still have a coherent musical movement.

Quality, of course, must be inherent in anything that a composer does, but his scope must be broad and his technical means flexible. Generally, complicated musical texture that might have interest in itself as music has a tendency to get lost in relation to stage movement. The music must help to make a direct impact and any complication that might be valid musically, but that would weaken the theatrical effect of the whole, is of dubious value in this medium.

It is sometimes hard for a composer to know when to compromise and when not. A natural feeling for theater and stage experience helps in these situations. A talented composer with these attributes knows at what point a choreographer's demands are justified or merely an attempt to find an easy way out. A musical adjustment or change is valid if it obviously heightens the effect.

Most composers understandingly view their music as a
mother her child. Choreographers, at least in the initial stages
of developing a ballet, very seldom have the same maternal attitude to the music. There are comparatively few choreographers
with a really highly developed musical understanding. By that I
mean an aesthetic response to and technical knowledge of music.
Their conception of rhythm and feeling of pulse is, for the most
part, symmetric. This applies even more so to the actual dancers.
A composer who writes rhythms in uneven patterns is apt to be
very confused, if not amazed, when he hears the dancers counting
the beats. They very often will count, for instance, "seven" on the
music's "one" beat, and blithely carry this through a whole sequence without any apparent confusion or disruption.

Complicated rhythmic patterns and uneven groups of
rhythm pulses usually result in confused balletic reactions. It takes
repeated hearings and very often explanations and, if necessary,
adamancy on the composer's part, before the choreographer and
dancers get the "feel" of the patterns. However, a composer's
sense of rhythms for ballet purposes must be of a very high order,
because this is one of the basic ingredients for this kind of music.
The reasons are obvious, but the most successful ballet music has
always been rhythmically dynamic and stimulating. Therefore,
the pulse might not be a simple one, but it must have a basic
natural propulsion. Choreographers and dancers can adjust and
react to complicated rhythmic patterns that they cannot necessarily count out, but that generate their reflexes through a basic
and positive validity.

Some aspects of contemporary ballet utilize a good deal of
pantomime and very often require corresponding music that does
not have any particular rhythmic vitality. This is a different problem, of course, and then the effect must be achieved through other
means. Musically these means can be melodic, or they can be attained through different textures, tonal resonances, and so on.

Choreography, like musical composition, runs a wide gamut

of expressivity and style, and it is naturally important that they match aesthetically, one to the other. There has to be a fundamental sympathy with each other's aims and an understanding of each other's possibilities and limitations. I say limitations, because often one element can serve to stimulate the other, or inspire new directions. A composer might convey through music an expression of mood that the choreographer did not think of doing, but is stimulated by the new perspective that the music conveys. On the other side, the choreographer will demonstrate a pattern of pulse and design that makes the mood immediately accessible to the composer and in a way that he might not have expressed before.

For the most part, the musical texture has to be of a kind that will sound with small groups of players. Even the commercial ballet companies, such as Ballet Theatre, when touring rarely carry an orchestra of more than twenty men. In places like New York the orchestra is expanded, but this is the exception, and for a ballet to remain in repertoire and receive consistent performances it must be, among other things, feasible for performance by a minimum number of players. The best practical solution is for the composer to score for a moderate size orchestra with the strings expandable, as the occasion arises, and cross-cue very diligently. This does away with the necessity for two separate scores— one for full orchestra and one for small. By combining both possibilities on the one score, through adroit voicing and cross-cuing, the composer will not only save a lot of time, but the demands of the basic small orchestration will tend to give his writing a clarity and directness that are an asset to effective theater music.

It is common practice to make a piano condensation of the score. This is really the first direct contact between composer and choreographer. There is usually a pianist who specializes in playing for dancers and he or she is engaged to work with the choreographer. It is very important that at this early stage, when the choreographer and dancers are absorbing and learning the music, the general tempos and dynamics be interpreted as closely as possible to what the orchestra will sound like. The composer must establish these fundamentals with the rehearsal pianist and choreographer. He must also be sensitive to any misjudgments or maladjustments between music and choreography, because now is the time to fix them and, if necessary, to re-evaluate and rewrite.

An accumulation of minor rhythmic and dynamic misunderstandings can be very annoying or disconcerting once a composer has gone to the trouble of scoring. A case in point would be a passage that the rehearsal pianist plays very loudly and stridently. The composer might visualize this passage orchestrally as quite the opposite. The choreographer, for the most part, only knows what he hears and choreographs accordingly. The first orchestra reading then is liable to cause great consternation, because the scoring conveys a completely different impression from the piano rendition. Here again experience counts. The composer must know what the choreographer hears and expects and how far one can deviate from the restrictions of the piano setting without confusing the dancers.

In starting a new work the question of which comes first, the music or the choreography, has often been raised. There is no set formula for this, but the general procedure is as follows: The choreographer and the composer discuss the idea of the ballet and the general texture. Certain high spots are developed, such as set pieces, a pas de deux, etc. For these, the composer very often writes a section of music that expresses the mood and the rhythmic feeling. If the choreographer reacts favorably, it is set balletically to the music. The movement might now have to be shortened or lengthened, or certain changes made to meet a choreographic requirement. On the other hand, there are other parts of the ballet for which the choreographer develops a specific kind of movement and the composer fits the music to that.

These different methods are used either separately or concurrently. As the ballet begins to take form and substance, another element enters, namely, the mechanics of the stage. If there are sets that have to be changed, one faces the technical problem of allowing enough music and movement to cover the time it takes to change the set. In some cases a bigger stage than anticipated might require adjustments in the choreography that very often affect the music. It takes a good deal of practical experience for a composer and choreographer to develop, in their own minds, a vehicle that will be consistently effective and feasible in terms of dance and stage.

Often glaring defects of one sort or another don't show up until the ballet is well into rehearsal in the theater itself. This stage is perilously close to the first performance and is the most likely place for drastic disagreements and changes to occur. Tempos that were satisfactory in the rehearsal room and that are an integral part of the music from the composer's point of view have to be changed to fit either the theatrical requirements or the dancers' needs. There might be drastic cuts or deletions. The answer to this situation, of course, is ample and long preparation and, if necessary, revisions over a long period of time and with all the facilities of the theater available from almost the inception of the ballet. Unfortunately, in most cases and certainly in the case of the commercial ballet companies, this is neither practical nor possible.

If the composer is fortunate, the musical by-product of the ballet can have a life of its own. Some of the most popular concert material in recent years have been ballet suites or extracts. The most successful of these are usually taken from ballets that have a maximum of dance and a minimum of pantomime, and they treat whatever story there might be objectively rather than subjectively. Composers should be diligently careful when selecting ballet suites for concert performances to use only the movements or parts of the work that are complete within themselves in form and content.

Music and ballet, both being dynamic, have their own motion and design. The ways of combining both are diverse and changeable. Every school of thought and style has its own problems and means. This makes writing for the dance an exciting task. Its greatest difficulties lie in the fusion of these two media into an artistic entity. It would make interesting reading to analyze the significant ballets of our repertoire in terms of the respective composers and choreographers and their manner of collaboration.

A genuine dance notation is the representation through the use of symbols, of ideas which are expressed by movement. The fact that the content of movement becomes understandable through its shape and rhythm is not surprising, since all that we can really see . . . in movement is its shape and the relationship between shapes as they follow one another. —RUDOLF LABAN

ANN HUTCHINSON

The Preservation of the Dance Score through Notation

HISTORICAL BACKGROUND

MUCH HAS been written on the development of dance notation through the ages, and the merits of one system versus another, but little has been said about the dance score as such. This is largely due to the fact that, with few exceptions, no system has been in use for a sufficiently long time or by a sufficient number of people to leave proof of its value in the form of completed dance scores.

The manuscripts and books which have been handed down through the centuries are the source of our knowledge of the dances of former times. Though much can be done through words and pictures, the contributions in the form of different notations, those of Feuillet, Zorn and Stepanov to mention a few, are invaluable. As Gaspare Angiolini, a contemporary of Noverre, said:

"Feuillet did more for the future by recording some of the dances in notation than Noverre, who failed to do so."

There is truth in this, but we are nevertheless indebted to writers like Arbeau, Noverre, Rameau and Blasis, who gave us such a clear insight into the thought and feeling of the day concerning the dance. Thanks to Arbeau, we know about the Basse dances of the sixteenth century. We also have many examples of the court dances of the time of Louis XIV due to the widespread use of Feuillet's system of notation, in which many suites of dances were published in different countries. During the nineteenth century Zorn perfected the notation system started by St. Leon, and published many examples of folk dances and ballroom dances of the time, the best known being the minuet. While these notations are sketchy—Zorn, for example, often took it for granted that the reader was familiar with the steps and so would omit a turn or other necessary detail—researchers have been able to reconstruct them. With a knowledge of the music and costume of the period and an understanding of the behavior of the people through study of the contemporary literature and painting, we can reconstruct the dances with a degree of authenticity.

Among the people well known for having so reconstructed the old court dances are Melusine Wood and Arthur Mahoney. Miss Wood has devoted years to research into the costume, music, ideas and behavior patterns of the day in order faithfully to reconstruct the movements. Mr. Mahoney studied the Feuillet manuscripts in Paris, and has since given many performances of the court dances of the seventeenth and eighteenth centuries. A recent example was the complete ballet he choreographed to Handel's score, entitled *Parnassus*.

The first complete ballets on record to be written in a dance notation were those in the Russian repertoire written in St. Petersburg by Stepanov. The notation of *The Sleeping Beauty* was used when it was later revived, the most recent instance being the revival for the Sadler's Wells company.

CONTEMPORARY SYSTEMS OF NOTATION

Of the more recent attempts to devise a workable notation, few are still in existence and even fewer have left any dance records of value. Little if anything is being done in the Margaret Morris movement notation, nor have we heard of its ever having spread beyond England. The system of Sol Babitz of California seemed interesting but proved impractical, and nothing more has been heard of it. Pierre Conté's method is clearly limited to ballet. A recent development is the as yet unpublished and unproven notation of Alwin Nicholais.

The one system on which fifty years has been spent and which has proved itself the most practical is that of Rudolf Laban, first published in 1928. The strength of the Laban system lies in its simple logical basis and its universality. In the early stages, any notation system can seem plausible, since simple steps will always be easy to write. It is not until every type of movement has been tried and every rule tested that the weakness or strength of a method is brought out. In the early years of its development the Laban notation, or "Kinetographie," as it was called, was used and spread by many teachers and dancers in different fields. Each person contributed to the notation from his experience and kept it from developing in favor of one particular type of movement or another. Among those who have done notable work in the Laban notation are Albrecht Knust, who has written several ballets of the Munich Opera Company; Sigurd Leeder in England; and in the United States Irma Betz and Irma Bartenieff and the Dance Notation Bureau of New York and its many associate members.

One of the earliest experiments in the Laban script occurred in Germany in 1936 before the staging of a mammoth presentation for a Dance Congress. The thousand dancers who were to take part in the presentation were spread throughout forty different cities, so to each city a dance score of the presentation was sent, to be used for preliminary rehearsals. When the dancers met for the first time, the parts fitted together smoothly and the show was given with only one dress rehearsal.

Since this early beginning the Laban notation has spread as far as Eastern Tibet where recorded Tibetan folk dances are to be found in the History Library at Kanting. Folk dances have also been written in Czechoslovakia, Hungary, etc., and it is hoped that one day all the available ethnologic material will be written in the Laban system, so that it can be studied by everyone.

CONTEMPORARY DANCE SCORES

Within the past two decades we have seen not only the recording of many full-length dance works in the Laban notation, but also the beginning of the practical application of the notation, particularly the reconstruction of dance works through notation. The first reports of a successful revival of a ballet through the notation was from Kurt Jooss, when he taught his ballet *The Green Table* to an entirely new company in Chile and referred constantly to the score, written in 1938. In the past decade he has referred to the manuscripts constantly, particularly when a number of new dancers have joined the company. On his recent visit here Jooss said, "If I ever entertained any doubts as to whether the notation was practical and worthwhile, they have long since been removed. The scores have proved to be invaluable on so many occasions, and have saved time, if only to settle the inevitable disputes among the dancers." In this country the first opportunity to use a score for reference occurred in 1949 when Ballet Theatre was experiencing difficulties in reviving *Billy the Kid*, since so few members of the company remembered the ballet. Zachary Solov, who was in charge of the rehearsals, called upon me for assistance. Though I had not looked at the score since 1943, I was able to reconstruct the needed sections without any trouble.

It was not until the score of the dance sequences in *Kiss Me, Kate* were commissioned in preparation to producing a London company that any real attempt was made to put notation on a functional basis. Apart from the desirability of having the dances faithfully reproduced, there was the additional factot of the easier working conditions and of the time and energy saved. Hanya Holm, choreographer of *Kiss Me, Kate,* was delighted with the results of working with the dance score. Being freed from the anxiety of trying to remember every detail, she was able to devote her time to perfecting the movements and making the few changes necessary due to the augmented company. The usual result of reproducing a Broadway success in London has been that, thanks to the written word, music notation, and drawings, the book, musical score and the costume and set designs have been faithfully reproduced. But not so the dances, for even when the choreographer is there in person many details are forgotten and much new choreography must be done. This is true not only of musicals but of all dance works.

Other dance works which have been written within the past few years are the Balanchine ballets *Symphony in C, Orpheus, Theme and Variations, Bourrée Fantasque,* etc., and in the modern field works by Doris Humphrey and Charles Weidman. There has as yet been no need to use these scores to any extent, other than the few questions raised each season by members of the company. When a ballet has been dropped for several years then there will be a real need to refer to the dance score.

THE BALLET SCORE

The score of a complete ballet consists of two parts: the floor plans and the movement notation.

The Floor Plans. The diagrams of the positions of the dancers on stage are written next to the movement score whenever they are needed. A set of all the floor plans is usually kept separate from the score itself and, since they will be used mainly by the choreographer or dance director, they are written from the spectator's point of view. A glance at the plans will give an idea

of the entrances and exits of the dancers, and the over-all movement and formations. They are indispensable whenever any complicated crossing or weaving of individual dancers or groups occur.

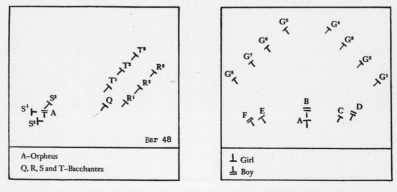

Floor plan for *Orpheus*.   Floor plan for *Symphony in C*.

The Movement Score. The score showing the movement itself is much more complex. Ballet or group dance scores vary according to the number of dancers on stage, and whether they work
independently or in groups. A separate staff is needed for each
dancer, unless there is unison movement on stage for any length
of time. A typical score of a formal classical ballet usually shows
the prima ballerina, her partner, two soloists and their partners
and the corps de ballet in the background. Thus the score will consist of eight staves joined together on one page, with the music,
if desired, placed at the extreme left, the bars of music corresponding with the bars of the dance score.

What factors must be stated in a complete score? Every
detail must be stated without which the reader would not automatically perform the movements correctly. The most natural
positions and movements are written the most simply. Here are
some of the factors which usually must be stated.

A. *The dancer's relation to space:*
Entrance or starting position on stage.

Relationship to other dancers.

Relationship to the audience—which direction the dancer faces. As the movement unfolds these relationships must be re-stated whenever necessary.

B. *The dancer's movement:*
We must know: the starting position, position of the feet, the arms, head and posture of the body.

When the movement starts we must know: Which foot moves first? What steps are taken? In what direction? In what rhythm? Small or large steps? Is there a leg gesture? What direction, level, rhythm? Is the leg straight or flexed? Is there any movement of the body and arms? Does the body bend? Into what direction? Is there also a twist in the body? Do the arms move fluently, or in a staccato manner? Are they stretched, or bent?

These and other questions must be answered before one can be sure that every necessary detail has been taken care of. We do not realize how many of these factors the eye automatically takes in at a single glance.

RECONSTRUCTING THE SCORE

The question "Are notation scores complicated?" often arises. Dance scores are as complicated or as simple as the ballet itself. Just as an intricate step took the choreographer longer to define and make clear to the dancer, who in turn took longer to learn and perfect the movement, so such a step will take more time to analyze and write, and more time for the reader to reconstruct in the future. This is no fault of the notation itself. In no notation can a complex and unfamiliar movement be written simply. Short cuts, labeling certain movements and steps, will work for those who know the movements, but will fail when memories grow dim or someone unfamiliar with that type of movement or terminology tries to read the manuscript.

This is the problem which has confronted each generation of notators. Are we to have a notation which will be a universal one, suitable to all styles of dancing and types of movement, or is it better to have different notations suited especially to the different needs—ballet, modern, tap, Spanish, Oriental, etc.? A universal notation must be one which is built on the anatomical possibilities of the body, and in which each step or movement is described by the basic elements of which it is made, the part of the body, direction, level, rhythm, etc. Such a notation will make any movement understandable to a person who has thoroughly studied the notation. This is the advantage, that one notation will serve for all, and that a student in China can read a score written in, say, England. The immediate disadvantage is that, since each step is written out fully, the reader must reassemble the symbols into a finished movement again. Whether this process is a facile or a tedious chore depends on the experience and ability of the reader. As with any kind of reading, practice is the necessary requirement to attain fluency. Just as a first attempt at reading words results in disconnected syllables, so the beginning steps in reading dance notation are equally mechanical and unrelated to real movement. The disjointed steps and gestures of the beginner are soon translated into flowing patterns correctly phrased when the relationship between the symbols on the paper and the movements they represent becomes automatically understood.

As with words or music, certain patterns become familiar, and the more experienced reader will read phrases rather than single words or notes. Since most steps are built on basic forms, they become easily recognizable, and it is possible to tell at a glance the general style of the piece. One of the advantages of the block symbols used in Laban notation is that they form patterns easy for the eye to perceive.

It is not so much the ability to learn a notation system, but the ability to analyze movement which is essential to a writer or reader of notation scores. It is because the student must delve into the various realms of movement, into the relationship of the body to space, and the dynamic and rhythmic content of movement, that notation training is of value to any dance student, whether he intends to use the notation himself or not.

THE FILM VERSUS THE NOTATED SCORE AS A RECORD

In recent years the film has often been used as a means to record dance. Some people advocate that the use of movies dispenses with the need to have a work notated, claiming that it is both easier to record and easier to reconstruct dance through motion pictures. These views are noticeably held by people who have never been in a position to compare the advantages and disadvantages of the two methods. It is those few people who have actually revived a ballet through watching a movie, and who have also experienced the use of notation in reconstructing a dance work, who can speak with authority for or against the one method or the other. The situation is clearly comparable to the record of a symphonic work and the printed score of the same piece. To study each individual part, the musician needs the written score. To obtain an idea of the finished work and how it should sound, he turns to the recorded performance. It would be unthinkable to ask an entire orchestra to learn their parts through listening to a record being played again and again. So it is in the dance world. The movie cannot take the place of the dance score, nor vice versa.

THE DANCE FILM

The advantages of a dance film are obvious; what are the disadvantages? The main problem is, of course, the financial one. To make a first-rate movie requires special lighting, a suitable studio, expert cameramen, sound equipment, etc. An inferior work-film can be made during a performance, to be used merely as an aid to the memory. Here we come up against the artistic integrity of the choreographer and also the cameramen. Many photographers will not make an inexpensive film since it is a poor example of their work, detrimental to their reputation. For the same reason choreographers, notably Martha Graham, do not wish to have their work-films shown outside the studio. In order to obtain results that are artistically interesting, certain liberties must be taken and the film will cease to be an accurate record of the original dance.

Among the choreographers who have had experience in reconstructing their works through films are Massine and Balanchine. As a result of his experiences, Balanchine has given up the use of movies as a sole means of recording and has commissioned the Dance Notation Bureau, through Ballet Society, to record all of his works. The results of Massine's experiences are known through the dancers who were involved in the process of watching the film over and over in order to learn their parts. These are the difficulties they experienced: The need to reverse right and left (the movie being shot from the audience's point of view); the problem of analyzing a movement carefully, since slow motion on the screen means the loss of the rhythmic beat; trying to determine the correct rhythm and counts when the film has no sound track; the visual loss of movement through the absence of the third dimension, for instance, when groups cross and dancers are lost from sight; the need to run through the whole film when only a section in the middle is needed. Some of the dancers who quoted these experiences have since worked in the New York City Ballet Company and have been able to see notation put to use. They were amazed at how easily their questions were answered by a quick glance at the notation score.

THE NOTATED SCORE

The obvious disadvantage in the use of dance notation to record a dance work is the scarcity of professional notators and of people who can read notation with ease. These are drawbacks which in time will cease to exist. The advantages of using a notated score have been experienced by only a few, but once experienced they wonder how they ever managed without it in the past. To record the work, the dance notator attends the rehearsals while the work is being choreographed. Whenever possible the score should be written right from the start. As each dancer learns his part and the steps are demonstrated and analyzed, the notator writes them down. Thus the choreographer's original intentions are recorded, not an individual dancer's interpretation. The cost of a notated score is low in comparison with that of a film.

The greatest advantage of notation is in the reconstruction. If there is doubt about an exact rhythm, arm movement, position on stage, it can be looked up in a few seconds. The section of the dance can be turned to, the right page found, the column for the dancer, the measure in question, and finally the part of the body, there being a separate column for each part.

When a ballet must be taught to a completely new cast, the process is similar to the original choreographing of the work, minus the time-consuming experimentations. The dancers are shown where to enter from the floor plans. Then the movement is taught from the actual notation. The notator can easily familiarize himself with any tricky sequences in order to demonstrate them to the dancers. On the other hand, the notator, like the choreographer, can read back and explain to the dancers sequences which he himself is physically unable to perform.

A good example of reconstruction from the score occurred during the rehearsals of *Kiss Me, Kate* in London. In reconstructing the Parade and Street Scene, in which each of the dancers is an individual character with individual patterns, I, being in charge of the rehearsal, proceeded to teach each dancer his part from the score. After each dancer knew the counts of his movements and where to go across the stage, the first attempt was made to run through the entire scene. It was amazing to see the choreography come to life, with only a few mishaps occurring when dancers did not know on which side to pass each other. This was soon straightened out, and the rest of the rehearsal time spent on polishing up details. Had the dancers been able to read the score for themselves each could have received his part, studied it at the same time, and when all were ready the scene could have been put together, thus saving more time. As it was, dancers had to sit by waiting until they had been shown what to do. The day will come when a dancer can take his part home, study it at his own leisure and come back for a group rehearsal needing only polishing and practice in dancing with the ensemble. Musicians do not learn their parts by ear, nor actors their roles by verbal coaching. It is a disgrace that dance still uses these medieval methods. To date we can quote only one example of a dancer teaching herself her part from the dance score and being able to go into the dance without even one rehearsal. In a few years this will doubtless no longer be a novelty.

Thus we see the idea of a workable notation becoming an actuality. We have as yet only isolated instances, but they prove beyond a doubt that notation can and does work. It has still to become more widely used; every dancer should have a working knowledge of notation, and in every company there should be a professional notator on hand to write down the new works.

As a start towards dance literacy, notation is being taught as part of the curriculum at the School of Performing Arts, a vocational high school where students may specialize in dance. Courses in notation are also taught at many of the leading dance studios in New York and in some colleges throughout the country.

We no longer need to prove that the answer to the dancer's and the choreographer's needs exists. We have only to hasten the day when all will benefit from the use of dance notation and the existence of a library of dance scores. In the meantime, future generations will be enriched by a greater source of knowledge of the dance works of this era than of any other in history.

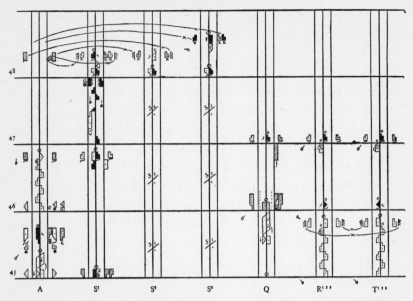

Orpheus to music by Igor Stravinsky. Orpheus being attacked by the Bacchantes. Choreographed by George Balanchine.

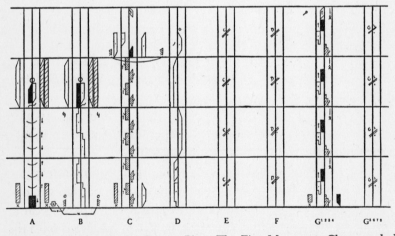

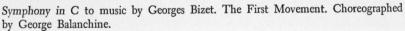

Symphony in C to music by Georges Bizet. The First Movement. Choreographed by George Balanchine.

There *is* no marking time or standing still. Nor *is* there a restless progress that aims at final, utopian perfectness and leaves to furnace and pickax all the once beautiful, now superseded, works of the past. But there is something better than progress: a ceaseless, ever-new adaptation of art to the changing needs of man. And in such adaptation, art slowly uncovers one by one the inexhaustible potentialities of human senses and souls, to which we bow in wonder and awe. —CURT SACHS

THOMAS BOUCHARD
(RECOUNTED BY THE EDITOR)

The Preservation of the Dance Score through Filming the Dance

I AM walking along Forty-second Street.

It is ten o'clock in the morning. The light still has the texture of softness, an inimitable caressive quality. Ideal to a photographer's eye.

Suddenly I see a paper flying in the air. It is floating with graceful majesty, without a single repetition in its movements, down along the walls of this gigantic masonry.

At the same instant, my eye catches sight of an old man trying to cross the street. Lifeworn, the incarnation of man's frailty. He steps down from the sidewalk. A jaywalker. A passing car at full speed just misses him. One jerk, he jumps backward onto the sidewalk. This backward movement, performed with unconscious intensity in fright and in his basic drive for self-preservation, is the muscular reaction of a split second. From head to toe complete coordination. The entire system—unaware of its powers, worn out by life, drained by age—suddenly concentrated in one little movement, in the one step backward, a step in harmony with itself, but also with the cacophonous world around him.

The paper. The old man. And also the girl.

While I see the paper glide down and the old man leap for his life, a girl is in the range of my vision. She comes towards me. She hurries. She must be late for her office. I see the movement of her body, the tender curves of her bosom, its hardly perceptible quiver under the tight blouse, her head slightly held sidewise—the image of natural perfection!

Thanks to my ocular perception, thanks to my two eyes I can see the paper, the man and the girl, absorb their movements and be aware of the rhythmic flow of an inanimate thing, of muscular motion, of grace and beauty per se, and be aware of all this at one moment.

The camera is at a disadvantage. The range of its vision is no match to ours.

It is most sensitive to any rapid movement. It cannot follow it as smoothly and as easily as our eyes which can adjust themselves to it without being subjected to a flickering image.

Spatial gaps are quickly absorbed by the human eye. But they shout at you from the screen and haunt you!

The three-dimensional image: the triumph of the human eye over the lens . . . The paper, the old man and the girl did not appear shadowlike on the invisible screen of my eyes. No. They were as plastic as the color of each detail was natural.

The camera—a mechanical cyclops in miniature! Its one eye in the middle of its forehead staring at an object. We must admit though, it is concentrated on it, well focused.

But in order to embrace the object in its entirety, it must move backward and each detail becomes small, indistinct. Can it still see the paper, the man and the girl?

The paper, on wings of illusion performing an unheard-of dance: yielding to gravity, catching its balance at the right moment, and again challenging its imaginary equilibrium! This paper becomes as small as the head of a pin and its wonderful dreamlike movements are lost. It is falling down, that is all the eye can see now. Its movement is stripped of the essential, of its artistic expression, of its individuality.

The old man's movement remains as unclear as its motivation. The girl, in such remoteness, loses the secret of her magic.

Only a close-up of each detail could restore all the intricacies lost. But this would be an entirely wrong approach. In order to convey the same intensity of experience and the same impact of drama and artistry as reality has given our eyes, we must use the inventive and imaginative qualities of the "camera" to recompose the entire event.

Technically speaking, it means to shoot pictures, to cut and to edit them. Artistically speaking, it means to compose the architecture of a symphony in the language of pictures.

This circumscribes the problems involved when dancing is to be filmed. He whose artistic vision goes beyond the desire to preserve steps and aims at the depth and message of the subject matter has already understood me. The others never will.

The dance is choreographed for the stage. Film in comparison to the stage is infinitesimal. The dance seen with the eye of the camera from a certain angle for any length of time is against the very nature of this medium.

A simple record on film of the goings-on behind the footlights from the stationary angle of the audience in the theater or concert hall is a mere carbon copy of the dance, and it serves its specific purpose.

Jean Erdman, young American dancer who, with an equal measure of emotional fervor and intellectual probing, continues on the road of the modern dance. *Photograph by Gerda Peterich.*

Hand-and-face study of Pauline Koner whose technical skill and emotional intensity give us some of the finest dramatic presentations of the modern dance. *Courtesy of Pauline Koner.*

Pearl Primus, a breathtaking dancer, who has done invaluable research on the African Negro dance, in one of her famous leaps in *Dance of Hate. Courtesy of Pearl Primus.*

Ruth St. Denis, the "High Priestess" of the dance. *Courtesy of Sally Kamin.*

We must learn to see with the camera. We must marry beautiful motion to beautiful pictures.

We must realize that our perspective with one lens is faulty, that we cannot avoid distortions.

I fully understand that the dancer is interested in the pure record of his movements, in the preservation of his dance compositions as a whole. It can be done. Certainly. But we must realize that we cannot mate two different artistic media and hope for an offspring of pure artistry.

The stage illusion is produced through the remoteness of an apparently different world. The film illusion is created through its immediacy, its closeness and life-likeness.

The dance must be recreated for the film. To begin with the beginning: In the film, there is no curtain that can be raised. Therefore, the opening must already differ from that of the stage performance. When I did *The Shakers* for Doris Humphrey, we introduced the dancers—and with it the entire atmosphere of fanaticism and religious ecstasy—by having the dancers ascend a staircase and gradually line up for the ecstatic dance.

Abruptness in the introduction of any artistic offering kills the very effect at which it aims. We were aware that it was our essential task to retain the spirit of the dance and those parts of the compositional movements which express it most vividly.

It is not the continuity of the dance—composed for the stage—which matters. The true sequence of steps and gestures is inconsequential. To the camera eye it is repetitious. The stage dance needs repetition for emphasis and for the connecting links of the various phrases of movements. On the screen, however, their effect is monotonous, the eye refuses to follow them. What may be a necessity on the stage or in the concert hall, what may even be effective there, borders on the ridiculous in the film.

The leitmotif of the dance composition must become the central piece of the film symphony. The repetition of this leitmotif—of course shot from various angles—is essential to the screen. It is comparable to the radiation of its message from a nuclear point.

Art cannot always be explained. It need not be, not necessarily. It often evades its logical conclusion without denying its emotional impact. (Its logic can be still beyond our own mental capacity which often takes decades to become conditioned to a genuine understanding and appreciation, sometimes it takes centuries: think of El Greco, or Hoelderlin.) But one can always analyze any creation of art and take it apart. And one must do so with the dance before filming it.

The variations of its main theme must be organically grouped around its leitmotif. That means organically from the camera point of view, which may seem out of context and incoherent as far as the original composition is concerned.

But one must not forget that the dance composition for the stage has to be turned into a *film symphony of the dance.*

Emphasis and climax must also undergo changes. The film accentuates differently, since its architectural structure is different. Though both the dance and the film are basically visual, the dance reaches a climax through other means than the film. What can be achieved through fluidity and a gradual growth there, is attained on the screen only through a dynamic blending of shots whose sequence may seem arbitrary and erratic from the dancer's viewpoint.

The camera can see one and the same movement from various angles. Instead of following its continuity, it can stress its meaning or heighten its beauty by seeing it from an angle which always remains inaccessible to the audience in the theater. The correct blending of these fragments must finally result in a total impression reviving content and form of the dance composition in its entirety, though with other means.

The camera can take a shot of a certain movement followed by a facial close-up whose expression highlights or even explains the inner cause for this step or gesture. The film can also superimpose one image upon another and thereby whip up the dramatic intensity of movements which the dance itself cannot do. The film can make good use of the counterpoint and juxtaposition technique of great painters. In fact, it must make use of it to overcome the major problems it faces: space and quick movement.

All this of course depends on the mechanical facilities, on the technical means at our disposal.

The ideal premise for the filming of the dance would be a semicircle arena, six cameras easily movable, shooting at the same time with 35mm films. In other words, if I must experiment with three cameras, whose mobility is greatly limited, and 16mm films, it is the mechanical inadequacy which cripples the experiment.

But experiment we must. The effect I have tried to achieve in Hanya Holm's *The Golden Fleece* can be considered only the first step in a series of experiments probing the many possibilities of the filmed dance. In *The Golden Fleece*—perhaps to a great extent at the expense of the original dance composition— I have attempted a synchronization of movement, color and content aiming at the architecture of a symphony in which the fundamental causes and processes of the presented dance ideas are resolved in visualization.

This may have been a step in the right direction, or it may not. Only the results of new experiments will give us the right to pass any final judgment. But all these experiments need the full understanding and cooperation of the choreographers and dancers. They must become acutely aware of the camera eye. They must be able to dissect their dance compositions and account for each movement in regard to (a) its meaning, (b) its importance per se and (c) its importance in relation to the entire composition.

Each fragment will then play that role in the screen version suited to its inherent quality as a part of the whole. Through such an analysis the dancer will help recreate the dance for the camera.

When I was walking along Forty-second Street at ten o'clock in the morning and saw a paper flying in the air and saw the old man and the girl, I was, at one and the same instant, aware of these three different phrases of movements, different as to their nature, their motivation and effect. Reality is a great painter of contrasts.

These three fragments, let us assume, may be part of a dance composition called *Broadway at Forty-second Street*. The choreographer can easily introduce all three movements on the stage at the same time and give the audience a threefold spectacle, the movements of which he can gradually dissolve or blend into an entity. The camera cannot do this.

The choreographer can give your eyes an artistic version of what I have seen on the street. But when I film the dance composition of this scene, I must approach it from the camera viewpoint. If there is no preceding scene to prepare the spectator for the event, I would first have to conjure up the atmosphere of Broadway and Forty-second Street with a few shots.

In the movement of the paper is freedom from speed, greed, danger, freedom from the anxieties of our age. I must draw a cinematic diagonal from these majestic movements, subject to nothing else than wind, air pressure and gravity, to the girl's movements, the incarnation of natural beauty. I must build up the old man as the tragic center, as the victim of his time.

A few shots of Forty-second Street. Cars, buses, people hurrying, harassed, haunted by the man-made specters of speed —superimposition—movements in opposite direction—gradually showing stone giants ready to swallow the people—shots of the tops of skyscrapers—and the endless depth and placidity of the sky—and then down again along the stone walls until we catch a glimpse of the paper.

The first shots of the paper taken from above (only accessible to the eye of the camera!)—leading straight onto the street—showing the sameness in graceful motion: the paper, the girl. From the girl to the old man, as he is about to step down from the sidewalk, and back to the craziness of speed. Counterpoint: paper, then girl again seen from other angles—both still in innocent remoteness from the bedlam in the street, but already drawn closer to it—down, and nearer, to the reality of Forty-second Street.

The movements of the paper seem to become more tired, those of the girl more harassed; the old man has stepped down from the sidewalk; a last glimpse of the girl's graceful movement—a last attempt at a *relevé* of the paper—the quiver of her bosom has already become part of the anxiety of Forty-second Street; a car speeds toward Fifth Avenue, the old man jumps for his life—close-up—the paper under the wheel of the car—the girl begins to run—the superimposition of several images leading to the introductory shots climaxed by the old man standing in the center, gasping, perspiring, joy in his eyes at still being alive.

I am walking along Forty-second Street. Just a few random thoughts that have come to my mind. I look at my watch. I am late. I must hurry. I am expected in my studio. I cross the street, a horn sounds frantically, I jump back, run to the next corner thinking of the girl and the magic of natural grace. Out of breath, I arrive in my studio and greet the dancer who is waiting for me.

While apologizing for being late, my look steals away from her to the window. A piece of paper is floating through the air on wings of illusion—a reminder of the inevitable in life, with the endless blue above it in that small square of sky cut out of this gigantic masonry, and the noise of a speed-drunken age below—I wonder whether the old man's coordination will work again tomorrow.

The young dancer smiles at me. Does she surmise my

thoughts? Perhaps. But what does it matter? Her smile has the beauty of a lost dream. She turns around to get ready. Her movements have perfect poise and harmony. I am reconciled with my fate and start preparing to shoot.

Our firmest convictions are apt to be the most suspect, they mark our limitations and our bonds. Life is a petty thing unless it is moved by the indomitable urge to extend its boundaries. Only in proportion as we are desirous of living more do we really live. Obstinately to insist on carrying on within the same familiar horizon betrays weakness and a decline of vital energies. Our horizon is a biological line, a living part of our organism. In times of fullness of life it expands, elastically moving in unison almost with our breathing. When the horizon stiffens it is because it has become fossilized and we are growing old. —JOSÉ ORTEGA Y GASSET

For the ballet to be in the least credible, it is essential to be entirely incredible. —THÉOPHILE GAUTIER

———

KURT SELIGMANN

The Stage Image

THE FUNCTION of the stage designer is to create, through plastic means, a climate favorable to a particular dance. Some choreographers consider settings and costumes a necessary evil—a concession to the public which does not aesthetically appreciate the pure form of the dance, and requires a visual stimulant. Their reluctance holds little inspiration for the stage designer who would like to employ bold means and give full freedom to his imagination.

71

Other choreographers less bound by misplaced purism accept new ideas enthusiastically. However, the most original costumes and the finest settings, like the best musical score, cannot make up for lack of inventiveness on the part of the choreographer, or of technical skill on the part of the dancer. If music and choreography are bold, then the designer too is enticed to use bold means, and the flight of his imagination is unhindered.

Any dance performance should be an entity. The composer, the choreographer and the designer should collaborate to fuse their work into a perfect alloy.

Such collaboration is difficult. The three artists at work must find a precarious equilibrium in which each enjoys full liberty in his medium, but with the implicit intent of working towards a single aim: the aesthetic unity of the dance performance.

Successful collaboration depends on many more people than the composer, choreographer and designer.

The deepest desire of the producer is a capacity audience, and if successful he will at times give his advice, asked or unasked. He will try to bend the performance to his routine and, because he depends upon the broadest possible appeal, he will be mildly shocked by all that does not immediately please the masses. What producer who is not a Croesus can afford to allow his three artists to experiment freely with complete disregard of popularity and cash receipts? Only a gambler risking his skin would speculate on the new and unknown. Fortunately, those gamblers have not yet died out.

Often a stage technician is assigned to aid the free-lance artist who does not have stage experience. This technician, or scenic artist, may be a valuable help, or involuntarily cause all sorts of obstructions. When working with a painter of repute, his inferiority complex may get the better of him. He may barricade himself behind all kinds of technicalities and create nonexistent difficulties.

The lighting technician can also contribute to the success

or failure of a dance performance. Unfortunately, he has little to say. Lighting is perhaps the most neglected of the various departments. The costume designer does not always attend light rehearsals, a reprehensible negligence. And often the decision remains entirely in the hands of the choreographer whose chief concern is the use of light as a means of grouping the dancers or accenting soloists. Light can do a great deal more.

For Hanya Holm's *The Golden Fleece* at the Mansfield Theater a white drop curtain was provided where a black one was needed. The lighting expert was able to remedy this error and produce a fairly dark background by means of his projectors. But he seldom has the opportunity to use his initiative so effectively. As a rule he does what he is told, and too often he is told the wrong thing.

Many hold the curious notion that a minimum of light produces the best theatrical effect. A dark stage makes me sleepy. When it represents the depth of night it may be justified, but then the stage designer must find a way to enliven the stage image. Dim light on drab costumes may rest the eye and the mind but is far from inspiring. I believe that objects and happenings upon the stage should be fully legible. And light is the means par excellence for legibility. If there are enough projectors at the light technician's disposal, he can use successfully even awkward gelatins, dark blues and greens, which are very unbecoming colors. For my part, however, I favor straw and cocoa.

Many excellent designs for costumes and sets look perfect on paper and are works of art in their own right. If the costumes and sets when executed are disappointing, this is usually the fault of the designer, not of the costumer. The costumer often has a strong *scenic* sense, an understanding based on experience, and can work effectively from a rough and apparently meaningless sketch if it has been well imagined by a stage-conscious artist.

This metamorphosis from costume design to real costume is crucial for the stage designer. If he has not made himself clear, the costumer is compelled to interpret the sketch in his own way, and such interpretation may completely contradict the original intent. The ideal solution is for the stage designer to remain closely in touch with the costumer and use the latter's technical knowledge and familiarity with various materials.

Legibility is the important factor for costumes as it is for lighting. The costume is a fragment of stage architecture seen from a distance. Costly ornaments, intricate details may become completely blurred in the limelight. In *The Four Temperaments* ballet a group of costumes executed in white jersey on red tights were finished with complicated drapings painstakingly done by an excellent costumer. At the opening performance these drap-

eries appeared as quite flat white cloth. The folds had to be
accented with black trimming which would have been effective
of itself, without the tedious work done previously.

Yet legibility should not to my mind be confused with simplicity. Simple costumes and sets may have an immediate and
startling effect on the raising of the curtain. They may be legible
at once. But more complicated forms may "wear" better, especially when the performance is rather long. In this case, the
spectators' eyes will wander around in a slow reading of the stage
image, as of a tapestry whose intricate designs and many colors
will never become tedious precisely because of their intricacy. A
theatrical mood of mystery may be obtained through fantastic,
mysterious forms more adequately perhaps than by means of
light effects.

A choreographer will seldom accept uncritically the result
of the designer's and costumer's combined efforts. Here a skirt
must be taken off and replaced by a tutu, there a wig is too heavy,
a sleeve too stiff. Often from the dancers' complaints of dis-
comfort one might think that they were made of eider down
rather than flesh and bone. In accepting their proposed changes
the designer may strip his costumes of whatever was interesting,
amusing or characteristic. Energy and tact are needed to win the
battle with a dancer.

Yet there are limits which the designer cannot transgress.
Then the dancers' complaints become legitimate. When, for example, headgear or head ornaments are too heavy and considerably
restrict the visual field, the dancer's sense of equilibrium may be
impaired. Oft-repeated rehearsals alone can remedy this evil.

It is frequently said that the costume should permit every
possible movement of the body—an idea all the more dangerous
as it is shared by many dance critics. The choreographer argues
that the dancer's legs and arms are his organs of expression, as
the throat is the organ of the singer. He may protest to the designer, "A singer does not adorn his throat with velvet and tas-

sels. Why should the dancer adorn his legs and arms?" One
could reply that not only the arms and legs but the whole body
is the dancer's expressive medium. Therefore, if arms and legs
ought to be bare, why not perform completely naked?

Dance, of course, has exhibitionistic connotations, and exhibitionism might imply denudation. Where the erotic element
should be underlined, nakedness is nefarious. The talent of a
Joan Junyer is needed to bring upon the stage girls with bare
breasts, or costumes suggesting bare breasts, such as were designed
for *The Minotaur*. The cancan can teach us a lot about eroticism.
From the music halls it has grown into French folklore and will
continue to fascinate the public. The discretion that underlies

the eroticism of the cancan has its opposite in the nude dance (*Nackttanz*) so fashionable in the Germany of the 1920s. Serious efforts were made to promote the nude dance, as taught for instance at the Menzendieck school which ultimately failed. Today the nude dance mania has disappeared. But exhibitionism is an important element in any dance performance. The stage designer must remember that the audience identifies itself with the dancers upon the stage, thus partaking in the performance. He must find the means to stimulate this participation. Moral objections are pointless; there is neither moral nor immoral art, but only good or bad art.

"Loose" material, flowing veils may give free scope to every movement, and yet this is not what I would call an ideal solution. They confine costume to the passive role of the "adaptable," whereas, in my opinion, the costume has an *active* function. It should underline, exaggerate, clarify and mystify. There is no need for the costume to permit every possible movement, because the choreographer will not use every possible movement for his composition.

This we learn from the art dancers of various nations. The Balinese elongate their fingernails with metal blades. They are not able to join hands with other dancers; consequently they avoid this gesture in their dances. Certain Japanese No and Kabuki players are harnessed with stiff materials in geometric shapes. Such costumes allow only well defined movements prescribed by tradition, while others are rendered impossible. Actors and dancers of ancient Greece wore buskins, footwear constructed to give them supernatural size, which made them walk majestically and slowly. Why then should our costumes be designed to allow more movements than are necessary for a particular composition? Before starting his work, does a painter prepare an immense canvas which would permit him to execute a painting of any size, even if the result is to be a miniature, an infinitesimal part of this colossal canvas? Is it not more logical to plan a specific size for each art work and make the canvas to measure?

The planning of the costume is a subtle affair, as is every form of artistic collaboration. The designer may surprise the choreographer with costume sketches which appeal to him so much that he wants to build his dance composition upon the designer's costume ideas. Even attitudes of the sketched figurines may give stimulus to the choreographer. On the other hand, the designer may get his inspiration from hearing the musical score or from watching dance rehearsals.

Costumes can express symbolic ideas connected with the dance composition, or carry the spectator further into the realm of the imaginary. It is not necessary for the costume or set to fit the choreographic idea as a glove fits the hand. It can deepen and amplify ideas which the dance composition desires to express. For my costumes I like to use symbols, symbols in the form of real objects, not stylizations; real eggs, candles, cymbals, umbrellas, facsimile hands, dice, daggers and all those objects which startled us when we played lotto in our childhood.

These basic symbols cause a chord to resound in our unconscious; they free the spectator's memories and create a dreamlike mood, an expectation of the marvelous. The shock element properly used brings about displacement or alienation. When placed where they do not belong, objects with or without immediate symbolic meaning may create a poetic mood. Surrealists have made ample use of this means: Dali's *Giraffe Aflame*, Man Ray's *Lips in the Sky*, Duchamp's *Mona Lisa with Mustache*, my own *Guitar with Epaulettes*. Such displacements can be effectively used not only for costumes and sets, but also as choreographic ideas. Would it not be an interesting shock effect for a ballerina executing classic steps to be suddenly attracted by a chalk drawing on the floor and fall into a hopscotch? Or imagine a whole corps de ballet performing in strait jackets!

Blending is in utter contrast to alienation. The current opinion among stage designers is that the costumes should blend, blend with one another as well as with the backdrop. I am strongly against this idea. It induces one to mingle every kind of "tasteful" halftone, sweet grays and brown drabs which are supposed to caress the eye but actually are so saccharine that the satiated pub-

lic is not stimulated by color to participate in the performance. True taste and creativeness speak more bluntly. It is astounding how many straightforward colors and sharp forms the stage can absorb.

I have used bright reds, sharp yellows, blue and purple, etc., in front of a drop painted entirely in gray tones. The brutal separation of gray background and vividly colored costumes did not disrupt the stage image. On the contrary, the tension thus created heightened the audience's awareness of the dance. Other designers have used bright-colored costumes against a very colorful background, as Francés did in Stravinsky's *Renard*. He successfully circumnavigated the danger of the bright costume colors fusing with those of the set into a blurred image completely deadening the dance composition.

There is a further difficulty of which the designer must be aware. He is expected to design costumes as "impersonal" as possible and sets adaptable to various stages. When watching rehearsals he is inclined to adapt his costumes to the physical characteristics of the performers—to "draw" the costumes upon each individual. Dancers are frequently substituted, but not necessarily the costume design. Consequently, to suit the individuality of any dancer the design must remain impersonal. Although this may not be ideal it is necessary. Similarly, since companies tour the country with them, sets must be flexible enough for use on stages of various size.

Such concessions should not prevent the stage designer from producing new ideas. There are many modes of expression and their values depend entirely upon the inventiveness and creative force of the artist.

THE DANCE IN RELATION

TO THE OTHER ARTS

*Between the adjective possible and
the adjective impossible the mime has made his choice; he has chosen
the adjective impossible. It is in the impossible that he lives; it is the
impossible he does.* —THÉODORE DE BANVILLE

ANGNA ENTERS

The Dance and Pantomime: MIMESIS AND IMAGE

IMESIS IS that form of theater in which a dramatist-
actor delineates characters of his own creation with
or without speech. The mime is not an imitator. He
enlarges, emphasizes, particularizes, accents, comments upon the
character he portrays; he is a dramatist who portrays his characters. Mimesis, or pantomime, is universal and in the classic
line because of an elasticity which can incorporate dance or any
other theater forms required for the realization of images within
the dramatist-performer's vision.

It is as though images, either in the creator's memory or in
flashes of vision, acting as catalytic agents in relation to aspects
of man's life in the world, suddenly decide to have a being of
their own. Then the creator as performer has to release these
images to take their own form, using whatever theater and other
art forms are necessary to their realization.

In that sense, these images-become-characters are symbols,
symbols natural to the reality of performer and audience; characters who are our brothers and sisters in whatever time, place
and theme—in the sense, say, that Madame Bovary is a character

created by Flaubert. Characters, that is, created to speak for themselves.

For this reason, it is preferable that the mime be the creator and integrator of all the arts essential to the fused crystallization of, and comment implicit in, his image's form: costume, setting, lighting, even music. For costume, whether contemporary, medieval or antique, is part of the image's design, with the other component parts fused into the whole composition. Thus, the costume is sometimes the accent as the key or clue to the mode, manner, theme, form, character. So with setting, lighting, music.

This is, of course, one mime's approach to the presentation of images of men and women in characteristic personal moments of their being in contrapuntal relation to a particular period in time, to crystallize a kind of similarity in human behavior down through the ages:

To give personal form to a general experience.

To make the present visible by using it to telescope what was present in the past. It was necessary to see the past through the present, for we see what has been in terms of our own being in the present.

Thus the past would emerge as present, disclosing the essential continuity of the nature of man. The modes, manners and rhythms were merely masks beneath which were the old familiar universal faces of man and woman.

A mode or manner can be concrete as a stone, which when dropped in the sea of human behavior makes a whirlpool in which is swallowed a whole generation and, in time, a civilization.

Yet there always is a thread in that past. In painting it is "the classic line" which always emerges as "modern." And in modes and manners it is always the human behavior which emerges as contemporary.

Topical telescoping of the past in terms of the present was characteristic of the Greek dramatists when they told the sacred myths in terms of their own time. Very faint was the allegory in their references to the political tyrannies, social foibles and idiocies of their own day.

Using a past period as a mirror one might succeed in seeing—showing—one's own time.*

Thus the mime is concerned not only with characters who are tragic or beautiful or noble or comic or pitiful, but also with the *apparently* trivial. Trivial moments in a human being's life, or *seemingly* trivial aspects of it, are sometimes the most significant of character, education and social period. There are trivial moments in a spinster's life quite as tragic, and not only to her, as an Isolde's death or a Cassandra's doom.

The arts are of life; they are not created in a non-objective vacuum. There are no arts without man, and his images are the touchstones of the art forms through which he communicates his vision of the world.

Despite all the definitions and the credos, what remains as the essence of every composition in any art is the image—the image of a color, a combination of color, form, line and space; the image of a sound, or a combination of sounds with silences and rhythms, the image of a smile—one which opens a world in which character is seen, and, through the character, his world.

Many aspects of life seem to me untouched in the theater or in the novel, because in a sense there are no words which quite convey these glints of a smile or a frown, these nuances of human behavior which are the subtle halftones in the scale of human emotions. My feeling was that mime best expressed those images characteristic of human physical movement and expression in the waking and dream states; those nuances of sensation, manners and mannerisms, languors, intonations of expression—the list is endless—which change their form when crystallised in poetry and drama.

---

* Angna Enters, *Silly Girl*, first part of *A Portrait of Personal Remembrance*, self-illustrated. Copyright 1944 by Angna Enters.

I do not impute superiority to mime. Far from it. I merely maintain that mime is a kind of abstract crystallisation of phases and transitions—before your eyes—of life for which words are merely descriptions, however illuminating.*

The description then of mime must be in its own terms, rather than in those of poetry, drama or prose.

For in this theater of pantomime and dance which I am discussing the mime is always his own dramatist. And he is concerned with those aspects of life which are best communicable through mime.

The first mimes were their own dramatists, and later the first dramatic poets were their own mimes.

Mime is the oldest and youngest form of dramatic expression, and the most generally universal. It lends itself in the theater to every form, even to those arts which are not directly of the theater, like some forms of musical conducting; yet it retains its own form. All human beings are more mimes than dancers, in the way in which they walk and smile and weep and dance; in the way in which they tell stories, imitating themselves or their friends or even imaginary characters in some anecdote.

It is *natural* for man to mime, and dance is part of his miming, as making poems and music and drawings are.

Mime, or pantomime, is not the only best means of theater expression. Mime is only best for that expression for which there are no words, or for which too many words would be required.

Yet though pantomime is the oldest and most universal form of theater communication, less is known about it today by most performers than about any other technical medium of their profession.

One reason for this lack is that there is no formula for

---

* Angna Enters, *First Person Plural*, A Chronicle of Self-Education, self-illustrated. Copyright 1937 by Angna Enters.

the learning of mime as there is for dance forms. The learning of dance forms is of no aid in performing as a mime.

There is a limit to what the human form is capable of in physical movement. As the "revolutionary" dance pattern becomes more common, it not only loses its appeal as an unusual design but it takes on an absurd, dated aspect.

Besides, it takes more than an eccentric style in any form to make a creative artist. Picasso is not an important figure because some of his many styles may seem extreme. In a creative work one could take away the seemingly eccentric style—and the form and meaning would remain. In the pseudo the so-called original style is actually a mannerism—for the pseudo-artist has nothing to say and is saying it with the most elaborate obscurity, shrieking all the while: "Don't you dare question me, because I am modern!"

Today, the persistent notion that pantomime is exclusively a matter of gestures and facial expressions meaning certain definite words has grown out of dance's attempt to form an alphabet of literal physical expressions to be used in addition to dance techniques. The failure of this union finally has led to the use of spoken lines—by narrators or dancers—with much high-toned palaver about "a new art." Actually, it is a hoary theatric device.

Gesture seems to have been first with the Greeks in mime and pantomime—the general distinction between mime and pantomime here being that in the former words were, at first, used. But the height of this form—mime—was reached, according to the Greek and Roman commentators, when spoken language no longer was used. Dance movement was subordinate in the highest dramatic forms. The Greek was never a professional dancer in our sense. His professionals were mimes and used dance movements only when necessary. Sometimes dance predominated; more often, mime.

The time came when a Greek mime-dancer was expected to "dance with his eyes." And when we reach Quintilian he grows eloquent concerning the nuances of which gesture without speech is capable. All of the strangulated restrictions of "abstract" dance in the contemporary sense were unknown. Any movement was permissible, provided the combination of movements and gestures communicated an intellectual and spiritual whole.

The Greeks were not interested in form without content— that is, recognizable subject matter in the representational sense. Greek audiences did not expect a performer to enact "set" dances but to elaborate on them. They expected invention and intellectual comment from the professional performer. And they expected the mime to accent the telling of his myth-image—to be a political and social commentator. When he enacted the sacred or profane myths, the mime had to do so clearly and without obscurity.

Articulateness, however, is not a formula. The "classical" school of acting and dancing probably came into being as a last desperate resort due to inability of actors and dancers—I mean those of the past several centuries—to create or recreate the character and period of each play or ballet. This stylized form of expression, whether in ballet, interpretive "classic" or "modern" dancing, "classical" acting or emotionalized gymnastic gyrations in the "Greek" (or neo-primitive) manner, is always the result of learned arbitrarily formulized expressions instead of movements natural to the human body. The easiest way to avoid creating a composition is to think up a formula to apply to all problems. The obvious stylized line is the easiest line to make in drawing, or in dance.

With the rise of the literary theater, in which actors were supplied lines which required little else than their recitation, pantomime settled into the various forms of the unliterary theater— from the commedia dell'arte down through the circus and vaudeville of our own day. The performers in these unliterary theaters retained and developed the faculty of devising their own theater material, or making contributed material their own, and through it achieving a communication with their audiences.

I mean mimes who created their own character, and form of presentation for that character—such as Debureau, Toto, Grock, the Frattelinis, Rich Hayes, Mr. Joe Jackson, Nervo and Knocks, Yvette Guilbert, the Arnaut Brothers, and of course the inimitable Chaplin.

Delsarte, in France, had tried to free the French theater of its stylized form but had only achieved a formula himself. His formula, adapted to opera, theater and dance, succeeded in all but killing mime as a legitimate form of theater expression.

By the first quarter of the twentieth century, mime, as a theater form, had as its only practitioners clowns, mimics and Chaplin. In the dance, except for certain "symbols" left over from Delsarte, mime was frowned upon as the lowest form of expression. In fact, pantomime was denied any place in the dance's sacred grove; it was a twin devil along with "literature." Is it possible that acceptance by audiences of a mime-theater which came into being in 1924 had something to do with the extraordinary about-face of the "pure" dance into every form of theatricalism plus literature?

Of course, even before 1924 there already had been new evidences of a resurgence of mime as a form. With the advent of the Russian Ballet certain great performers again made mime history. Bolm, Nijinsky, Massine—and, in the theater, Feodor Chaliapin.

For, as in the instance of Chaliapin, there were and are other figures in the theater who used mime together with words or song to delineate character, but for reasons of brevity these notes on mime must be concerned only with those who perform without speech.

The mime, incidentally, does not sink into copying or impersonating, which is mimicry. Mime and mimicry are confused in the public mind, but there is no more resemblance between them than between painting and photography. Chaplin is a mime, but those who imitate him are mimics. A mime does not copy another person's actions but invents characters who have their own life, a life quite apart from their creator.

Lucian brilliantly summarized the ideal toward which the mime can only strive, arduously and endlessly:

> You will find that his is no easy profession, not lightly to be undertaken; requiring as it does the highest standard of culture . . . and involving a knowledge of not only music, but of rhythm and metre . . . the exposition of human character and human passion claims a share of its attention. Nor can it dispense with the painter's and sculptor's arts . . . in its close observance of the harmonious proportions that these teach. But above all Mnemosyne and her daughter Polphymnia, must be propitiated by an art that would remember all things. The pantomime must know all "that is, that was, that shall be"; nothing must escape his ready memory. Faithfully to represent his subject, adequately to express his own conceptions, to make plain all that might be obscure;—these are the first essentials of the mime.

Unlike the formulized dance there is no key set of movements of life expressions for mime. Acrobatic virtuosity plays no part in its projection. Mime is too flowing and subtle, too personal a medium to be imprisoned in a system. Of all the theater forms, mime is most dependent upon the performer for its form; it is the projection of his image. In that projection there must be, above all, a clear, direct conception of what is to be expressed. There can be no nebulous strivings for decorative effect.

In the theater the outward form is projected out into the visual sight line of the audience. In a sense, it is like an architectural drawing in line perspective, with color accents added. Thus, mime is not a theatrical form in which a series of steps and gestures are combined in a variety of movements to make what is generally called a dance.

Because of its nuances of meaning, mime requires in its pro-

jection a progression of many forms, some in movement, some
non-movements, silences and pauses, all in timed rhythm similar
to poetry or song. Actually, mime is very like poetry and song in
its composition and presentation.

Performed by a group it necessarily becomes a stylized skeleton to hold together the dancers. A kind of opera libretto. I do
not mean that an opera libretto is not a legitimate device but
merely that mime does not reach the height of its possibilities
in group performance because pantomime is an individual expression and cannot be taught by a director or choreographer.

Stanislavsky, the director of the Moscow Art Theater, realized this in his efforts to make mimes of his actors. I believe it
may be said that he was the most successful of any theater director
in this medium. But the test of the players of the Moscow Art
Theater would have been their ability to project the characters
they were portraying without the use of words—of Chekhov or
Pushkin.

How then, if mime cannot be taught, is it to be learned?

It would be possible, to be sure, to work out a syllabus, but
its value would be relative. For one thing it would be personal
to the mime who evolved it, a method of working personal, that
is, to one certain performer and, as a result, probably unsuited to
others. Chaplin's mime is personal to him and that is why no
one has been able to do what he does. His mime has been plagia-
rized over and over again, but these plagiarisms have failed because they are copies—copies of the outside of a form personal to
an originator. Many actors have worked with and been directed
by Chaplin; it hasn't helped them.

For what is good for one artist need not apply to another
and may only set him on the wrong road to finding himself. This
is not a popular opinion, but it is a fact and awareness of it
may be the means of making an individual performer or just an

Study for beginning of a gesture.

impressionable pupil-member of a group. No one can teach another how to think.

Schools, and theories taught in them, are the result of art forms and not vice versa. Schools and theories are devised by those who try to discover what it is that makes a given art expression. But they are traps except when a worker in the arts discovers a form for himself through his own experimentation. And this form, because personal, is not transferable.

The young student with a yearning to crystallize his unformed images goes naturally to a teacher he believes can show him the way. Therein lies his first pitfall. If he falls into the downy pit of following his teacher he will be a good pupil but a lost artist. If he questions or discards or accepts only what he can use he will be a disobedient pupil but he is on his way to individual expression.

In the arts, the real culprits are not those who break the "rules" and ignore the "classifications" but those who make them.

Because of the nature of its form, no individual expression has suffered more from rules and classifications than has the dance in which some teachers and performers-become-teachers have tried to impose formulas as "the" dance. Those teachers and certain pundits have unloosed a murky morass of aesthetic gibberish, clichés in which muscular gyrations are entangled in "symbolism."

No one worker in the arts can create universal symbols. He can only crystallize the experience all men and women are heir to. A performer or artist never lived who by himself created universal symbols, but artists always have *recognized* the symbols, and each one gave the symbols his form, so that in his particular form you can see the universals. The modern art movement of the past hundred years has made ridiculously easy the foisting of much that is incomprehensible. Incomprehensible because too many arcane boys and girls have nothing to say. But one is an artist only if able to express in concrete form the image in his

vision. What is "subjective," "unconscious," "beneath the surface," "symbolical," must be made objective, especially in the
theater. Symbols are the result of the experience of the race.
Symbols are communicable or they are not symbols. And it makes
no difference what devices are used to bolster unintelligible symbols—whether these are "functional" stage sets or masks.

In its use of "symbols," the puppet or mask theater has had
its ups and downs. Its downs because after a time audiences tire
of stylized expressions—the mask's bloodlessness, whether an actual mask is used or not—and long for communication between
living human beings, for *living* image-ideas which are part of their
own experience.

In the ability to do this, mime is supreme.

That dancers, both ballet and "modern," recognize this is
evident in the change that is taking place. In the past twenty
years there has been a complete reversal, especially by the "pure"
dance, in the direction of mime. Even Isadora Duncan, towards
the end of her life, planned to venture into mime, perhaps because she sensed that movement without it could lead only to
a blind alley.

For, even without the simplest mime, dance soon palls. To
say that dance must be "pure" or need not mean anything is
nonsense, for the body itself is a symbol of its own meaning.

Leonardo da Vinci said it with his customary clairvoyance:

O mathematician, throw light on this error. The spirit has not
voice, for, where there is voice there is a body, and where there is
a body there is occupation of space which prevents the eyes from
seeing things beyond the space, consequently this body of itself
fills the whole surrounding air, that is by its images.

The approach to mime is just the opposite of formalized
dance because in mime self must be forgotten. Self-expression and
mime are at contrary poles.

Because of this there can be no extraneous movements or

gestures for sake of pattern. There can be no fill-in movements separating the continuity of thought in the composition of the image.

In *First Person Plural* I wrote that "dance is composition in movement." This is equally true of mime, but in mime the movement is often seemingly static, is frequently composed of non-movements.

Mime's image-themes should be projected with reservation and good taste; by good taste I mean the appropriateness of each gesture, expression, movement, of the character being composed in the audience's vision. Reserve indeed is one of the prime requisites of pantomime. Florid expressions of the personal emotions of the performer have no place in mime. Thus where mime is used as an adjunct to a set dance form or style it, too, is best in a stylized form.

While it is partly true that it does not matter how one gets one's effects in the theater, this does not mean that a deficiency in one expression should be bolstered by a pastiche of others, any more than in painting a lack of line or form is remedied by spatterings of color. To illustrate, a background of words should not be necessary to convey a pantomime which, I repeat, in its purest form deals with those expressions for which words are unnecessary. There are exceptions, to be sure, especially when the work is a form created wholly by one artist, but the lapsing of extraneous non-related forms, one upon the other, results in chaos.

Clarity is another requisite in mime. It is easier to pretend depth of meaning by obscure pattern, bolstered with poetics, than to achieve simple statement.

To sum up: The mime does not present himself but his idea-image. For this exposition the mime must use recognizable symbols.

These are performed in measured rhythm called "timing"— a rhythm established between himself as performer and himself as audience. If his composition is interrupted by effort on his part to force meaning on the audience in that black cavern beyond his frame, then his continuity, like a spider's web spanning two points, is broken and he falls into an abyss of confusion.

Therefore physical acrobatics and technical showing-off must be foregone. A too strenuous projection coarsens mime as a medium of expression. Leaps, stretches, whirls or contortions—those automatic standbys of dance—may make momentarily exciting and decorative patterns but, like all decorative arts, their patterns, repeated, soon pall. And then another stunt must be devised. Art is not a stunt.

In the Van Gogh still life "Grapes and Apples" one sees the accents which are that painter's endeavor to find for himself the form of his expression. Because of the violence of his strokes this is clearer in Van Gogh's work than in more subtle painters. The bold pattern is not made for the spectator but is the inevitable result of the artist's search for the realization of his own image. And this too is a difference, in painting, between the academic—no matter how "modern" that academic approach is—and the original, the artist and the stuntist.

The same is true in mime. A theater composition in mime must be recreated for oneself at every performance. The accents must be inherent in this re-creation, and not be merely flash to impress onlookers with difficult stunts. The arts are a communication between human beings. Mime is one of those communications, a magic cord of illumination through which the performer transmits images of our world into the past become present. Mime is of the "classic line"—the classic line which is the true and perfect and variable line of life no matter how it is employed. Like a child learning to walk one must find it for oneself.

La Meri, the uncontested queen of the ethnological dance, in the Farruca (Ritual Fire Dance) from her setting of *El Amor Brujo*. Photograph by George Philcox. *Courtesy of Dance Magazine.*

In the late twenties Doris Humphrey and Charles Weidman broke away from the Denishawn dance group and became the foremost pioneers of the modern dance. Today America claims Charles Weidman as her great dance pantomime and Doris Humphrey as her leading choreographer and teacher. *Courtesy of Charles Weidman.*

Helen Tamiris, next to Martha Graham and Doris Humphrey the most daring and pioneering dancer of the twenties. She has greatly helped to bring Broadway and the dance together. Here we see two of her dances from the musical *Touch and Go*: (*top*) "Mr. Brown and Miss Dupree"; (*bottom*) "Hamlet." *Photographs by Eileen Darby-Graphic House, Inc. Courtesy of Dance Magazine.*

(top) Hanya Holm, a perfect integration of European background with the spirit that is America, choreographing a Broadway musical with Ray Harrison as leading male dancer. *Photograph by Ed Carswell-Graphic House, Inc. Courtesy of Dance Magazine.*
(bottom) "Exercises in Technique" in a class given by José Limón in the Connecticut College gymnasium. *Photograph by Philip L. Carpenter. Courtesy of Dance Magazine.*

The filming of a scene may be likened to the construction of a sentence. If you like you can regard the standard long-shot of an object as the noun. Pans, changes of angle and distance, trick-shots or what you will, these are the verbs, adjectives, adverbs, prepositions, and so on which when put all together make up a coherent sentence. —BASIL WRIGHT

MARY JANE HUNGERFORD

Technological Progress and the Dance:
THE DANCE IN THE MOVIES

THE ART of motion pictures and the art of dance, both familiar to everyone, are equally difficult to define in precise terms. Within each there seems to be a dualism, a division according to purpose. Dance is done sometimes for the purpose of recreation and fun, sometimes for spectacle and communication.

Even the most cursory observation of film production reveals that the entire field is dominated by two main approaches: the fiction-entertainment film, promoted internationally by commercial interests; and the documentary-educational film, promoted by individuals and organizations interested in social reform, visual education and cultural dissemination.*

---

* From an unpublished article by Maya Deren, "Cinema as an Art Form."

97

CINEMA

Artistic Levels

There appear to be degrees of expressive creativity in motion picture production. The lowest level consists of simply selecting something which moves, choosing a lens speed for the camera and a point of view from which to shoot the action. Most films of the works of stage choreographers are on this level.

The next level involves causing action to be performed especially for the camera, photographing it many times in an effort to register the best performance from the best points of view, and selecting and combining the most effective shots into a continuity. Much of the Hollywood output falls into this category, although some ethnic and social dances from the preceding one are used.

The ultimate development requires a complete conception aimed at the communication of an idea or feeling through the expressive use of all the above techniques. This level is especially difficult to attain in a medium which involves the efforts of several individuals.

The method of cinema is by nature complex. On the colossal Hollywood scale its complexity is overwhelming. Attaining the highest level of artistic expression in the film medium is probably easier when two or three people work together with sixteen-millimeter equipment and a modest budget than on the scale on which the major production companies operate.

Movement Types

The motion picture, like dance, consists of movement in time and space used expressively, but it is movement of a much more complicated sort. As Nicoll points out, cinema movement is of four kinds.*

---

* Allardyce Nicoll, *Film and Theatre*, Chapter Three, "Methods of Cinema," New York, 1936.

The first is the movement which takes place before the camera eye. This includes the actions of human beings, possibly dance, together with any other movement in the field of vision. It may be that of nature such as rain falling, wind blowing, grass and trees or clothing and hair, smoke rising or fire burning. It may be the motion of some vehicle or machine, the action of animals or combinations of all these things.

A second type of movement is that of the camera in space. Changes in camera angle have the effect of motion on the part of the observer. Abrupt changes are achieved by cuts, gradual ones by panning, tilting or trucking. This type of motion may be used by itself as when the camera moves about to show the contents of a room in which there is nothing moving. Or it may be used in combination with the first type as is the case when a dancer is followed and kept within the frame.

The third type of movement is involved in the manipulation of the photographic and developing apparatus. The speed of shooting may be increased or decreased, producing the opposite effect when the film is projected at the standard rate.

Slow motion has been used occasionally for dance sequences. In the picture *Irene* (RKO, 1940) Anna Neagle does a dance of longing on a terrace at night in a long, filmy gown. The dance opens in slow motion with powerful effect which is lost when a more normal speed is resumed. The man who loves her comes upon her dancing there. Unaware of his gaze she continues to dance. The slow motion has the effect of making her dance an idealization seen through his eyes.

Extreme speeding up, often used symbolically to indicate the passage of time, for example the burning of a cigarette or fading of a leaf or flower condensed in time, is achieved by printing a series of stills taken a fixed time apart. This is a form of natural animation. By the same method any inanimate object can be made to move at any desired rate of speed. Not long ago an amateur made a color film in sixteen millimeter in which four pillows do a sort of square dance using this technique.

Unique expressive quality is possible through relating the speed of the camera to the speed of the action being photographed. Certain movement is produced only by fast action, for example the reaction of a skirt or long hair to a jump or turn. Shooting this action, performed with abnormal rapidity, at an accelerated camera speed for slow motion compensation, registers a sequence of movement with normal speed but with an abnormal quality.

Reversal is achieved through turning the camera upside down or cutting in a given sequence backward. Incredible physical feats are possible through this means. Many have seen the newsreel joke of having the diver return to his perch, which is accomplished by the use of reversal. Extremely slow motion can be accomplished by printing each frame two or three times. Startling effects can be produced by freezing frames, using a split screen and similar devices.

The fourth type of movement depends upon the linkage of the separate shots. Shots vary in duration and their succession may thus proceed at different rates. The duration of a shot controls the pace and rhythm of film continuity together with the type of transition. In montage the shots are very brief and follow one another in rapid succession with no transitional device, sometimes even with overlap. The dissolve, fade and mix may take place very slowly or more rapidly and thus influence the rhythm of this fourth type of movement.

The art of cinema, involving these four types of movement separately and in an infinite number of interrelations, is clearly an extremely intricate form of expression. A dance film cannot avoid concern with them and can scarcely be successful unless the persons responsible for it are reasonably familiar with each of the four types of cinema movement and with the whole realm of dance in addition.

DANCE AND CINEMA

Relation to Drama

The arts of cinema and dance are probably more closely related than cinema and stage drama. The essence of stage drama is objectivity. The essence of screen drama is subjectivity. Cinema is constructed much the way the mind works. Its form resembles observation, memory and imagination. The strength of the film lies in fantasy and psychological insight. Are not these also the essence of expressional dance?

Time and space dimensions of the stage drama are actual and cannot readily be abridged or extended. In film art the camera controls time and space. One sequence may be composed of shots photographed hundreds of miles apart or with lapses of many days between bits of action. On the stage, action must be artificially localized in time and space.

Time

Five minutes on the screen may cover five decades on the calendar. In a dance, two crossings of the stage may represent many miles of travel, as in the fugitive sequence in *Brigadoon*. Things happening simultaneously can be shown one at a time in a film. It is awkward if at all possible on the stage. Large lapses of time are believable only between acts or scenes. Quick shifts back and forth between different locations present problems of almost prohibitive sort in the live theater. Much action must be indicated through dialogue on the stage which can be shown directly on the screen.

Space

The camera further can alter size at will. It controls the selection of detail and the focus of attention without resorting to the subterfuges of facing, pointing, spot lighting or dialogue references on which the stage drama must rely. This control of spatial and temporal magnitude and concentration is a major distinction between film and stage. In this area the film can broaden the scope of dance art immeasurably.

Summary of Similarities

Dance and cinema art, then, are very closely related. The purpose of each is communication, the content dramatic, the substance is movement, the method uniquely psychological. Cinema combines visual and auditory symbols, using sound, color, light, movement and language expressively. Except for language and auditory symbols so does dance, and even this distinction recedes if we include new developments in combining dance with prose and poetry.

Differences

There are nevertheless some differences between these two arts. Cinema is broader in scope and more complex than dance. Dance belongs to the first type of movement of which cinema is compounded. When expressional dance is used in a motion picture its function is similar to that of other movement registered by the camera. The actions of characters are not always realistic or natural. They are often selected and arranged or stylized for symbolic effect. This is the case with most of Chaplin's work. It is also true of much of Disney's work in the field of synthetic animation.

Abstraction, the Meeting Ground

Clearly there are degrees of abstraction in both arts. When film is most abstract it is closest to dance. If the cinema frees itself of words entirely and uses only images and sounds, it is difficult to distinguish it from dance. Maya Deren's silent film *At Land* is a case in point. When dance is least abstract it is closest to pantomime of which the film makes liberal use.

Spectacle, whether of a religious, military or social sort, brings dance and film expression to a point of virtual unity. Stylized expressive movement such as that characteristic of Chaplin and Fairbanks in the silent films is the individual counterpart of spectacle and is sometimes synonymous with dance.

Relation to Music

Both dancing and motion pictures utilize sounds and musical accompaniment in comparable fashion. Few persons are kinesthetically sensitive enough to grasp the rhythmic form of movement through the visual channel alone.

The film does not use music throughout. But when it does not, it uses natural sounds produced by visible action, or symbolic sound, or else it uses silence expressively. Recently a number of dance artists have performed parts of dances without accompaniment except for the sounds made by footfalls or the rustling of a costume material.

Sometimes a director achieves a greater effect through a-synchronism or non-coincidence of sight and sound. A simple illustration is showing the listener with a bit of dialogue, instead of the speaker. In creating a dance accompaniment an emphasis on contrast and counterpoint with a minimum of parallelism is used and recommended by most composers.

A-synchronism is of great artistic value in cinema dancing, giving an enormous advantage over stage dance. As Eisenstein is aware, "Art begins only at that moment of synchronization when the natural connection between the object and its sound is not merely recorded, but is dictated solely by the demands of the expressive work in progress."* The noise of landing from a great jump, the patter of hard-toe ballet slippers and the labored breathing of dancers can be eliminated entirely from the sound track.

---

* Sergei Eisenstein, *The Film Sense.* Copyright 1942 by Harcourt, Brace and Company.

Technical Possibilities

Dance artists have much to gain through embracing the film medium. A large amount of artistic expression is possible by use of special processing and cutting techniques and by the manipulation of the camera. These, however, should not be devised after the choreographer has created the movement. The movement of the dancers to be registered by the camera, and the cinematic movement of the other three types, should all be part of the original conception. Even without adventuring beyond the most common cinematic devices, a dancer can create works in this new medium which are free of many limitations contingent upon human performance on a stage.

Some of the possibilities should be mentioned. Continuous action of a vigor and duration impossible to sustain in a stage performance is one of the most obvious. A costume or make-up can be changed gradually before your eyes without the necessity of an exit, lapse of time and another entrance. Limitless elevation and soundless landings, identical repetition and absolute perfection of performance, magnification of detail by means of slow motion and close-ups are a few other techniques that are well known. Attitudes for recovering balance and preparations can be eliminated or exaggerated for special effect. A movement may begin in one environment and end in another.

This is a device exploited by Maya Deren to a far greater extent than by Hollywood so far. In her first dance film she does it by an apparently continuous pan to the left, approximating a complete circle. The dancer is discovered and passed four different times, each time somewhat nearer the camera. The spiral movement which he begins on his first appearance continues uninterrupted from where it left off each time he is seen. Its tempo is consciously related to that of the turning camera.

When the film is properly cut so that the movement is

matched exactly, the integrity of a movement itself can bring together different environments in a significant relationship. Later in the same film the dancer does an idealized leap, taking off from the floor of a room, sustaining the elevation over twenty seconds, and landing out of doors. It was constructed actually by photographing in reverse the dancer's drop from a height into a spiral fall, with purposeful manipulation of camera speed and angle, expert editing and cutting.

Perhaps accidentally synthetic animation has also made a significant contribution to the art of dance. Since it has shown the film medium to be ideal for the creation of choreography based upon impersonation of animals or the presentation of natural or mechanical movement, there ceases to be any excuse for human beings to try to do bird, wave or machine dances. For a long time the art of dance has suffered from a concern with such subject matter. It can now be relegated to primitive ritual whence it sprang and where it still belongs. The limits of our contemporary stage dance are thus more clearly defined. Doubtless it can achieve greater refinement of expression through concerning itself with truly human movement adapted to theater space and conventions.

Cinedance

At the same time a new art form has begun to emerge, born of the union of dance and cinema arts, which offers a challenge to the uninhibited choreographer. I have coined the word *cinedance* to designate it. The fundamental characteristic which distinguishes a cinedance is its cinematic quality. It is constructed of a series of shots of expressive movement, usually somewhat stylized to achieve a rhythmic and spatial coherence. The choreographer, relying upon a unique type of mental imagery, plans the content of each shot. He considers the camera placement, lens type, shooting speed, transitional devices and related cinematic techniques quite as carefully as the dance movements and costumes.

A cinedance cannot be reproduced by photographing a dance conceived in a stage-like space, no matter how extensive or how irregularly shaped, and regardless of how many times the camera angle is changed. Furthermore, a cinedance could not possibly be performed on any theater stage. It is so completely cinematic in its form that it can exist only by way of the projected film. When a cinedance is used in a feature production it is an integral part of the structure of the photoplay and in no way "incidental."

CONTRIBUTION OF DANCE TO CINEMA

Incidental Dancing

There is no doubt that the art of dance can contribute and has contributed enormously to the art of cinema. We shall list the chief contributions briefly. Bulking largest are incidental dances of four types: social, ethnic, theatrical and expressional.

Incidental dances at minimum lend atmosphere and production value to any sort of motion picture. Any dance adds variety of costume and of the rhythmic and spatial patterns of movement.

Social dances are used to establish place, period and social level, personal characteristics and mood. Both social and ethnic dances can explain some of the values basic to cultures different from ours. They can illuminate the motives of different kinds of people under different circumstances.

Theatrical dancing serves chiefly to provide splendor to awe the spectator. Elaborate settings, breathtaking numbers of beautiful girls and handsome men, gorgeous costumes and richly orchestrated music are at least a feast for the senses. At best, theatrical dancing evokes in addition an emotional response to forms which have aesthetic quality, sometimes even expressive overtones.

Absolute perfection, even virtuosity, is almost commonplace in both theatrical and expressional dancing in the entertainment feature film. However, in expressional dances splendor of production and proficiency of performance are beginning to be placed where they belong; that is, secondary to developing the plot of the drama and integrating the dance structure with the architecture of the photoplay. Thus the cinema follows the stage trend started with *Oklahoma!*

Tap, toe, character, acrobatic, adagio and exhibition ballroom dances are the inevitable components of stories about people who work in or attend theaters and night clubs. Ballroom and square dancing are essential features of social intercourse in America and as such are usually required where social gatherings are involved.

Ethnic dances provide part of the atmosphere for pictures set in foreign countries. They are beginning to exhibit honesty and simplicity with greater frequency. Audiences already surfeited with the sensuous writhings of scantily clad stock girls are forcing Hollywood to a more responsible approach to the treatment of foreign backgrounds.

Fantasy

Fantasy has most often given expressional dance its opportunity to function in feature films. The motion picture is the ideal medium for fantasy because of its power to create a convincing illusion. Fantasy is a logical link between the arts of dance and cinema, because it discards colloquial movement and dialogue for stylized movement and manipulation of the cinematic tools.

There are degrees of fantasy, however, and the most expressive dance art is possible when the freest fancy is required. For example, in a feature based upon a musical subject there are frequent opportunities. Movie audiences long ago tired of being shown close-ups of instruments, players, conductors and the dental equipment of vocalists.

Ideally some substitute should be found and a variety of devices have been tried. Best of all, however, beyond the immediate demands of the story, would be a visualization of the inner meaning of the music in the manner of "Ave Maria" in *Fantasia* (Disney, 1940).

Dream sequences and similar fantasies have employed expressive dance in many instances, in silent as well as sound films. Many attempts in recent photoplays have fallen short of the highest achievement, although the example in *Yolanda and the Thief* (MGM, 1945) with choreography by Balanchine shows significant progress.

Horizons

Finally, the highest artistic level is achieved when the dance director ventures beyond the limits of incidental dancing into the realm of cinedance. To date most cinedances have found their way into photoplays through fantasy: dreams, visions, hopes and memories. A beginning has been made in expressing the deepest and most complex feelings of human beings, in externalizing the form and content of musical compositions through a visual accompaniment. Long strides have been made into the realm of cinedance in exploring the vast possibilities of synthetic animation.

"The Skeleton Dance" (Disney, 1929), arranged to the music entitled *Danse Macabre* by Saint-Saëns, is a good example of animated cinedance. The peak of development in this field was probably reached with the audio-visual concert *Fantasia* which opens up even more extensive areas for the unprejudiced choreographer.

The churnings and eruptions, the flow of molten masses depicting the beginning of our universe which accompanies Stravinsky's *Rites of Spring*, besides being scientifically plausible, are laden with emotional overtones. The stylized movements of the mythical creatures and the rhythmical phenomena which are the visual expression of the Beethoven *Sixth Symphony* are artistically eloquent.

The exquisite movement of snowflakes, milkweed seeds, leaves, thistles and even mushrooms set to the music of Tchaikovsky's *Nutcracker Suite* is molded into expressive choreography of great variety and richness. The colors and forms seen with the *Toccata and Fugue in D Minor* by Bach, sometimes resembling musical instruments or the motion of sound waves, more often purely abstract, externalize on the screen the inherent rhythmic and dynamic structure of the music. This is cinedance at its abstract pole.

Here is an art to tantalize the creative capacity of the most imaginative choreographer and to make him forever impatient of having his fancy chained to the comparatively narrow range of action which humans can perform. Through the magic of animation any movement is possible. The variety and depth of expression of which cinedance is capable can only be guessed for the present. But soon more qualified dance artists may turn their attention to this field.

CINEDANCE AND THE FEATURE FILM

Several years of intensive study of the role of dance in the American motion picture has brought to light a few examples of cinedance. True, the surface has barely been scratched. Many dancers and dance directors are entirely oblivious of the nature and possibilities of cinedance, emerging as a new art in its own right. Others, either accidentally or more or less consciously have been producing examples of cinedance, and the lay public, without having a name for it, is already familiar with the new form as well as the artistic conventions which are a part of it.

Gene Kelly's "Shadow Dance" in *Cover Girl* (Columbia, 1944) was among the first and has become a standard example. In it the camera follows the dancer down a city street cluttered with familiar impedimenta. Always he is pursued by his Conscience, a slightly distorted image of himself reflected in the windows he passes. His inner struggle is expressed through stylized movement and that most cinematic of film techniques, double exposure photography.

The Spanish Toreador sequence in *Anchors Aweigh* (MGM, 1945) is pure imagination—the audio-visual expression of a wish. The fairy story in the same motion picture is another example, involving a combination of human action and synthetic animation. This is the newest branch of cinema, now being exploited extensively by Walt Disney. The roads along which cinedance may go in the future are many and fascinating.

PAULINE KONER and KITTY DONER

Technological Progress and the Dance:
THE DANCE IN TELEVISION

TELEVISION, ONCE a fantastic dream, is now a reality and will in a short time have lost its sensational effect as a technical novelty. It is fast becoming part of our daily life, accepted and assimilated by everybody as one of those devices without which one cannot very well exist in a button-pressing world. As every invention proves the necessity of its existence by the beneficial merits of its functions, the importance of television will be borne out by the influence it will exert on our way of life socially, culturally and artistically.

The dance has already been recognized as an ideal form for this new medium and it may prove to be as vital to television as music has been to the radio. At last the dance will be able to reach a vast new public—a public which has had little or no opportunity to develop a discriminating taste for this art. The fragmentary moments of dance represented in moving pictures, or the occasional vaudeville and musical comedy shows have hardly sufficed to develop a basic understanding and appreciation of the dance in its full scope.

Now, with the advent of television it is to be hoped everyone

111

will become acquainted with this art form. The repeated viewing of dance presentations will create a gradual awareness not only of mere showmanship and the outer form, but also of fine artistry and the inner significance. It is only through such a slow process of conditioning that the public will develop a sense of discrimination for the dance and a specific taste for one or more of its many facets, be it folk, popular, ballet or modern.

Television is an intimate art form. With its close-ups of particular movements it can highlight detail which is generally lost in the theater. Thus the teledance audience will undoubtedly become more sensitive to and aware of artistry than the present theater audience.

Besides being presented as entertainment, the dance can also have its place in television as an educational force for the development of mental and physical coordination. The numerous amateur dance groups and classes all over the country are proof of how many people seek the joy and satisfaction of expressing themselves in dance movement either for the sheer physical elements of exercise or for an emotional release. Imagine the effect that dance classes given on television programs will have on a greatly magnified public. First, it will reach those to whom live classes were never before available. Secondly, it will bring them highly equipped teachers both for adult and children's classes. People may even get together in different homes to participate in teledance classes.

But beyond these mere social implications, the cultural effects of television dance may bear far-reaching consequences. People of different nationalities and races will develop greater sympathy and understanding for each other, if they become more familiar with each other's idiosyncrasies. Ignorance and our lack of imagination breed misunderstanding and hatred between groups and nations. The visual closeness and intimacy brought to us by television may eradicate our indifference and prefabricated intolerance towards other people. This could be a first step in the direction of sympathy and understanding. The ridiculous ceases to be ridiculous when differences are no longer differences but mere variations. A ring in the nose is after all no different from a ring in the ear; they are both variations on the same human desire to attract attention.

Through television each individual is made subjectively aware of the rapidly shrinking boundaries of the world, both in time and space. The little Balinese dancer with her face powdered white, her quivering headdress, her fluttering hands will enter our living room and, by her charm, her delicacy and shyness, will give us a greater understanding of the real inner qualities of the Balinese people. There is no other medium in existence as yet that can create such lasting effect as the visual immediacy of television. The realization that this Balinese dancer is performing in Bali, while being seen in New York at the same time, leaves a strong impression because of its element of aliveness. The more we shall see of the folk dances of other nations and the more they shall see of ours, the greater will be our mutual understanding. The dance having no language barrier can play an important role in replacing fear and distrust by tolerance and sympathy. It can also be a stimulus for new reflexes and associations. What is more, active participation in the folk dances of different nations will create a kinesthetic affinity as well as an appreciation of the various emotions and temperaments of the many peoples of the world.

Just as television must affect society in general, so it must also affect the artist in particular. It is a synthesis of certain elements of the theater, the film and the radio, but it also has something very definitely its own, namely its electronic properties. Television involves the transmission of "constantly flowing" electrical pulses, while moving picture film is actually a series of "stopped" moments. This constant flow in television creates a fluid quality of movement which, while the difference is not definable in a special sense, is nevertheless felt in the over-all impression. Furthermore, many unusual effects can be achieved electronically, by the turning of a dial, that can never be presented on stage and can only be done on film by a long and arduous process.

Television has a great many possibilities to create such special effects as superimposing one image upon another, or combining live action against a filmed background, showing the tele-actor in the clouds or under water, or the willful distortion of an image. These possibilities challenge the imagination and can make of television a new art form. It must, however, be approached with all the care, thought and understanding that an art form demands and should not be regarded as a medium for mere reporting. Aristotle says, "A work of art should aim at form, and above all at unity which is the backbone of structure and the focus of form." How can television achieve this all-important element of unity? There are three essentials: content focus, compositional focus and camera focus.

Of course, different programs will demand diversified camera treatment with a specific sense of style and a feeling for rhythm and dynamics, relative to the subject and mood being televised, in order to create a unity of presentation. The planning of the camera shots is equivalent to film editing for moving pictures, the difference being that tele-editing must be carefully plotted before and actually takes place during a performance, whereas film-editing is done after the film is shot. Once a teledance is on the air there can no longer be any corrections or retakes. All of these considerations inevitably affect the choreographer and dancer. The dance as presented on stage cannot be simply transferred to television. It should either be entirely readapted or specifically choreographed to retain its artistry, integrity and interest on the television screen.

The choreographer must develop a new reflex, he must forget the element of design in relation to space and think in terms of a new dimension, namely the camera, but not of its physical presence, only of its visual potentialities. He must forget his theater conditioning where the audience is beyond the footlights. The television audience sees the dancer from any position the camera chooses. The position of the theater audience is fixed, that of the tele-audience variable, as variable as the mobility of the camera. During a performance the cameras move freely, shooting from contrasting angles and distances, even moving among the dancers.

This mobility of the camera compensates in some degree for the lack of space which, at present, dancers find to be the greatest handicap. If the choreographer creates in the terms of "camera," space limitation becomes negligible. Furthermore, such a limitation is not permanent, since space is only a "conditional" element and will be expanded as tele-studios grow. But camera is a "constant" element.

Dance composition for television must change its form. It must be "cameragraphed" as well as choreographed. What is cameragraphing? It is the planning of specific dance movements for specific camera shots and electronic effects, which form an integral part of the basic choreography.

Let us take a simple example. Suppose you are planning a slow development of a rhythmic pattern for a mounting hypnotic effect. You may start it just with a hand, then transfer it to the feet, finally allowing the whole body to take up the rhythmic pulse. Should the camera shoot this entire sequence with a long shot (i.e., a shot taking in the entire figure), the whole effect would be lost. The tele-screen is small, therefore the detail of the hands or feet would disappear in a long-shot. This movement, instead of building in excitement, would seem long and dull. However, if you plan for the camera to shoot in close-up—first the hands, then the feet, and finally the entire body in long-shot—you direct the viewer's eyes to the important focal point, you highlight the individual detail and create a montage of camera shots in relation to the movement which is part of your basic choreographic conception.

Cameragraphing ties the composition together and, though there is mobility and change of camera shots as well as special effects, demands a planned sequence which should be developed along the principles of true compositional form. The viewer will not be disturbed by arbitrary camera switches which break up the flow and continuity of the dance composition. On the contrary, a well cameragraphed teledance should so blend the camera changes with the movement that the viewer will not be conscious of the camera as a separate element, but will only be aware of an unusual and exciting new kind of dance.

Cameragraphing, of course, is not simply the planning of shots. If the dance wants to retain its art form in television, then cameragraphing must respect all the demands of compositional form, such as dynamics, style, framing, montage, balance, transition and finally motivation which is most vital. In order to achieve unity and coherence camera shots should be motivated. To shoot a dance from any angle for no other reason but its mechanical effect may create confusion.

Aside from the basic importance of camera, there are several other considerations which the special nature of television requires. First, there is the small size of the viewing screen. This lends itself better to the use of small units in group composition. In a long-shot the figures are small, in fact, the more people included in the shot the smaller the figures, with the resultant undistinguishable movement. It is much wiser to limit the groupings to three or four people at any one given moment, so that the screen will not look crowded. It is also of great significance to check on the transparency of design. The groupings must be so planned in relation to the camera angle and framing that the dancers do not cover each other and spoil the intended design. This does not mean that an occasional shot of a larger group is not possible. On the contrary, if used with discretion such a shot can create an interesting effect and accentuate a following close-up of a single dancer by sheer contrast.

Secondly, there is fluidity of movement which is of prime importance. This fluidity does not necessarily mean slow movement, for fast movement can also have a smooth rhythmic flow. It is the sharp, jerky staccato movement in quick succession which looks bad on television and tends to convey an exaggerated impression. Such movement should not be developed in long sequences, but should be properly spaced, punctuated and used sparingly for maximum effect.

Thirdly, the choreographer must constantly visualize how his work will look on the viewing screen rather than on the studio floor. What may look very dull to a studio audience may be a high point on the receiving screen. Sometimes a very simple movement holding little or no interest on the studio floor is a planned simplicity to enable two or more cameras to shoot simultaneously and thus create a superimposed image of the dancer's face and full-length movement. A very slow turn of seemingly no importance may have been planned for a dissolve shot from one camera angle to another. Such a dissolve causes a momentary overlapping of the two images and gives the turn a quality of movement which has never been possible on the stage. Dissolves on slow, spiral and turning movements become part of that movement, thus creating a new and exciting dimension. As a matter of fact, the true teledance will rarely make a good stage dance and an exciting stage dance will rarely make a good teledance, unless it is completely readapted. The basic principles of each are, in some ways, directly opposed to each other.

The influence of television on the dance is felt not only by the choreographer but also by the dance performer who will have to condition a whole new set of reflexes. Extreme mental alertness and flexibility will be a necessity. Readjustment in spacing and direction may be made even at the final rehearsal.

The dancer must be ready to cope with any emergency such as a breakdown of a camera during a performance, necessitating an instantaneous readjustment of all the dance patterns towards another camera. Also the ability to improvise will help the performer out of many an unexpected situation.

Every performer must also be completely aware, yet unaware, of the cameras. He must always be conscious of its direction so that he can project his movement to that direction, yet he must never show recognition of the camera as an object. The moment he does so the change is recognizable on the screen. In other words, never look "at" the camera, look "through" it.

Television is a very penetrating force, perhaps because of its electronic properties. It has an uncanny power to reveal insincerity and superficial emotions. No longer must the performer think of projecting to an audience at a distance. Now with the closeness of the tele-camera he must tone down. Perfect control and simplicity, ease and smoothness become dominating factors. Restraint in the sharpness and accent of movement is essential. If presented without restraint such movement can take on the quality of the old-time "flickers."

Undoubtedly, television will demand the development of greater artistry in performance. A small detail which is completely lost in a stage performance can become a high spot in a television performance. Pure brilliancy of technique is not enough. The ideal television dancer should move with controlled fluidity, be aware of the smallest detail and never overproject. The sensitivity of performance and the mood created are of basic importance.

Although the dance is, of course, only one aspect in the yet unforeseeable development of television, it will undoubtedly play a leading role in its artistic department and will greatly contribute to entertainment and education. If the artistic integrity of the art will be preserved in its presentations on the tele-screen, television will be able to do for the dance what no other medium ever could: it will popularize its many forms of expression and help reestablish the forgotten truth that "the dance is the mother of the arts."

In drama it is particularly important that the course of the action should not only build up an idea of the character, but also should build up, should "image," the character itself. Consequently, in the actual method of creating images, a work of art must reproduce that process whereby, in life itself, new images are built up in the human consciousness and feelings.

—SERGEI EISENSTEIN

———

WALTER SORELL

The Actor and the Dance

MOVEMENT AND rhythm are at the root of all artistic expression. They are also inherent in man as his most individual manifestation, and therefore in every fictitious character as well.

We all move and gesture in our private lives, and these movements have a certain rhythm, the rhythm created by our emotions, or, in a broader sense, by our personality. Unaware of our posture and gait, unconscious of our gestures, we have a certain pattern of movements, rhythmically definable. We react to certain events under certain circumstances through physical manifestations in a manner which could be predicted with almost uncanny precision, were we to possess an exact blueprint of our past and our habits, and the objectivity of interpretation.

The actor whose task it is to make a fictitious character live

———

This essay does not attempt to embrace the rather complicated problem of these two interrelated arts. It is part of a book (as yet unfinished) dealing with all aspects of stage movement.

for us must reorganize his most personal pattern of movements to fit it to the fictitious character he portrays and must synchronize his own rhythm with that of the person delineated by the playwright. He must realize that the movements of the character are a complete entity and must be performed as unconsciously as his own; that every business on the stage is clearly defined as to movement, since it portrays part of the character's mentality as conditioned by his past life; and finally that his character's movements convey from the stage the emotional motivations of his actions and reactions to the audience who may understand his words better, and the idea which these words express, if his movements explain them properly.

To be able to do this, he must have learned to isolate the various parts of his body and to control each part separately.

When the dancer releases his movements, he tries to fill spatial dimensions with the dynamics of expression. He must carefully plan and organize his movements to convey his idea. He has little more than his body to make himself understood. Costume, décor and musical accompaniment help him create an atmosphere and stimulate the spectator's imagination. But these are only attendant means of support for his artistic endeavor. He must be able to carry across the footlights as a visual person and project his ideas through movement, through gesture. He can only achieve it through complete control and coordination of each part of his body. Only then can full harmony of movement be attained.

The actor is inclined to forget that every theatrical performance is basically a "show." This word alone underscores the importance of its visual as well as audible effect. He lacks resourcefulness in gesture, in fact, he is afraid of movement because he is afraid to overact. His first attempts on the stage have been etched in acid letters into his memory. How sure he was of his words, but he did not know what to do with himself: his hands, his arms, his legs, his head, his entire body had suddenly become alien to him! He has so many excuses for drifting into a state of underplaying, of non-acting. He does not realize that he denies theater when he fails to animate his character with gesture and movement, when he fails to project through them emotion and thought. He does not realize that, by not doing it, he renounces the very thing he is trying to do.

". . . do not saw the air too much with your hand," is good advice Hamlet gives the players, "for in the very torrent, tempest, and, as I may say, the whirlwind of passion, you must acquire and beget a temperance that may give it smoothness." Shakespeare knew his hams, he knew the pitfalls of acting, he knew how difficult it was to achieve a true characterization. And since no character can live in an intellectual and emotional vacuum, the actor feels impelled to fill the arising emptiness with empty gestures.

"Art is a product of imagination," Stanislavsky said. "The actor must feel the challenge to action physically as well as intellectually . . ." If he does not, he is unable to read the blueprint of his character's personality, or he lacks the imagination to interpret it, or he has never learned to move.

The actor must learn that he has a body. As he does not take for granted that he can speak a part correctly because he has no speech defect, he cannot very well assume that he can move correctly on the stage without learning how to move. He learns to modulate his voice, to place the right stress on the right word, to accentuate phrases. So can he learn from the dancer the right emphasis and pressure in movement, the smooth flowing of gesticulation, the faultless transition from phrase to phrase.

Only the full integration of drama and the dance leads to complete unification of the spoken word, which is the most powerful medium for the expression of ideas, with the emotional motivation and resonance which lie in movement and rhythm.

When we speak of good casting we actually mean that the director or producer found a type of personality which will be best fit for a certain character, or comes closest to the character's physical and mental structure. The rest is then up to the actor's ability in characterization. This ability depends on the range and intensity of his expressiveness. It is erroneous to assume that expressiveness is confined to the word. Though the word projects the idea, it only begins to live when the actor's entire physical impact gives it the resonance it needs. "Words are the design upon the outline of movement," Mayerhold said. "We must put the body back."

Movement is the silent manifestation of emotion. In its rhythm lies the actor's conception of his character. How he enters upon the stage, how he breathes, how he walks, how his own rhythm becomes one with that of his co-players and the rhythmic pace of the play, is the essence. Profound characterization needs of course more than muscular coordination and the reproduction of a gesture pattern. It is the actor's awareness of the underlying rhythm of his character which actually directs his movements. A great actor must be a great dancer, however unconscious he may be of it. He is a "frustrated" dancer: we do not see him leap or turn pirouettes, but these are specialized technical achievements. What we do feel is the radiation of expressiveness coming from his body which he controls and whose coordination is perfect.

Movements on the stage are only seemingly attendant factors to words and action. Movements carry the words and crystallize action. Words which are not backed up by the right movement or gesture have no resonance. Action must have an inner justification which cannot be explained but must be "acted." Only then will it be logical, coherent and real. To copy or photograph life is still not the creation of artistic reality. What makes action appear real on the stage is its atmosphere which may be in the texture of the playwright's words. The reader of the drama can feel it, since his imagination will rebuild it for him. The actor on the stage must take the place of the reader's imagination and rebuild this atmosphere for his audience. It is here that the actor must prove his ability. Silence on the stage is more important than the spoken word. The slightest pause filled with a gesture, or the restraint from movement—but even then one must feel the restraint!—can create a mood which a hundred words could not conjure up.

Body and mind are fused into one, and no actor can hope to reach the mind of his audience by neglecting to project the expression of the body. A Shakespeare can only write that his character "enters," but the actor's entrance is a physical revelation and it is only through the medium of his body that he can create an emotional response. A single emotional experience can be simplified or magnified through a gesture, where the word alone would mislead the actor into pathos.

Instinctive motor-response alone is not enough. Conscientious efforts and systematic training are necessary to attain physical harmony. It is deplorable that the actor no longer has any contact with the most elementary artistic expression, namely, dancing. This is all the more deplorable since he has thus no longer any contact with the most elementary instrument of artistic expression, his own body.

Ideal acting would demand from the performer not only to forget his personality, but to change his character and appearance for that of the portrayed person. We cannot very well expect such complete metamorphosis of the actor, night after night. Otherwise, the new person alive in the actor would take possession of the actor's thoughts and feelings so intensely that the actor, with every new part, would become a fully changed personality and the stage a seat of reality instead of a world of illusion.

"It is impossible . . . for an actor to disassociate himself from his own self," Lynn Fontanne said. He cannot forego his own inner personality, he clothes it with the cloak of a fictitious person and attempts to inspirit it with his own thoughts and feelings. In other words, he animates his part as he understands the character's thoughts and feelings. This is a highly individual process in which the actor cannot easily separate the gesture and movement pattern of his own ego from that of the fictitious character.

When we speak of a part as fitting an actor like a glove we wish to convey our impression that the actor's characterization made the fictitious person so alive that his own personality went unnoticed. In this case, he was able to make the fictitious character his own, or bring about an almost complete fusion of his own being with the new character.

Too little or no attention at all is given to the unconscious process of blending the two individuals, the real and the fictitious. Harmony in characterization can only be achieved when the actor is conscious of his own self and arrives—through whatever channels, emotionally or intellectually—at a well-defined realization of the nature of his part.

"If the actor really feels an emotion," George Arliss said, "there is no sensible reason why he should continue his performance on a confined stage. He should rush into the public square and play out the scene there." He is seconded by Katharine Cornell who denies that the actor "lives" his part. Nor does she believe it necessary for an actor to have experienced an emotion in real life to be able to portray it.

Helen Hayes is of a different opinion. She thinks that "an actor must have experienced in some matter, even if only in a vivid imagination, an emotion corresponding to the one he has to portray, if his conception of the part is to be right in feeling."

Can both be right? In fact, they are. This is not a question of an intellectual viewpoint, because it is not their viewpoints that clash but their personalities, their mental structures, which finally decide the actor's approach to his part. The blending of one's ego with the fictitious character is a gradual process until final identification in the actor's mind is achieved. Whether it is a purely intellectual or a rather emotional approach matters little.

What matters is the realization that words, movements and

character form a natural and irrevocable entity and that the search for the right pantomimic expression must come from within. To set up generally valid rules or to prescribe definite gestural movements for certain parts, feelings or styles defeats their purpose. How far the misconception of movement and gestures can lead is shown by the example of Helen Hayes who certainly knows better when on stage than when she says in *Players at Work* by Morton Eustis: "In comedy, I have found that I must keep myself up, arms must be held higher, gestures must be of an upward nature. In tragedy just the reverse."

How very effective movement as an instrument of characterization can be is proven by the following report by Constance Smedley:

> The American actor Frank Bacon, famous for his phenomenal success in his play "Lightnin'" . . . was confronted in the court room by his old wife who has been persuaded to apply for a divorce. His hands held the audience by playing up and down the lapels of his coat. They expressed his desire to do what he wished, his reluctance, his groping for the right decision, the whole play of his emotions, so when the short word came, the audience had sat enthralled in dead silence, following his thoughts and feelings, and knew all that the word did not say . . . The hands had been hidden, they came out at the right moment . . . This is synthetic drama . . . I still can see his hands clenching and working on the arms of the chair. How they held the position, or wavered, or turned over the problem, and then finally gripped hold in one final convulsive direct movement!

As soon as an actor has found the right movement for an emotion or a given situation, the word following the gesture will be just right because it is borne by the movement itself. It is an established fact that the human brain, through a muscular chain of reactions, makes us perform involuntary gestures or expressive movements a fraction of a second quicker than our tongue is able to form words. This is understandable when we consider that the gesture is the expression of the underlying motives of reactions, whereas speech is the result and effect. Therefore, it is only natural that a gesture should precede the spoken word at least by fractions of a second, heralding the reaction before it actually takes place.

In his search for the right movement pattern of his character no actor should think he can free himself from his ego. On the contrary, he should be aware only of hiding his personality behind a mask, the mask of another individual. As he grows into his portrayal of the character, he gradually substitutes a second skin for what was originally a mask only. His personality will remain a magnetic power if he succeeds in subordinating it and giving the character he interprets priority in thought and feeling.

But he can only achieve genuine harmony of reality through a synchronization of gesture and speech, of movement and idea. Mime and diction are the two expressive means of acting. The one cannot exist without the other, and only the crystallization of the combined visual and auditory sensations into a unity will bring forth the effect of lifelike acting.

When the Ten Thousand things are
viewed in their oneness, we return to the Origin and remain where we
have always been.   —SEN T'SEN

JOSEPH GREGOR

(translated from the German by the editor)

Panorchesis

THE DANCE is not the oldest, most primitive of the arts, nor is it so linked with the others that it is difficult to draw a line of demarcation. In fact, the dance is inseparable from them, because it contains all of them and constitutes their common root. Would we wish to enter the realm of ideas with Plato, then the dance could be the idea of art, changeable into any form, from the lowest to the most sublime, but also changeable into quite different forms of expression, into music as well as sculpture, into architecture as well as poetry.

It is the only form of art which, with self-assuredness, embraces the whole world and of which our own efforts, the man as dancer, is only a poor image, a human appendage. The conception of the universe in full movement, yet with this movement composed as to its direction and speed of innumerable, not accidental but coordinated, single components subject and related to rules—this notion is one of the greatest our minds are able to conceive. Here the thoughts of God and the dance are close neighbors. He who is able to comprehend the one thought, or at least to absorb it with his feelings, will also possess the other.

It is a fitting simile that our look at the starry sky is, at the same time, directed at a macrocosmic dance stage: the endless variety of distance and movement does not only create the image of recurrence (rhythm) in the spectator, but also of ingenious form (dance pattern). It seems unnecessary to speak about rhythm; with every hour, in fact, with every breath in our life, from the very first sunrise we experience to the sunset of our last day, we are completely included in the macrocosmic rhythm. The movement of the planets, to use a simple example, contains objective and subjective dance patterns; an objective dance pattern is the planets' composite motion, revolving around a central sun, while simultaneously rotating on their own axis; a subjective dance pattern is the movement of the planets as we become aware of them in the sky. In their orbital paths they assume different but recurrent positions to each other, they move in one direction, but seem to come to a standstill and even to retrograde. The objection that these are only similes, or images, is at hand, yet it is strange that this image of the "dance of the stars" is used by both the astronomers and the dance theorists.

Ideal dance, however, is presented to us in a most gigantic manner through the nebulae which seem to be formed of light and rhythm only, but in reality are probably formed of totally mysterious qualities, in which matter and spirit are equally far from each other, or equally close. The wonderfully regular nebulae of the Great Bear—a distance of two and a half million light years—is a dance formation whose two spiral arms, perfectly symmetric and in rhythmic movement, reach out of their radiant ecstatic nucleus into the light phenomenon of brightness and darkness. Both arms are a multitude of suns, with their nuclei still a mysterious mass of fire, and the whole nothing else than a single dancing turn in the universe.

It is here that the great formative imagination of Greek antiquity tried to attain a connection between the dance (if I may so continue to call the macrocosmic events) and music. The planets move in epicycles, the relation of these circles to each other result in their "dance" (Apollonius). The greatest achievement of coming close to the conception of modern astronomy is the theory of Eudoxius from Knidos: 27 concentric spherical surfaces circling around the earth in 24 hours, yet each of them also possessing its own independent movement. The outermost brings forth the movement of the fixed stars, the movement of the planets is caused by four, that of the sun and the moon by three spheres. The spheres are not only in optical but also in acoustical harmony with each other; the prevalent relations between them penetrate not only the celestial inaudible, but also the terrestrial audible music. The harmony of the optical-acoustical system of the cosmos is thus achieved, permeating our being in dance and music. I know of only one similar instance of such an all-embracing scientific notion, and this belongs with our century. It is the modern theory of the atom, according to which the dance of the stars is found repeated in the microcosm of the atom, and thus the entire universe is harmoniously complete with it.

Rhythm arises out of movement which is regulated by laws; in the macrocosm, the Halley comet has a cycle of 76 years, and we assume that an extraordinarily rhythmic regularity exists in the microcosm. In contrast to the orbits of the planets, the distances between the electron shells within the atom can be relatively expressed in small whole numbers, and the velocity in these orbits is constant. Comparatively speaking, the dance in the atom probably has a classic simplicity similar to the dance in the above described spiral nebulae, in spite of the hardly conceivable difference in size. The physical largeness however becomes reduced to completely secondary importance. Even if we imagine the hydrogen atom, as a whole, to be as large as the earth, its nucleus would not be larger than a tennis ball; the electron at a distance of about half the radius of the earth would have the size of a toy balloon. Despite the incredible "emptiness" of the universe we occasionally find enormous masses: in the star Betelgeuse (in the constellation Orion) the sun and the earth would have enough room and could move in the actual distances from each other without reaching the circumference of this star.

Rhythm as a law of movement, as the obvious result of universal forces, is everything; matter is nothing. It may be possible and it is even very likely that a new theory will change these conceptions, as Copernicus revolutionized the Ptolemaic system, but it is inconceivable that the basic law of "energy-movement-rhythm" will ever be disturbed. Our latest notion of it has become so ethereal that we can conceive the dance as taking place independent of matter and only in fields of energy.

This titanic picture has its counterpart in nature everywhere, a phenomenon which I would like to call *panorchesis* and which has not yet been investigated. Let me give you an illustration. We are standing under a linden tree, heavy with leaves through which the wind passes. Every single leaf performs rhythmically recurring movements which can be compared to a dance design, but the entirety of the foliage is an immense orchesis which we can perceive with our eyes and ears and which changes with the direction and intensity of the wind. But the wind too is part of the current of air wherever we happen to be, and this current, in turn, is part of the current of air of the entire hemisphere, in fact, of the globe! In my opinion, there is no constantly recurring movement in nature which could not be included in its panorchesis; with it belong the tides as well as the smallest ripple of the waters, also the flight of birds however planless it may seem to us. He whose eyes follow the movements of swallows, their loops and turns and figures, will admit that this is dance whose "purpose" to only a small degree lies in the search for food and mainly in the *ecstatic union with the panorchesis of nature*. Every child realizes that a swarm of gnats gives the illusion of an entire ballet.

In the realm of animals we can stop using the dance as a mere rhetorical image or simile and speak of it in terms we are

used to. The Grallatores on Cape York (Australia) dance a qua-
drille which is said to excel in rhythm and grace the one danced by
men. The chimpanzees perform a round dance whose rhythm embraces the entire body, even the lower jaw. It is a round dance in
which these animals not only move rhythmically in a circle but
also perform turns—certainly not a simple dance movement. To
see man included in the panorchesis is, after all these observations,
a foregone conclusion. The infant lying prostrate executes a sequence of rhythmically recurring movements with his arms and
legs, movements which have the "purpose"—as far as we can speak
of purpose in nature at all—to give his limbs the necessary ability
to move which is gradually extended to the whole body. Those
movements however are not erratic, they are meaningfully coordinated and accompanied by sensual pleasures, which is an implicit part of the notion "dance." From here on, most people are
included in the panorchesis, the clumsy as well as the graceful,
the swift runner as well as the slow-walking, shaking old man.

The human example makes us face the peculiar fact that
the dance is an art form which is executed exclusively with the
body and, in fact, with the whole body. Though as part of its presentation costumes and décors are used, the dance remains limited
to the body alone, because the body is its sacred means of expression for all time. The participation of the *entire* body is very essential, including the whole physical and mental personality behind
it, whereas the art of singing, for instance, makes use of certain
parts of the body only, although with rather far-reaching participation of the singer's mind. There is an inseparable link between the
dance and music, its most closely related art form. The movements of the kicking infant are not only coordinated to each other,
but also in their entirety to his babble with which the rhythmic
expression is transported into the second, the acoustic, realm.

The dance without music is unthinkable. Though music for
the dance may be limited to a percussion instrument, it can be

all the more intense. Even in the very few cases, which impress me as omissions or exceptions to the rule, where certain panto-mimic moments or sometimes entire dances are presented with-out music, it only seems as if they do without it; in reality they carry the music in themselves. For music is the root of the two strongest functions of the dance, of which one is physical, the other mental; it is rhythm and ecstasy. Without these two neither the simplest social dance, nor the most magnificent ballet is im-aginable, inasmuch as these and every dance variation between these two means of expression are considered works of art. Besides rhythm, music contains the germ cell of the dance *form*, as far as the body receives from it the impulse to move in a well defined manner.

A chorus of the Marquesas (Polynesia, as described by Handy and Winne) holds one pitch and is only different in rhythm: two eighths and a fourth, on one tone, recurrent in various arrange-ments. In other words, a movement in anapaests, as we know it from simple choral passages of the ancient tragedy. A death song of the Pueblos (as described by Stumpf) is limited to the range of a tenth, changes between two-, three- and five-four time and has a highly complicated melodic line; nevertheless, in this case also the creative dance urge emerging out of the music is clearly manifest: the melody moves in a *descending* stepwise progression and stays after two short outcries in a low register. I do not know any more magnificent primitive "death motive!" The formation of the steps, their rise and fall, is inherent in the music; in fact, they are born together with the music.

Mass ecstasy through music: on the Solomon Islands, a host of men are dancing; the older men in the middle form the shape of a star, the rays of which are formed by younger men; at the outermost ends are the half-grown boys. A muffled howling of the old men marks the start and is taken over by the rumbling of the younger men's weapons; the sounds become gradually organized into rhythm, then the entire star begins to turn . . .

now the howling and rumbling has already become melody, being translated into movement . . . the tempo grows, the star turns faster and faster until the participants, overcome by ecstasy, roll on the ground in rapture. I know of no other example than this, described by R. Parkinson, which would better convey the entire "music-dance" process from a simple, sung rhythm to mass ecstasy, all the more since it is a visible phenomenon reaching up to the nebulae as far as sublime primitivity goes!

We know of innumerable cases of the ecstasy of individual dancers, such as the shamans of the Sakai (Sumatra, as written about by M. Moszkowski): two sorcerers uninterruptedly mumbling prayers and formulae of exorcism. The beat of the drums, supporting and stimulating them, organizes the rhythm. One of them rises for the dance. First, gracefully, with fan, sword and a bracelet of little bells. The rhythm grows livelier and more intense, the dance toward the sick man and away from him gradually grows into turns; faster and faster, until the tempo becomes frantic and, in complete frenzy, the dancer collapses.

We would know what dancing is, if psychology could give us an exact analysis of the ecstatic experience of the shaman. But this will never be possible. We are limited to observations and descriptions, also to drawing conclusions, to gauging and registering, but, in the main, we can do little more than guess. Thus we know that the spirits of great ancestors as well as of demons and totemic animals take complete possession of the ecstatic dancer, and even our modern learned explorers only conceal that they too are convinced of it. He who has ever had the good fortune to be present at such dances becomes convinced of it.

But to know this we do not have to search the gloomy dark of the African jungles and the fires and storms of Polynesia. Every dance demands ecstasy. The ecstasy of the waltz is well known; it is not only rooted in the music and the sliding turns whose sensual effect is unquestionable, but also in its immensely erotic component of this self-forgetful and close dance between man and woman. But before the waltz came into being, the minuet—and before the minuet, the gavotte—must have had the impetus for ecstasy, in a rather modest, restrained or, so to speak, stylized form, but it was unquestionably part of it. These transitions from the greatest, primordial ecstasies to certain style-limited movements are akin to the transitions from musical to pictorial ornament and have a common root or relationship between the dance and painting. A minuet by Mozart, with its wealth of musical ornaments, most easily directs the inner visualization of the dancer on a detour along pictorial ornaments, linear designs, tendrils and spirals, onto the final road to the creation of movement.

With the "suite" the dance has made a wonderful gift to music; music, in turn, has shown its gratitude, since even the greatest and most perfect symphony retains a great deal of dancing in its scherzo. It is understandable that the dancer is tempted to widen the range of music to which he can dance. Though I must admit that Beethoven's *Seventh Symphony* has arisen from a celestial, dancing gaiety, it seems nevertheless desirable that such an attempt as Leonide Massine's to translate it into balletic terms (1938) remain isolated. It cannot be doubted that originally every song is created for the dance too, but the lieder by Franz Schubert or Richard Strauss are as remote from the dance as are the magnificent, primitive creations of sung dance music. On the other hand, there are important and highly distinguished composers who possess such a strong dance spirit that, time and again, they return to the dance: Chopin, Tchaikovsky, Debussy, Respighi, Stravinsky and many others.

The deep-rooted relationship between the dance and sculpture is proven by the incontestable supposition that the dance is sculpture in movement created with the dancer's body. The human body is the eternal theme of the sculptor's art whose creations of bronze and marble are in repose; the dancer's creations coming out of himself are in motion. This process, rather difficult to explain psychologically, is elucidated in a wonderful way by the poet, Hugo von Hofmannsthal, in his "Conversation of the Dancers":

> My foot strikes against a sere branch of a tree, Hymnis, and its miserable existence enters my being, as the beauty of violets and roses enters my own existence through my eyes and enslaves me; and at night I must lie there waking with open eyes and must think of this miserable piece of wood, be at its will, imitate its misshapen body with my crooked rigid limbs, so that a night bird watching me would take me for a Thessalian witch or for someone obsessed—must one not fear?

The conception of the dance as a gradual awareness of the visible world, born out of fear of the world's existence, is noteworthy and will certainly play its role in a future aesthetics of the dance, as already presented in sketchy contours by Spencer and Schopenhauer. He who was fortunate enough to have seen the silent tragedy of Pavlova as a dying swan will realize its meaning beyond all philosophy.

We must imagine that the dance, in its fulfilled and perfected form, must also contain *liberation*, a more sublime existence as a necessary counterpart. We dance to free ourselves from the fear of life and we dance *only* if we can set ourselves free. In Hofmannsthal's dialogue a sailor tells the dancer of his adventures; the lasting after-effect, shaped with plasticity, is this:

> She begins to sway her hips. Somehow one can feel that she is not alone, that a great many like her are around her and that they all dance together before the eyes of their gods. They dance and move in circles, and dusk falls upon them: shadows loosen themselves from the trees and merge with those many who dance, and from the tree-tops emerge big birds in whom the deceased dwell and the birds move with them in circles, and the island shakes under them like a boat full of drunken people. And nothing on this island can escape the power of the dancers; at that moment, they are as strong as gods; the arms, hips and shoulders of the gods

are with them in their movements: from nowhere the blue net of death or the coral red sword of their gods can fall upon them. They are those who give birth and those who are born on this island, they are the bearers of life and death.

The dance mask is the strongest plastic expression of the dance, it is ecstasy transported into and held captive by sculptural form. Therefore, the good dance mask will, in silent communication, instill the dancer with movement, and it matters little whether the mask stems from a primitive tribe whose members create masks, or from a great artist of a high culture (Greece, Italy [commedia dell' arte], Japan, Siam), or from present-day artists.

The laws of movement must also emanate from the costume. Here is another bridge leading to painting. In the same way as a minuet by Mozart finds the dance expression of its musical ornament in certain movements, positions and steps, so must a certain costume fit best the basic musical and choreographic form of the Mozart minuet. The artist who designs a costume for the dance must have the imagination that can visualize movement which is in accord with the dancer, he must be able to create his material for the dancer, or let us better say, to drape the dancer's body with it. This kind of imagination is implicitly manifest in Callot and Lancret, it is strongest in those artists who have lived in the climactic epochs of the ballet, in the mannerists at the court of Louis XIV, in L. O. Burnacini at the court of Leopold I, in A. D. Bertoli at the court of Charles VI, and in Léon Bakst when the Russian ballet was at its height. These artists as creators of the ballet costume have not yet been surpassed, their vision of form and color, of wool and silk and ornament was as purely coordinated to the ballet of the seventeenth, eighteenth and the beginning of the twentieth century as an African ancestral mask made of wood and bast reflects the ecstatic expression of the dancers.

If the individual dancer establishes the link to sculpture, then the relationship of the dance to architecture—one of the strongest radiations of the dance in general—is created by the dance group. Music cannot divide space and arrange it methodically; this is left to the dance, the art of mobile sculpture. Different space-thoughts arise from a group of dancers who move either in a straight line or in circles. But besides the lineal and circular ballet, motion in space can be so manifold that it has its macroscopic counterpart only in the starry sky. (From whatever angle one contemplates the dance, the idea of the panorchesis becomes obvious.) The circular line turns into an elliptic orbit, already known to the primitive tribes when they no longer danced around one but two wooden poles. If the circular line opens without ever closing again, it follows a parabolic course.

The architectonic function of the dance can already be found in Homer (Odyssey, VIII). Young men of the Phæacians in glistening armour dance in a circle in a quick waltz step. Odysseus, who, first at war and then during his long adventurous wanderings, had been away from all culture, could hardly get over this surprising impression. Then, two dancers get ready for the dance with the balls and place themselves in the center of the circle. During their performance the other dancers around them provide them with the percussion by clapping their hands and stamping their feet. Thus, the antique orchestra, one of the most important forms of the dance stage, was created.

In this manner, every eminent dance epoch shapes its own stage out of the inner architecture of the dance itself. The lineal movement of the festive procession, in combination with the movement of two dance fronts, created the dance stage of the sixteenth and seventeenth centuries, a very long trapezoid with its shorter base in the rear; out of it the procession unfolded approaching the spectators; the two dance fronts could be developed fanlike without any décors being in the way. In fact, this architectonic type remained in use for two centuries and is still alive to some extent.

Max Reinhardt tried to form the mass movements and dances in A Midsummer Night's Dream in such a manner that, in a sequence of dense circles which alternately moved into the rear of the stage and downstage, all functions of a dance stage, depth as well as height, arose out of the movement of the performers without resorting to technical means. The dances of the elves, that phenomenon of "dancing trees" moved by the wind, thus created out of themselves their surrounding architecture, and thereby their own stage image which consisted of nothing else than a dark round horizon in which the imagination of the spectators could visualize an abundance of phantoms.

This was the exceptional case of an extraordinary, almost suggestive, director. We can only hope, however, to reach new architectonic functions of the dance when the style of dancing will have renewed itself as a whole, as happened in Reinhardt's case with the histrionic style. Since our dance stages are essentially based on the technique of the Russian ballet, that is on the expressive forms which are a century old, it can easily happen that the most magnificent stage settings for our ballets convey the impression of something that had been *accidentally* added to the dance instead of having grown out of it *organically*. This became manifest in the Russian ballet when Derain and Picasso began to work for it. While the Russian artists, Benois, Dobuschinsky, Gontcharowa, Larionow, but above all Léon Bakst, possessed an extraordinary understanding and feeling for the ballet of their country, the stage images of a great many of the younger artists had the appearance of idealistic claims on the ballet, claims which it could never fulfill since its aims are basically different from those visualized by the artist.

Let us only compare the sketches which Burra designed for the *Miracle in the Gorbals* with the actual stage settings of this pantomime on the stage of the Sadler's Wells Ballet! I am afraid that the highly individual imaginative stage designer and the natural preliminary conditions of the dance as rooted in the human body and in the dance technique can easily fall apart. This was certainly *not* in Noverre's mind when he demanded the ideal union of the painter with the dancer. But, on the other hand, we must admit that in his epoch the techniques of dancing and painting were not a hundred years apart from each other. I very well understand choreographers who, like Helpmann in *Adam Zero*, leave the stage completely empty in the most essential scenes with the exception of a few necessary pieces of décor, steps, sloping boards, etc., but otherwise work with light and shadow as was done on the Russian stage in its splendid period of rejuvenation thirty years ago.

The more alien the fantasy that penetrates the realm of the dance, the greater are the dangers it encounters. Nowhere can it be better observed than in the close net of connection between the dance and the art of writing. Here everything could be enumerated, everything from the touching idea of dancing the death of a swan to the extensive pamphlet which Lord Byron devoted to the waltz—for even the denunciations of its opponents serve the dance. I think that "imageless dance" exists in as little degree as does "imageless music." The image however is the first step to its interpretation. Since there are arresting and liberating, climactic and anticlimactic movements, *humor* and *tragedy* in both art media, no spectator or listener can be denied the right of letting his imagination continue to work and to play with those similes closest to them and to search for the drama.

But there is more to it than mere comparisons. It is uncertain as to where ecstasy leads; it can lead to the highest elevation of existence as well as to its destruction—as the examples of the shaman and the dancing star on the Solomon Islands prove, it is ecstasy itself that contains drama (from δράω, to do, to act, but also to do good and evil). The Viennese dancer Rosalia

Chladek danced a short *Prelude* (Liszt) which, carefully avoiding any literary influence, is composed of conflicting movements and clearly leads to ecstasy. The entire dance lasting about five minutes becomes the symbol of fate. I see the strongest drama in this or similar compositions, a drama never presented on any stage with greater intensity.

It is certainly understandable that the dancer is inclined to yield to poetical analogies and to let them influence his dance creations to a certain degree. As the dance is a constant struggle with the spirit of gravity, it is only too understandable that the dancer leans toward the poetical image and dances in his ecstasy the fate of Icarus (Lifar). As Hofmannsthal's dancer becomes one with the "body of a piece of wood," these dancers become one with the bodies of demigods; in this manner has grown a magnificent art, the Roman solo pantomime, and one could experience with the mimes—no matter whether Agamemnon or Odysseus, Helena or Hekabe was danced—how the drama during the development of the ecstasy took possession of the dance.

The growth of solo pantomime is by no means a singular phenomenon. Lifar developed the leap almost into flying; the limitation "almost" means everything; the necessary return to the earth can be interpreted as the fall of Icarus, in the same way as other dance dramas drew from this "rebounding to earth" the symbol of the dancer's lifts, jumps, his rise and suspension in air. In the first case the interpretation is negative, in the latter positive, buoyant.

The motive of arrestment and liberation is very popular on the dance stage, because it is so very natural to depict in repose and movement. It appears in the oldest libretti: as chained Eros, as Renaud fettered by Armida, as Andromeda liberated by Perseus. It reappears as the knight of the Renaissance processions who, imprisoned in a rock, is liberated by his lady. In a later period we find it in the petrification of the living and in the liberation of the enchanted, the speaking and dancing statues in innumerable baroque ballets and operas. Why has *The Sleeping Beauty* been so popular for the last half century, from Petipa's first creation in Russia in the nineties of the last century to its latest version in Covent Garden, in 1946, by Sergejeff? Simply, because Perrault's fairy tale is basically a ballet, and the enchantment and revivification of the Princess hovers over everything. The *Victory of Light*, danced in innumerable variations, is derived from the medieval miracle play and has its greatest model in the Christian idea itself. The Soviet Ballet which frequently used the same motive, only giving it social significance, also follows the idea of the miracle play. Even the primitive sanctification of activities and the songs connected with it, songs of fishermen, hunters, lumbermen and of many other professions, can be found in some form on the ballet stage, only we no longer surmise that, in these cases too, the panorchesis makes itself felt.

The text or idea for a ballet will be the best which takes these age-old connections into account. It is said that the technique of the dance, particularly of the ballet, is strongly based on tradition, all the more as there are certain movements which have been handed down to us from ancient Egypt and a great many from the Middle Ages. The strong infiltration of the so-called "old" school of the ballet by new forms of movements and of expression, particularly in the last decade, makes it appear very likely that certain technical aspects of the dance will change in the next decades. Unchangeable, however, will remain the connection of the dance with the celestial bodies. The dancer is the last priest at the altar of mankind.

THE DANCE IN THE MAKING

Nothing so clearly and inevitably reveals the inner man than movement and gesture. It is quite possible, if one chooses, to conceal and dissimulate behind words or paintings or statues or other forms of human expression, but the moment you move you stand revealed, for good or ill, for what you are.

—DORIS HUMPHREY

RUDOLF LABAN

The Educational and Therapeutic Value of the Dance

LET ME say this at the very outset. The dance, as it is traditionally understood in our time, has no intrinsic educational or remedial purpose. The dance today is an art form which can be appreciated and enjoyed either as a spectacle, if performed by professional dancers, or as a recreational activity, if performed by laymen. Why its beauty and significance are appreciated and enjoyed is a question seldom, if ever, answered. Certainly, the answer will rarely include the mention of educational or remedial purposes.

The teaching of dancing or of the applied history of the dance in schools is desirable. As one of the subjects of education it can be compared with the teaching of other art subjects, such as music, painting, designing and modeling. Such teaching will enlarge the horizon of the pupil and will enable him to admire dances with more understanding. The adult having enjoyed art education and thus also dance education in his school days will be better prepared to use one or several of the arts for his recrea-

145

tional purposes with some taste and discrimination. The fact that
the dance is probably the primary art of man might give it a certain importance and preponderance over the other arts.

The oft proffered opinion that the dance is of educational
or therapeutic value, because it is the only art in which the human
being is involved as a whole, seems to me to be based on a mis-
comprehension. The fact that the dancer performs large and
clearly visible movements does not indicate at all that the whole
person is involved. I have seen many dancers who throw themselves into the air without any sign of inner participation. On the
contrary, such large movements are frequently very externalized,
comparable to hollow shells in which not the slightest indication
of an integration of body and mind can be discovered.

Yet there exists a part of the dance which, if purposefully
applied, can have an eminent educational and remedial value. It
will be expected that this part of the dance consists of nothing else
beyond the visible movement. The only trouble is that, although
highly valued and appreciated, it is rather difficult to catch its
real nature. What is the fascinating "something" which distinguishes the dances of a Pavlova from those of the members of her
company? Why are the star dancers and artists of the stage or the
screen so deliriously admired and able to earn fame and wealth?
Is it their outstanding technical perfection? No. Many acrobats
and acrobatic dancers can be found who have a far more highly
developed body technique than these idols of the public who, if
observed objectively, frequently do not show much more than an
average mastery of movement. Yet, they have this apparently indescribable "something."

We find this curious part or feature of movement in ordinary
life as frequently as we do in the art of dancing. Some people
move with a charm which is similar, if not identical, with that
of great artist dancers. Ordinary people do not associate their
charm of behavior with any acknowledged or unacknowledged
stage technique. They would never dream of dancing in a ballet

and yet, I am sure, they are quite conscious of and probably cherish and love the particular charm of their movement. They may even cultivate it. Now, if this is not the quintessence of dance I do not know what else it can be. Everybody who dances strives after this "something," even if sometimes unconsciously and perhaps clumsily. Dancers are often trapped by external skill which is indispensable for a theatrical career, but their guiding star is, without doubt, the charm of movement.

If one could call the humble striving after this radiant quality "dancing," I would have to refute my initial statement. I should have to affirm that the dance has the most eminent educational and remedial possibilities.

Because of its inexplicable influence on adolescents and its mysterious effects in healing certain illnesses, the dance was considered a magic art in remote epochs in the history of mankind. Present-day educationalists, addicted to fashionable intelligence tests, and doctors who believe passionately in drugs, might ridicule and despise the magic dances which to this very day permeate the education and medicine of the so-called primitive tribes.

The rediscovery of the dance as a means of education and therapeutic treatment in our time originated from the aesthetic pleasure which some teachers, doctors and industrial welfare workers took in watching modern stage dancing. They came to the dancers with the question: "Can you do this with our children, our patients, our workmen?" The dancers did it and with quite unexpected results. Not only did the children, patients and workmen enjoy themselves, but some of them seemed to be changed in an inexplicable manner by dancing. The headmistress of a school in which such dances had been arranged was surprised that a child, considered to be "dull and backward," suddenly became lively and interested even in intellectual studies. His sudden progress in such subjects as reading, writing and mathematics, where previously he had appeared hopeless, was astonishing.

Another remarkable fact was the improvement in the community spirit of whole classes. Cliques and solitary individuals, who had hitherto been competing and quarrelling tiresomely, became friendly and sociable.

A further surprising effect was that the health of some of the children improved. Weaklings who always had a horror of gymnastic exercises, and with whom drugs and other treatments had proved entirely ineffective, became stronger and more vital through dancing. Nervous children became less frightened, quieter and more open to advice and correction.

Now this might seem to be magic, since it cannot be explained. It took a considerable time to investigate the background of such effects. It has been observed that an old working woman, twisted by rheumatism, can have the essence of dance, this charm of movement, as well as a beautiful girl. A man can have it as well as a woman, no matter whether he is old or young. Moreover, this feature of movement can be acquired, developed, regulated and mastered. The only question is how, and this is a question deeply concerned with problems of education and recovery.

Education and remedial measures have a common factor; both have to deal with individuals who, through various causes, lack some inner or external qualities needed in the struggle of life. They must be helped to rediscover certain powers and functions. It is relatively irrelevant that education develops dormant qualities of a growing being, while remedial measures have to re-awaken qualities lost in the struggle of life. In providing powers and functions, both educational and remedial measures are greatly helped by the charm of movement.

Modern dancers, investigating this charm and seeking a new basis for their artistic expression and technique, took great trouble to study not only the external forms but also the deeper effort-content of working movements. Motion study in industry as first advocated by Taylor and his followers, protagonists of scientific management, awakened the keenest interest of modern dancers and found as much stimulation and help in them as they did in the exercises of traditional dancing.

The first occasion on which I could clearly see how dance and work were not only able but predestined to meet was a great pageant of crafts and industry, the organization of which was entrusted to me by the municipal authorities of Vienna. The idea was to call the attention, not only of the city and the country but of the whole world, to the great wealth of industrial tradition dying away in the aftermath of the First World War.

The task was a tremendous one, because all the working organizations, old and new, from the almost medieval guilds of handicrafts to the most complex groups of modern commerce and industry, felt it necessary to remind their contemporaries of their existence, their needs and their hopes. My idea of putting the rich traditions of industrial customs, and especially of the songs and dances of the crafts, in the center of the procession, soon caused it to be known as the dance procession of industries. It brought forth a wave of festive enthusiasm, the intensity of which surprised me.

Many thousands of different operations with all kinds of material and varying from the one-man shop to monster combines revealed to me their common denominator which was rhythmical effort in the flow of work, the charm of movement.

I learned to consider all the hammering, drilling, filing, assembling, transporting, as well as maintenance, repair, supply and distribution as one great unit, the overwhelming rhythm of which cannot be better described than as a symphonic ballet of human brain work and hand work.

The tragic background of this gay festival was the struggle— a life-and-death struggle—of people who were fully alive in their productive energy but had to face the rapid decline of all possibility of work. Craftsmanship was still cherished, and work, as far as it was available, was performed with real affection. On one of the four hundred floats of the cortege a forge was installed and the ancient methods of forging horseshoes in the Alsatian, Scottish and Italian styles were demonstrated, each with its special rhythm and accompanied by dances of apprentices and girls in similar rhythms. Another float of gardeners and agriculturists showed the origin of the well known Vienna Waltz, which is, as students of the history of the dance surmise, the primeval threshing of corn with the feet. Yet another float contrasted the bizarre old professional dances of medieval grocers with the gigantic rhythm of the modern department stores. The factories—producing objects of iron, glass, leather and all kinds of other materials—were represented by machine dances. The pride in work and the love of perfect rhythmical performance was visible everywhere. The whole festival revealed a gigantic poetry of movement and a traditional knowledge of the laws of motion ruling both dance and work. Expressed, as it was, in living practice, it gave an excellent example of how vocational education and recovery in festive recreation can be achieved through dancing.

We know today how primeval tribes accompany their work with songs and dance-like body rhythms, and this old spirit is by no means dead; movement training is at the root of almost all industrial education, and, in a new form, it is the fundamental idea of reformers like Taylor. In all the measures evolved to improve industrial efficiency, such reformers paid the greatest attention to human effort, without, alas, penetrating to the heart of the problem of rhythm. For this reason they failed to introduce its beneficial effect into contemporary work.

In earlier days when individual workers asked modern dancers to help them improve their skill and relieve the strain of their work it soon became obvious that the similarity between popular dance forms and working procedures offered a valuable basis for the study of the educational and therapeutic value of the art of movement.

There are repetitive and free dance forms very like repetitive and free working movements. Although most repetitive work is done with arms and hands, and the dance with legs and feet, the movements require, as a rule, the same kind of inner efforts in both fields. In spite of the fact that the spirit of the dance is usually light and quick, while that of work is heavy and slow, and in spite of other similar differences in the use of the elements of effort, it soon became evident that exactly the same elements are used and combined in both work and dance.

The exercise of the complementary character of these two ways of moving is extremely salutary in its effects when working movements are taken as the basis of movement exercise, or artistic movements as a recreation and a stimulus for working people.

The workers seeking relief from the strain and pain of their work in the unique experience of the dance pageant, pointed unerringly to the unexpected but fundamental possibility of restoring lost energy and of improving working habits through the use of artistically harmonized movement.

Dancing, as a means of recovery from the strain caused by work, developed in much the same way as it did in schools. The only difference was that in the case of schools the teachers and heads of schools sought such advice and help, while managers and industrialists remained indifferent for a considerable time. It was actually the workmen themselves who, after seeing some performances by modern dancers, expressed the desire to do something similar. When they subsequently studied some dances selected for the purpose of recovery the result was the reduction of fatigue and pain in those parts of the body which were overstrained by repetitive activities. The workmen affirmed that they had become more interested in their work and especially in the rhythmical content of certain operational movements. Incidentally, a few charge hands, foremen and even managers joined in the dancing, but methodical application of rhythmic, dance-like exercises in the factory was a relatively later outcome. It was only when workers' dance clubs and movement choirs had been established that this came about.

The study of the harmony of movement differs essentially from the traditional technique applied to the performance of some set steps. When man dances he may develop dormant as well as lost qualities, just as occasion arises. He penetrates into a realm of hidden treasures, some of which he may collect while others he rejects or disregards. What are these treasures? Expressed briefly they are all experiences of the charm of movement. Or shall I say they are valuable life experiences gained in movement? An example might make this clear.

Dance has often been used in olden times as a means of improving human relationships. Dance considered as a school of behavior is expected to develop a deeper-rooted harmony of social friendliness beyond external politeness. Our enquiring mind asks, however, what is the mechanism of such achievement? This mechanism might be revealed if we consider that people using freely flowing movement become more open-minded than those who are bodily cramped and wrapped up in themselves. This opening is visible; when people gather together they can see and discern more than the simple process of opening. They learn to know one another through the reciprocal observation of their movements. Traits of movements common to all human beings are experienced and compared. Individual differences are noticed. In everyday life certain peculiarities of movement may arouse suspicion; aggressiveness, selfishness may be seen in them and provoke defense and aggression. Here, in communal dance, this fear is abolished. There is no cause for immediate fight; fear is abolished, tolerance is awakened.

Such are the treasures discovered by the experiences made in communal dance.

Individually, it is especially the control and mastery of one's own movement which is felt to be beneficial, for fear and suspicion are not restricted to the relationship with other people. One can be afraid or suspicious of oneself. Human behavior and its inner motives are surrounded by a great number of taboos and conventions which are apt to tint harmless inner stirrings with a shade of noxiousness or even danger. The self-conscious person is mostly not conscious at all of his self. Consciousness cannot be acquired by thinking alone. One must become familiar with one's own movements and the intentional stirrings mirrored by them. This familiarity is gained or, at least, promoted by dancing. To learn all these and many other similar things is without doubt an educational process. Dancing of the kind described has thus certainly an educational and perhaps even a therapeutic value.

The reluctance of some people to join in communal dances or to move freely for themselves cannot be exactly called an illness, but it is very near it. If the impregnation of suspicion with fear is too intense, so that a simple opening of the personality through free movement cannot take place easily, special forms of remedial dance exercises will be helpful. An adequate knowledge of human nature is an essential precondition for devising such exercises and dances. Here we come to the important question as to whether the dance teacher who wishes to apply his art to educational or remedial purposes can gain the necessary insight into human nature through his dance experience alone or whether he needs some additional studies.

The wealth of experience which dancing offers is illimitable. Yet, it is just this wide range which may be confounding. It is therefore a help to discern various types of dances. It is easily understood that dances of a more gymnastic or acrobatic kind might be of greater help in physical education and physical recovery than expressive dances which contribute to the education and the treatment of the emotional sides of man. It must, however, never be forgotten that dance in its deeper meaning involves both physical and psychic experience, though one of the two may prevail slightly in certain types of dancing. It is in any case not sufficient to subdivide dance steps into physical-acrobatic and psychic-expressive ones.

The methods to be developed for the application of the art of movement in education and therapy are closely linked with the recognition of the social aims of theatrical art. In recent years, institutions have been built up in which valuable research work dealing with contemporary movement habits is carried out. The training of artists, industrialists and teachers on parallel lines is undertaken in schools like the Art of Movement Studio of Lisa Ullmann in Manchester.

An important question is whether the theater of the future will be willing and able to follow the present trend of modern dancers and draw from the same sources of life which are becoming evident in our industrial civilization. In the first place, a greater consciousness of the importance of movement in the corporate effort in all works of stagecraft is needed. It should also be realized that the knowledge of the contemporary form of using movement differs greatly from the dance forms of ancient times.

The entertainment provided by the spectacular dance or the recreational pleasure of the dancing layman of our days is not sufficiently concentrated on the intrinsic features of the inner efforts and their conscious and purposeful application to human development and welfare. The educational or remedial effect of the dancing of today, if it ever arises, will be haphazard. In some individual cases the right effort might be awakened in the right person and at the right place. Yet how rarely this happens is shown by experience; otherwise all professional dancers would be perfect angels of an incredibly high level of inner balance and health. It cannot be too frequently repeated that it is nonsense to attribute to dancing itself any intrinsic educational or remedial value. It is the charm of movement for the sake of which dances are invented and selected which finally determines their effects.

Take, for instance, the motives behind traditional folk dances.

Every community that sets great store by pride of race and hero-ism will have dances which display proud and heroic gestures. These will be essentially different from the dances invented and cultivated by peoples of a languid or melancholic temperament. The ideal Spaniard, as figured in the dance imagination of his an-cestors, will differ in many respects from the ideal Russian, as fig-ured in Russian dance movements. So that dances show the differ-ence in the racial idealization of personality.

The motives of which these dances consist are rhythmical sequences of efforts which can be considered as the phrases of the language of movement. The educational and remedial effect of dancing resides in whatever is expressed by such phrases of movement.

The educational and remedial value of the dance is often compared with that of sports and games. The movements in sports or games such as in the outstanding technique of tennis, football, hockey, etc., developed in England and the United States not so long ago; fencing in France and Italy. They show that a few typical efforts were cultivated and refined in these countries with no reference at all to those larger selections of rhythm contained in the national dances of, to name a few, Scot-land, Russia, Hungary and Spain.

The rhythmical intelligence of the peoples who have a living tradition of communal dances is certainly of a higher order and their rhythmical repertory is far more comprehensive than that of peoples who have cultivated only sporting efforts. Dancing con-sists not only of more but of longer sequences of varying move-ments and efforts which distinguish it from games. The dancer must use his rhythmic ability during longer periods of time. He uses whole phrases of the language of movement, while the games player has in general only one cumulative action to perform—for instance, a hit—after which a pause occurs. The games player's effort-expression is not one of phrase or poetic sequence but of single exclamations.

Using the analogy of language, dancers are able to repeat certain poetic sequences and some of them are even able to use the entire vocabulary of rhythm in any desired combination. The dance is in this sense a rich and free poetry of movement, which can help to develop rhythmical intelligence and sensibility and thus bring man nearer to the physical and psychic balance of his capabilities. The disintegration of rhythmic sense frustrates all attempts to master life and the instinctive as well as intellectual desire to regain the lost rhythmicality is, partly at least, an appeal to the educative and therapeutic power of the dance.

Everybody has seen children jumping around happily. This might be considered as one of the natural forms of dancing. Children may even instinctively feel that their rhythmic jumping or dancing contributes to their bodily and mental well-being and to the development of some of their inner capacities and powers. This hidden self-education and self-remedy have both been studied and the knowledge acquired hereby forms an essential part of modern educational dance.

The performing dancer who exhibits an especially skillful variation of primitive jumping impulses is without doubt driven by the conviction of the deeper significance on the one hand in the recollection of his past experiences of exuberance from hilarity to sadness, and on the other hand in the anticipation of future excitements. A child can dance because of latent vitality, but can also dance in the expectation of food or of other pleasures in view. Sexual dances or war dances of olden times were anticipations of mating or killing. They produced without doubt an integration of bodily and mental functions which enabled the dancers to fulfill the expected activities with the whole power of their personality. It is, of course, a far cry from this primitive integration of function to the purposeful application of dancing in today's educational and remedial science. Yet, all we understand by the word "dance" today is, alas, mostly the rhythmic excitement of the child or of the man of primeval civilizations brought into skillful and aesthetically interesting shapes which have no appreciable educational or remedial influence in themselves.

The dance as a genuine means of education and recovery is an entirely different proposition. The application of dance for this purpose needs a special study of human nature and of the inner efforts shown in movement behavior.

It seems as though racial memory preserves certain primeval instincts such as were used and needed by man living in a virgin forest. In our times such instincts are not really needed; industrial man can survive without hiding himself behind symbolic behavior. And yet sometimes these old inherited instincts seem to demand an outlet and appear then in the symbolic gesture of a dance.

The wafting charm of Fokine's *Les Sylphides* may perhaps be the expression of more domesticated instincts than those shown in the demoniac impersonations of savage dances. Man has many layers of inherited instincts in his body-mind and each of these layers finds its expression in particular forms of movement. The most primitive layers might be mirrored in almost animal-like impulses, while the human and humane movements surge from more recent deposits of racial memory. Older layers are on the whole forgotten, even if they sometimes try to rise to daylight.

The modern dancer tries to embrace the whole content of all layers of the human psyche and this fact might explain the liberating and therefore beneficial effect of this kind of dancing on people in whom the various layers of the personality have become unbalanced.

It is the struggle of instinct-driven behavior, illustrating as it does all the variations of human efforts, which forms the charm and the real content of dances. This is also—so it seems—what the modern psychiatrist might be able to use in curing certain cases of neurosis. Some remote and primeval instincts dwelling deeply hidden in man might give rise to movements which are an expression of the wild and almost indescribable frenzy typical of primitive races in their first savagery. Some movements might spring from the behavior inherited from a less remote and more domesticated ancestry. These ancestors might have cultivated certain social and individual virtues which could give rise to movements of a more gentle and less exaggerated type. We can learn much from the themes of the struggles and tales which we see on the ballet stage. Coming as they do from the depths of racial memory, they illustrate many of the finer shades of humorous and tragic moods in human behavior. In many ballets historical pictures are built up of periods of wild and reckless living in which the perversion of natural instincts is shown. In other ballets whole groups of dancers are transmuted into spirits. In *Les Sylphides* the wafting and floating of a whole company of ethereal dancers is brought into relief by one human who, himself, is lost in a dreamlike sea of emotional sentiment springing from the delicate instinct of tenderness.

It is not beyond the bounds of possibility that the line of development of the language of movement as well as of the ideas expressed in this language will lead to the scientific dance of a scientific epoch. The vision of the world as an arrangement of rhythmical vibrations on a vast scale of waves and dynamic streamings might prove a powerful incentive for future choreographers. Biophysical powers, effective in movement, will then be more consciously applicable to physical and mental recovery and regeneration through dancing.

Modern anthropology and psychology might provide as a background an amazing chemistry of the instincts underlying human behavior and of the transformation of their various manifestations throughout the ages. Today we know more about the human organism and its functions than in the days when the first dances were created.

But there is more to be considered than the present enlight-

ened view in regard to body and mind. For Art cannot be separated from Life, and the survival of the dance in everyday life is
one of the conditions for the survival of the dynamic arts as a
whole. It may be that well-meaning people who hate ballet might
be driven into this attitude because ballet, as they see it today,
appears to be separated from life. At least from life as they know
it, namely, the dreamless life of scientific man. One side of life—
the world of the dreamer—is so hidden from them that they can
no more see its meaning and beauty. But, if the question be asked
what happens to the minds of people who cherish the beauty of
the dream world, the reply will be that not only will such people
enjoy this beauty, but they themselves will contend that dream
life is the necessary compensation for the waking life. This opinion is, of course, one which is more commonly held in civilizations
other than ours. But amongst us can be found a few people who
see in the lack of coordination between the dream life and a waking life the cause of many of our individual difficulties and illnesses and cultural crises.

Love of the art of movement has a practical motive and it
is perhaps foolish of the artist to deny it and to hide the fact of
its usefulness behind the screen of pure aestheticism. There are
many comprehensible connections between dance and life and
one of these is the use of the art of movement as a means of education and therapeutics.

Because people cannot see the color of words, the tints of words, the secret ghostly motions of words:—

Because they cannot hear the whispering of words, the rustling of the procession of letters, the dream-flutes and dream-drums which are thinly and weirdly played by words:—

Because they cannot perceive the pouting of words, the frowning of words and fuming of words, the weeping, the raging and racketing and rioting of words:—

Because they are insensible to the phosphorescing of words, the fragrance of words, the noisomeness of words, the tenderness or hardness, the dryness or juiciness of words,—the interchange of values in the gold, the silver, the brass and the copper of words:—

Is that any reason why we should not try to make them hear, to make them see, to make them feel? . . .   —LAFCADIO HEARN

CARMELITA MARACCI

The Symbolic and Psychological Aspects of the Dance

I N ANY appraisal of the dance today one should be aware of the two elements which comprise this form of expression, the inward and the outward. The inward aspect of the dance, that is the creativity of the artist, is at its strongest point of productivity; this in spite of the terrific outward pressure against keeping alive an art form so specialized and so little understood, because each dancer brings to it a very personal, and altogether subjective, psychological approach. This is the American modern dance, not

Katherine Dunham, a great student of Negro dance and folklore, a great choreographer and—last but not least—a great and entertaining performer. *Courtesy of Sally Kamin.*

Ruth Ann Koesun and John Kriza in Herbert Ross' *Capriccios*, perhaps the most successful ballet in the last few years from the youngest generation of American choreographers. This ballet was first shown by Trudy Goth's Choreographers' Workshop, then an improved version of it by the Ballet Theatre. *Photograph by Eileen Darby-Graphic House, Inc. Courtesy of Dance Magazine.*

The New York City Ballet: Maria Tallchief and Jerome Robbins in *The Prodigal Son*.
Photograph by Ed Carswell-Graphic House, Inc. Courtesy of Dance Magazine.

Iva Kitchell, the great dance humorist, in *Soul in Search*. Photograph by Dwight Godwin-Windmann. Courtesy of Dance Magazine.

in any wise to be confused with the more prevalent Freudian, Daliesque ballet accomplishments. Symbolism in the former reaches back to the Greeks; whereas in the latter, symbolic gesture seems to spring in the main from efforts at browsing in the direction of Freud.

Though generalizations are dangerous, and I recognize exceptions, I believe that the over-all approach of the dance is derivative. Therefore, we cannot speak of the dance in America without taking into consideration two distinct groups, the commercial ballet theater dance which, whether it feeds on private capital or not, is a working organization that we, the audience, can attend, or the non-commercial modern theater dance which we can attend if we are privileged enough to be on the mailing list.

The psychological aspects of the American ballet are sometimes manifested in a decorative externalization, and it is much more "fun" than the American modern dance which is dynamic and troubled and not so much "fun."

The American modern theater dance suffers in greater proportion from the outward pressure than does the ballet theater school. What is the outward aspect of the dance? It is the social-economic circumstances in which each individual artist finds himself. The outward pressure limits, hinders, turns inward upon the creative talent, and this in turn, like an ever-flowing flux, turns outward to produce a strident trend of disturbance in expression. The latter is conclusive proof of a kind of psychological frustration, and actually produces a dance which shocks present-day audiences who do not recognize their own time, have no ceremonial attachment and have always felt the dance to be only a diverting experience of no great importance.

This trend of disturbance is found in Mary Wigman as a manifestation of the disillusionment of the post-World War Germany of 1918 and later in America; it is the result of the age in which we live, an age brought about by scientific discovery, progress and social revolution. The American modern theater dance is concerned, as much as is the scientist, with this changing world. The American ballet theater school is either stuck in the bend of the turn of the century's poetic niceties or concerns itself with grubby vulgarisms clothed in beach costume and phallic symbol décor. The wholesome American-scene dance is loved by both camps. The ballet treats it decoratively; the modern, with greater awareness as to the social and economic reasons as part of the pressing necessity of living. The latter school digs deeper and therefore is more dynamic than linear.

To make a general observation on the dance without mentioning names is, for me, impossible. The dance of Spain, for instance, we remember through performances of a few artists; and in the case of La Argentina, the greater the demand, the greater her outward success—and the less demand she felt to search for a true expression. Her glorious smile was the symbol to people of a sunny, carefree Spain. Commercialism in the dance is rarely a blood brother to creative awareness. In Argentina's case, people mistook her personality for representationalism. She was Spain. Because she danced few regional dances, her gesture had the grace of a diplomatic mission and she could be at ease in London, Paris or New York. Hers was the universal symbol; she was a lady, and a commercial triumph. Her wardrobe symbolized Paris; her dancing, the gardens of Spain; her bows, the envy of any Russian ballerina; and her gentility, that of an English lady. Argentina offended no one who could afford the price of a ticket. Argentina's dancing, therefore, was the genteel aristocratic symbol of a wilting social order. So individual and so subjective is dance expression that I have chosen, purposely, a Spanish dancer whose troubles were masked in an overwhelming smile. This was not a symbolic expression of Spain but rather a tasteful, acceptable expression of one woman's gentility. A dance so rooted in strict form was, strangely enough, an international diplomatic bow to our peace of mind. We still envy those who can afford champagne, orchids and all the other accoutrements of a special class. Argentina danced—what every woman wants—elegantly with the greatest degree of perfection. She was the essence of Spain if you could afford it.

The dance can only be a symbolic expression within the limitations of the individual's personal beliefs and his relation to society.

When we approach the symbolic aspects of the dance we must keep in mind the danger in connection with the use of symbol. For symbol in the dance is often misused to express something that is totally without coherence and arises out of a lack of information as to how to handle the symbols used. This misuse, in turn, brings forth confusion and a further reflection of "misrepresentationalism," as in the example of the Freudian ballets so prevalent today; in Argentina's case an unconscious use of superimposed meaning; the other—in the Freudian ballets—a conscious, half-baked use of symbol without adequate knowledge of the meaning.

The symbolic, contemporary American modern theater dance uses few symbols, relatively speaking, that can be understood nationally, even fewer universally. The import of such esoteric symbolism shrinks with the growth of a "one world" philosophy.

Symbols spring from antiquity, and the contemporary dance, unless it follows faithfully the direct purpose and fulfillment of ancient gesture, is weakened and loses its significance. Symbol is a telling shortcut to the written and spoken word. In antiquity, symbolic gesture was necessary for the understanding by large masses of their part in the spectacle and its relation to communal happiness. The barren expression of symbolism in our time was proven by the coincidental use or rather misuse of the first theme in Beethoven's *Fifth Symphony* as a symbol for victory. This is a dangerous clinging to antique methods of provoking mass excitement, in utter contrast to a genuine manifestation of symbolism.

Modern dance has concerned itself with primitivism much as the Left-Bank painters in Paris did with their jump back to African sculpture, and another jump to Japanese prints. Then it found itself confronted with the psychological genius of Freud. This is an unhealthy historical process. Natural historical progression was overlooked in ignorant sensationalism to provoke stylish response. The dance has not led. Its sycophancy feeds on literary, graphic and scientific trends. In the jump—a dynamic, frenetic, misdirected jump from antiquity to Freud—the American theater dance schools shockingly overlooked the evolutionary process. Nietzsche was fashionable. Isadora's bible, *The Birth of Tragedy*, was inherited by Martha Graham. Perhaps that is why Curt Sachs mentions only one dancer—Isadora Duncan—in his book on the history of the dance. In the past the dance was a leading art form, today it only follows other art forms. Isadora stripped away décor and elaborate costume, and gave to the dance the place it once held, that of an expression, in an art form, solely of the spirit. Her dance had a naturalistic simplicity closely akin to the great historical past.

The ballet brought people into a world of unreality or retreat, while the modern dance tried for a long time to bring people into the light of revealment. Prior to Freud, symbolic expression was subconscious, and with Freud, symbolic expression for the first time became conscious awareness as sexual expression of man's inner needs.

The dance remains more violently separated and more national than any other art form, mainly because it is not as highly developed as literature, music or painting. This lies in the fact that dancing has been—except in antiquity and where the dance is a necessary part of life in the community—a diversion to living, a theatrical tour de force. Work in progress for a dancer is polishing the bow without questioning the soul. We can go even further and say that the reason the dance is arrested is because it has forsaken its organic meaning, its joy in becoming. It is bogged down in meaningless symbols. The dance should not interpret words. It should discover and find, with humble questioning, and not feebly adhere with minimum effort to man's other mighty works. It isn't outside influence that warps the dance, it is the whole-hearted capitulation in blind, opportunist following of ignorance. If the dance is to assume any stature, it must spring forth from immediacy and embrace universal experience.

"Not the brow, but the experience; not the eyes, but the look; not the lips, but the sensuousness," said Spengler. The dance has been afraid of revealing the depth of human experience. The one art which could afford to be honest has preferred camouflage and confusion. I grant that the dancer reveals himself, and in many cases what he reveals he might well keep to himself. The problems that have beset more searching individuals are forgotten in the dancer's interest in his sex life. It is as if his coming of age was the most important and only event of his life. He can't get over it. This revealment concerns itself with murderous, incestuous, labyrinthine gloom, side by side with nasty, twitching, minute hands and feet studies. It is sodden, not soaring. It is knee-deep in the quicksands of gloom and fast sinking into total oblivion.

I am not in disagreement with this attitude except to find it a sorry situation if the artist feels at one with the spectator in projecting this despairing dance, and is shocked to find there isn't a large audience for it. Perhaps the audience's reaction, or lack of enthusiasm, for the psychological trend in the dance has provoked the dancer to turn more inward; this in turn has provoked, ironically enough, some enthusiastic response on its part, and the audience now considers sensationalism the important aspect of the dance and might regard more humanistic gentility with a scoff. Argentina would be old-fashioned. The danger in the dance field is its adherence to the prevalent mode. It is ashamed of heart and in the name of surgical dissection produces studies of personalized maladjustments. Granted this is the psychological age. Then why

the renewed and ever-growing interest in chamber music, rooted
as it is in romantic nineteenth-century thinking which embodies
man's development up to Freud? Why, then, in this frayed-nerve
period, the realization that we must do other than display our
sickness without at least a working hope?

Albert Einstein and Thomas Mann, to name but two outstanding figures in the contemporary world, recognize the strin-
gency of our times and the possible impending horror, and are
seeking through active participation to do what they can to pull
us out of man's present dark dread of the future. We cannot think
universally if our scrutiny is turned inward and we say: this is an
interesting neurosis; all else is hopeless. It is hopeless if we are
concerned with ourselves in one direction only, our sex life. Does
the artist of today assume that Beethoven, Goethe, Goya hadn't
any sex life? I think it is high time the dancers took it as part of
living and realized that that is how we got past the nineteenth century, and let it go at that.

Even now it is old-fashioned to dance of possible better conditions. The New Dance Group's fist-shaking *Vanderloub's Head*
is wearing a tutu these days. In the matter of muscular activity,
they are neck and neck. Ballet dancers wear leotard, rubberized
fishnet hose and ballet slippers; the modern dancer wears leotard
and slippers. The ballet dancer is still more concerned with legs;
the modern dancer with the torso. Both schools ignore the hands,
but the face in the ballet department feigns sweet, sickly nausea,
while the modern refuses to recognize the face as anything other
than a nuisance with far too many unnecessary, busy interruptions
of the fluid body-movement whole. But then you can't keep up
with these things. What is fashionable at this very hour, I
wouldn't know. I wouldn't be at all surprised if the ballet dancer
had thrown away her toe-shoes and the modern dancer had caught
them in mid-air and had found how delightful, if naive, it is to
try to soar.

I don't wish to sound trite or malicious, but I have never felt that Martha Graham would have been greater in *Frontier* or *Primitive Mysteries* if she had been the product of the Cecchetti-Legat schooling. Nor do I feel that Escudero's *Farucca* would have benefited by the *entrechat ricaduta* or *ascendenza*. Not that the ballet dancer remembers that the pink slipper should only support the soaring, but unfortunately the toe-shoe is used as a crutch and a brace for almost anything but an ecstatic quality. In fact, there are many times when the modern dance could use to advantage (and has recently) a slipper, and many times when (*Saint Francis of Assisi, Facsimile,* etc.) the ballet could have—as in these instances—used the unshod foot to great advantage, or, in the second instance, at least recognized the implications of Freudian symbolism attached to the slipper. In the case of *Saint Francis of Assisi,* the incongruity of ballet slippers offended me as much as if one of the religious paintings of El Greco were to wink.

Specifically, the forms of the dance seem to restrict honest, good, straightforward approach in compositional method. Modern dance's approach to the *Sarabande*: long hemline, full bow to authenticity in the neckline and sleeves, to give you the feeling of the period, ruined by bare, calloused feet. To suggest country, if not always time, when the modern dance—in attempting Spanish themes as inspired by Lorca—presents a modern dance matador with knee-length tights (which he evidently finds comforting to his purse and his leotard technique), there is just a faint hint of costume so that we, the spectators, say, "Oh! Spain!" In the case of modern approach to female Spaniards, a piece of red cloth tied around an austere bun with perhaps a bit of rope rakishly placed to suggest a bolero is a sufficient bow in the direction of Spain. I have always been highly amused to find that four little pieces of wood and two pieces of string and shoes are never the accoutrements that modern dancers use in their comments or observations on Spanish themes. The American dancer dances everything and everybody.

The ballet dancer also loves Spanish themes on the more

sensational theatricalized level, because ballet dance stresses dexterity of feet. Ballet dancers can do rudimentary heel work rather rapidly; case in point is *Tricorne*. But again they use fancy hands instead of castanets. The ballet dancer's lack of dexterity of hands is equal to that of the modern's. The constant stress of *port de bras* and not *de mains* makes the ballet dancer forget that the hands are second only to the face as a means of fuller expression. Modern American Russian themes are done in the same manner, dispensing with extraneous detail. One likes to feel that this is a process of elimination rather than a lack on the part of the composer and executant. These works, when performed by the modern group, are done as a friendly expression of good will, but rarely are they as moving as when the modern dance adheres to its own American folklore or primitive dance movements. Such a highly integrated dance as the Spaniards possess will reach fruition, I hope, in a truly creative native Spanish dancer.

The ballet theater dance has not been concerned with Lorca, Goya, El Greco, friendly salutations to countries, but in a highly undisturbing way (unless you are as composed as I am) with a nod at past ballroom attitudes of these countries and their people. I mean, of course, the people in the ballrooms. The graduation balls; the lilac suffering of the privileged few; the flower-plucking pains of the maiden and a prince who suffers with her and after her; this never-ending theme and variation in a day when most of the world's royal courts have crumbled. Very seldom is this courtly obedience given a slap on the derrière. The one exception was Agnes de Mille's *Tally-Ho*. The latter may not have been a great work, but it had a point of view and was done by a person who didn't let slipper satin stand in the way of genuine comment and wit. Perhaps Miss de Mille understands her source material better than most dancers, and then invests her composition with a lively, provocative point of view. Perhaps it is best to say that Miss de Mille does not come from any single school of dance and never follows a cult-like formula which blinds most artists to the essential ingredient in any work of art: a wide comprehension of humanity, its frailties as well as its nobility.

On the one hand, the dance suffers from its derivative nature in its adherence to final formal pattern; on the other, from its separateness in that it does not join hands with the great developments of man. It is obedient to symbol insofar as its patience for research goes. It is hindered by fashion and its doubts are greater than its beliefs and it is afraid of its honesty. The modern dance is a truly successful form of movement-expression. It has lived inwardly so long because of the public's lack of interest that its contribution is of far greater importance than that of the ballet. Within the last few years it has admired the gloss of the ballet in a dangerous manner. So strong is the prejudice on the part of the public that managers call the works of the leading modern dancers "ballets." That the modern dance survives at all will be testimony to the genuine sincerity of the few who believe that the dance can do other than entertain.

It is a curious situation that in a country such as ours the dance has made such determined strides. It is a theatrical achievement in a country where folk dancing is kept alive by as small and determined a group as is the creative dance. This unhealthy situation is not the result of the dancer's ethics. The serious creative dancer survives despite public indifference towards an art expression it probably considers old-fashioned. The dancer, in many cases, has been forced to seek dance forms of other countries where such expression is a vital part of the people's lives. It is to be hoped that the rich vitality of the modern dance will not find its fate to be that of the folk expression of this country. Something so much a part of our times can live only if the participation of entire people is enriched by this earnest contribution.

And this dance will have nothing in it of the inane coquetry of the ballet, or the sensual convulsion of the Negro. It will be clean. I see America dancing, standing with one foot poised on the highest point of the Rockies, her two hands stretched out from the Atlantic to the Pacific, her fine head tossed to the sky, her forehead shining with a Crown of a million stars. —ISADORA DUNCAN

I am certain that movement never lies . . . I am not saying that a good person makes a good dancer or that a bad person makes a bad dancer. The motivation, the cause of the movement, establishes a center of gravity. This center of gravity induces the co-ordination that is body-spirit, and this spirit-of-body is the state of innocence that is the secret of the absolute dancer.

—MARTHA GRAHAM

WALTER SORELL

Two Rebels, Two Giants: ISADORA AND MARTHA

THE GREAT creative artist who breaks away from the traditional concepts of his time and tries to find a new way of expression is no accidental phenomenon. There we see him walk far ahead of us, off the beaten track, unique in his appearance, in this underlined dramatic otherness of his, willful and capricious—and yet, in spite of such apparent isolation and self-imposed solitude, he remains part of the total, akin to the pulse-beat of his time. But an urge so great that it seems inescapable forces him to break out of the cobweb of conventional ideas and forms; and because of this desire, however inexplicable even to himself, his vision is able to carry him beyond the lines demarcated by his contemporaries.

This urge to seek new ways of expression is conditioned by cause and effect, by action and reaction in the development of society. It seems that whenever a cultural phase reaches its peak of saturation, it creates in itself the spirit of its own antagonist. Thus, at a certain point of history, the revolutionary artist anticipates a new form and content of life which, at that time, has become ripe for him as he has for his time.

No time has ever been more ready for decisive changes than that of the turn of the century. When we speak of the "gay nineties" we visualize women with wasplike waists sweeping the city streets with their froufrou ruffles; women on bicycles and men with monocles; the air filled with the effervescence of champagne and the echo of cancans from dancing halls; overstuffed rooms with bric-a-brac from the orient which the white man was just about to divide and exploit; everything was "fin de siècle," and one recited poetry in cozy Turkish corners with the divan half-hidden behind a bead portiere. But behind all this sham glitter and laughter was an uneasiness and weariness and a meaningful "after-us-the-deluge" attitude. One was not sure of whether it was the end or a new beginning. One began to see that not all was well. Ibsen's Nora had just then slammed the door of her doll's house behind her. The machines caused unrest, strikes. One was frightened by Hauptmann's *Weavers* and shocked by Zola's *Nana* and *Germinal*. One could not help reading Oscar Wilde, Dostoievsky and Tolstoi, and about man's growing awareness of his responsibility toward man. In short, one was frightened, and cushioned one's fear with plush.

On the other hand, the turn of the century, to be more exact the decade between 1895 and 1905, clearly shows the revolutionary trend in man's feeling and thinking as an antidote to his "all-out escapism." His dissatisfaction with the old concepts of the world he lived in led to a fervent groping for new form and content in all spheres of activities. The revolutionary changes were, so to speak, in the air.

Materialistic science received its death blow. Madame Curie, Professor Roentgen, Koch and Pasteur kept the world breathless at the time when Edison electrified it; Freud began to probe the underlying sources of our way of being; Einstein dented the old basic concepts of physics, Schoenberg questioned the bases of the tonal system, and, somewhat later, Picasso tried to reduce figures and objects to their fundamental geometric forms and to turn the abstraction of these forms into new artistic designs.

Only when we recall that time to our mind, that condition of man's mental and physical state, can we understand the new era of dance which began with Isadora Duncan. In retrospect, her daring and deed appears, first and last, as the utter negation of her time. The affirmation came later, actually came after her. She was not the irresistible performer whose technical form of expression would still be remembered many generations later. No, she was the torchbearer of a new idea, the rebel who laid the groundwork for the dance of the twentieth century.

When Isadora "rediscovered" the dance, the Russian ballet was chained and paralyzed by an autocratic bureaucracy and its artistic output was tagged "Mental Stagnation." It had then become stereotyped in the expression of form and idea, or, as Lincoln Kirstein said, it had "petrified into a formula for technical display."

Isadora rediscovered the dance through the discovery of her body. She worshipped nature and her first dance masters were "wind and wave and the winged flight of bird and bee." She felt the immediateness of nature expressed in her own body and was out to evolve her "movements from the movement of nature." How can any body function when it is not free from the constriction of whalebones, the stuffiness of the tulle ruffles and the gaudiness of jewels? The nude is the noblest in art, she cried out. The right conception of beauty can only be "gained from the form and symmetry of the human body." And what is dance if not beauty awakened in the human body? And from there one step further: body and soul must grow so "harmoniously together that the natural language of that soul will have become the movement of the body."

First came her negation of the then dominant type of ballerina with the frozen coquettish smile, the negation of decadence and imitation of bygone times, the negation of meaningless, machinelike movements, of outdated acrobatics. Then came her enthusiasm for the Greeks which was her detour to find her way back to natural body expression. When she used the Hellenic freedom of the body, she was looking for some kind of prop, and for an incontestable ally in her fight for her ideals and for recognition.

What she danced was not really what the ancient Greeks might once have danced. She realized it herself when she said that her dance was American, that it was born of the woods and the sea and the eternal spring of California. But she maintained that to find the dance again as free movement and as creative force, one must go as far back as the Greeks in history and the instinctive movement of child and animal in life. Because they, and they alone, move according to their form and frame, their organic structure—not artificial, not construed and contrived, not angular.

Angularity was the one thing she could not perceive at all and which she detested most. And here again she proved to be of her time, imbued with the neo-romantic spirit of those days no matter how far ahead of her contemporaries she actually was. She saw no angular movement in nature, no full stop put behind any movement to denote its end. There were only undulating lines which never came to any stop.

Her art was lyrical and, as such, highly personal. She believed in "the divine spirit through the medium of the body's movement." She believed that "spiritual expression must flow into the channels of the body, filling it with vibrating light." But where can it come from if not from the "soul"? For her, all emotional experiences were the origin and seat of expressive movements. We must not forget the time had then come to make man stop and probe his self.

That was what Isadora Duncan did in her own way. She probed her self. She may have meditated in front of a mirror (and did she not stand before an imaginary mirror her entire life?), seeking the physical release for all that went on in her spiritually. She waited for the moment of emotional stimulation to find the right expressive movement for what she felt. The stimulation had to come mostly from outside, from music. But she did not interpret it. Its function was to make her creative impulse function. What she interpreted was nothing else but her inner feeling, her unconscious stream of thoughts, her tumultuous physical desires. Such expression could hardly be stimulated by the then prevailing custom of dancing to cheap Italian tunes. She did away with them and turned to serious music: to Gluck (who was her favorite), Wagner, Beethoven, Chopin. It was their music that inspired her "soul" which, in turn, flew "into the channels of the body." As she said in one of her lectures (Berlin, 1903), it was precisely at such an inspired moment that she tried to find the *key movement* which every dance needed and from which the other movements would emanate, like a motor phrase from which the power of movement would evolve its own forms.

But was her main merit to "recover the natural decadences of human movements," to fill and shape them with emotional content? That she gave freedom and content to the expression of her body was but the first step into a new direction. To see what she did from an artistic viewpoint only would limit the scope of her deed which was not merely the deliverance of the dance from the shackles of the past. She aimed at the deliverance of man through the dance. This became clear when she spoke of how astonished an intelligent child must be

> to find that in the ballet school it is taught movements contrary to all those movements which it would make of its own accord. This may seem a question of little importance, a question of differing opinions on the ballet and the new dance. But it is a great question. It is not only a question of true art, it is a question of race, of the development of the female sex to beauty and health, of the return to the original strength and to natural movements of woman's body. It is a question of the development of perfect mothers and the birth of healthy and beautiful children. The dancing school of the future is to develop and to show the ideal form of woman. It will be as it were a museum of the living beauty of the period.

The ideal form of woman as Isadora saw it was not the Gibson Girl of her time. Small wonder that the America at the turn of the century—then in the last phase of her "Gilded Age" and dragged into McKinley's imperialistic adventures—rejected Isadora. The feelings were mutual, and as if into a self-imposed exile she went to Europe where she finally triumphed.

That she shocked the people wherever she went was in the nature of her personality. When she rediscovered the dance through the discovery of her body, undoubtedly sex was at the root of her drive to dance. She always remained the apotheosis of sex, vacillating her entire life between the purest maternal instincts and those of the adventure-seeking woman. Only the dignity which lay in every move she made, in every word she uttered, kept her from slipping into the cheap and profane. And it seems that this most primordial of our instincts was the very source of her strength and greatness.

Whatever she did was a slap in the face of all established norms and codes. She was a rebel who stormed the barricades of law and order, of rule and regulation. It was a time for rebels, and she was one of them. In the utter negation of the past lay the realization of a new era. She opened the door on the threshold of this era, and a new vista became visible, different from what was known before. It matters little that she was unable to really fulfill her creative task. Perhaps her character—the same character which gave her the impetus and strength to rebel—defeated her in the final fulfillment of artistic creation.

When it is true that every century may have its Napoleon, but not every Napoleon his century, Isadora found her time ripe for her. She restored the human body to its natural rights, after man had neglected it for two thousand years. She delivered the dance from the fetters of mere entertainment and recreated the art in its oldest form of expression: the expressional dance. And with the return to the freedom of movement and with the discovery of the awareness of our self, Isadora Duncan anticipated the conception of modern man.

2

Martha Graham dances the modern man: his personality in the abstract, his hopes and failures, his frustrations and inner conflicts, no matter whether she uses American folk material or goes back to Greek mythology.

About the same time Isadora gave her last recital in Paris (and shortly afterwards lost her life), Martha Graham gave her first recital in New York. A mere coincidence? No doubt. And yet it carries symbolic significance.

To set these two great dancers in juxtaposition is an attempt to draw a painting in contrasts, though there are, sociologically seen, threads leading from one to the other.

If Isadora was a beginning, Martha was its fulfillment. In retrospect, it seems that Isadora's method was, as a most personal expression, limited to simple walking, running and leaping. It was soul minus technique, while Martha is technique plus soul. What was still a never-ending groping for new form and content with

Isadora—vague, however impressive it may have been—has found in Martha its master.

Opening her soul; seeking her inner self still with the help of a mirror; turning her feelings inside out in uncontrolled effusion, with her sex somersaulting: that was Isadora. Martha came of age with psychoanalysis; she had the advantage of a whole generation's experience over Isadora; she is sparing in her expressive language to such an extent that she only communicates the essence of her innermost feelings; she is all restraint, complete integration.

In imitating nature, Isadora tried to give the impression of wind and wave and bird; it is true, she no longer escaped the ground as the ballerina did, but she merely made use of it, since it was inescapable. Not Martha; for her the floor is vital, she has used it as an expressive area and has thus added it as a new space to the dancer.

Martha Graham revolutionized the dance vocabulary, and expressional dance as well as ballet have received a durable contribution through her technique. She broke completely with the idea of the flowing movement of the ballet and the lightness which is out to conceal all effort. She also felt that the undulating lines of nature, their rounded-off beauty—in which Isadora still so fervently believed—were a mere photographic repetition if expressed through dancing. Not unlike Picasso, or modern architecture, she tried to find the basic geometric form of the object, or idea, which she wanted to shape, and from there she went one step further to give the abstraction its new artistic form and face.

In revolt against the flowing movement she evolved a new language of symbols and finally arrived at what she termed percussive movements which take hold of the entire body in form of a beat, of contraction and release. She also evolved suspensions and falls from different positions and in a variation of accents and speeds which she applies to the expression of different emotional stages. Her entire body became a most articulate instrument in a fully coordinated manner: legs, shoulders, hips, face and hands welded to an entity which can only be achieved through the highest form of technique. And "technique," Martha Graham said, "only services the body towards complete expressiveness."

After a process of thorough elimination, after trial and error, she always tries to find the rudimentary expression of her inner experience. In its almost epigrammatic conciseness it loses its pictorial effect, becomes angular and, through the newness of its image, remains sometimes as obscure, or not immediately fully comprehensible, as a passage of one of T. S. Eliot's poems.

She was often criticized for appearing intellectual or even cold. It must be said that some of her dances strike us as unfamiliar, but everything ceases to be unfamiliar after a certain time. Her dances have inner passion, since the urgency to create is, with her, always emotional, never the result of mere thought processes.

Only the essential is tolerated, in movement and stage sets. And having reduced everything to the movement necessitated by the inner feeling, she arrives at the intensification of her self. Of her earlier period, it can be said that her approach had much of the American landscape, of purposeful soberness like the American cities—and is just as impressive. It is modern Gothic, made in the u.s.a. Martha said that

> nothing is more revealing than movement. What you are finds expression in what you do. The dance reveals the spirit of the country in which it takes root. No sooner does it fail to do this than the dance begins to lose its indispensable integrity and significance.

More and more, her compositions gain in poetic insight and are driven by an intense feeling. But there is so much awareness in this insight and feeling, such a complete delineation of psychological processes and such a wide range of symbolic images that we can often only grasp their depth and meaning after seeing and re-seeing these compositions many times. It may sometimes seem to lack clarity where, in fact, she has reached an expression that is the most concise presentation of what she has to say.

Lately, her compositions deal with emotionally complex situations and conflicts which can be termed psychological dramas. We can easily see how she delves deeper and deeper into the intricate problems of the inner processes of man: From her *Letter to the World* in which she portrayed the alter ego of Emily Dickinson to *Deaths and Entrances*, the tragedy of frustration, to *Judith* in which she tries to communicate the inner struggle of the woman who feels called upon to rise to the greatness of her deed.

It is this constant probing into what motivates human conduct, her total introspection into character and her characterization with all deeper psychological implications which sets her apart from all other dancers of her time and makes her exert such great influence on them. Martha Graham found the dance image of our "age of anxiety."

3

Isadora may well have been the initiator of the idea of the expressional dance, but her method was so personal that no school could continue where she left off. On the contrary. America's modern dance leads back to a dancer whom John Martin called "the antithesis of Isadora's" nature and art.

With the establishment of the colonial empires at the turn of this century, white man not only profited by the exploitation of the colored races, but the opening up of a new and exotic world also stimulated his imagination. Dreamlands had been found for those who wanted to escape the industrialized pattern of life without necessarily having to part with its comfort.

The oriental influence on literature and the arts in general had never been greater than at that time. Ruth St. Denis became entangled in the rich embroidery of oriental movements. She was not as dramatic as Isadora, she was spectacular. She knew how to give a great show, she reveled in light and color, in costume and scenery. But what gave St. Denis' dance the individual imprint was her ardent belief in mysticism and her desire to transplant the exotic and ritual dances of the Far East to America.

Her art, her lavish theatricalism was one form of escape, it was entertainment and stood in utter contrast to the growing problems of her time. The first quarter of this century was seething with all kinds of "isms" in the arts. The machine had changed the pace of man. Restlessness and riots were everywhere, and the growing awareness of a looming disaster. The First World War whipped the emotions up to a high pitch: the war to end all wars; hope for freedom, and the League of Nations. And then the great contrast of two worlds: Europe, the sea of disillusionment, frustration and fighting ideologies; America, an island of safety, security and wealth. Man lived in an atmosphere of stark realism and materialism. In utter confusion and fear of himself, he looked for relief into *himself*, searched for new self-expression and threw himself into new adventures, politically and artistically.

Martha Graham grew up in this period of growing strife and awareness, with the world's problems and man's predicaments piling up higher and higher. She was the first dancer of the Denishawn group to make herself independent. When she rebelled artistically against the artificiality of Denishawn, she felt forced to seek the adequate expression of what was then going on in her and around her. If "movement never lies," as she said, then she had to find her own language, the idiom and image that would express, in her medium, her own self and the self as reflection of her time. In other words, it was finally impossible for her to continue with the impersonation and representation of Hindu gods and Aztec warriors and oriental stories. Martha turned against the "music visualizations" and the rigidity of alien concepts which were not only alien to the American spirit but also to the problems of her age.

When Isadora Duncan dreamed of the great American dancer who would raise the dance to "the most noble of all arts" again, and when she saw "America dancing, standing with one foot poised on the highest point of the Rockies, her two hands stretched out from the Atlantic to the Pacific, her fine head tossed to the sky, her forehead shining with a Crown of a million stars"— then she must have visualized the image of Martha Graham.

*In the instinctive and organic life,
in the mental and spiritual life of man, characteristics make themselves
felt which demand communication. Man turns to man. Man needs
man. Art is communication spoken by man for humanity in a language
raised above the every day happening. What would be the sense of an
art that robs itself of its communication and arrogantly believes that it
can turn away from man?* —MARY WIGMAN

HANYA HOLM

The Mary Wigman I Know

ART GROWS out of the basic cause of existence. From there
it draws its creative and constructive forces. From
there it receives strength to renew, rejuvenate, transform
itself. And there only is it imperishable, eternal."

These are Mary Wigman's words. It is her belief that the
artist must absorb the primordial elements of life during the process of creation, that he must lose himself in something that is
greater than himself, in what she calls "the immediate, indivisible
essence of life." Caught by life's majestic current, the artist becomes excited and stimulated to express his experiences. His existence as an individual may be extinguished in the midst of life's
current, but he is rewarded for it by the singular gift of his participation in the all-embracing, universal happenings of his time. He
readily absorbs the energies flowing into him, but this steady flow
of energies will, at various points of culmination, force him to
action. These forces discharge themselves in the dancer as move-

ment—as the dynamic and rhythmic visualization of his life experience.

To Mary Wigman the dance is a language with which man is born, the ecstatic manifestation of his existence. It is the entity of expression and function, pellucid corporeality, a form made alive through the pulsebeat of experience. To know is not enough; where knowledge can no longer reach, where only the inner emotional experience becomes sole and supreme law, there the dance begins, the dance in which body and soul become an indivisible entity, or "the body, visible manifestation of its being, turns into the truthful mirror of its humanity."

2

Mary Wigman's dance creations emerge out of her awareness of her time and her almost demonic urge to give artistic form to reality, as mirrored within her, and to animate this form with her breath. Although man, arrested in his time, creates his most personal and specific form, it is never an arbitrary form invented by one person for any individual purpose. It develops with the individual, unchecked by any borderlines, reaching beyond oceans. The expression of the dance, its style and content, its intellectual basis and emotional impact, is the symbolic image of its time. And the artistic creation of the individual himself gains importance only through the establishment of a relationship between his ego and mankind.

But does Mary Wigman express mere "feelings"? She would say no. They are not feelings we dance; feelings are already too clearly delineated, too obvious. We dance the constant change of mental conditions, as they are alive in man as a rhythmic flow. The dance content must be like the content of any other artistic medium: its nuclear point must be man and his fate. Yet, not "the fate of man of today, yesterday, or tomorrow," but of man as the immortal phenomenon that arises, grows and dies, that is always the same and, in spite of this sameness, always different. It is not the personal problem, but the universal-human problem which becomes her main motif.

She strongly believes in any great work of art as growing out of a necessity. Every idea has its own inherent law, the rules of which develop during the creative process of each composition. Therefore, it becomes impossible to make them fit any other composition, should they not deteriorate to mere formulas. And formulas strangle the creative spirit.

With her, every creation seems to be a spontaneous, almost volcanic eruption of feelings suddenly freed and turned into visual images. But this suddenness is deception. She said once that "the idea for a dance comes to the creative dancer, so to speak, in his sleep, in other words, suddenly it is here. As a musician hits upon a melody without knowing where it comes from, thus the dancer's movements come spontaneously to his mind." Yet the dancer may have carried the idea around with him for a long time without finding its visual shape. Set into the world by an experience, of which we may or may not be conscious, it is a wearisome process until the foetus-idea grows and develops in our mind only to be set free, to take the form of an independent artistic life after much labor and final discharge through inner friction and tension.

While molding and shaping her inner experience she tries to purify what is most personal by making it impersonal and valid for everyone. What she demands from herself and every artist is the feeling of responsibility for form and content, for the absolute clarity of the visualization of his idea and for the ideal postulate that every genuine composition must be a confession, must bear testimony of the artist's own being and, beyond that, of mankind as reflected in him.

Her creations are unsophisticated. She draws from rich sources of symbolic-primitive origin. Although her dance compositions show a strong leaning toward mysticism, they are never cryptic; they may be "heavy" with symbolic meaning, but never get out of hand nor lose themselves in obscurity. Here her intel-

lect works as a moderating, controlling factor. It elevates her
topics to a level of universal importance.

In her *Witches Dance* (1926), for instance, it was not her
idea of visualizing broomstick or Walpurgis Night, but the deep-
bedded darkness in man, the wicked and witch-like trends in the
human character. In this dance as well as in her *Ceremonial Figure*
and *Dance of Death* she uses masks to underline the symbolic
power behind the reality of the dancing figure. In her opinion, it
becomes necessary for a dancer to hide his face behind a mask,
if the creative spirit forces the performer from a realistic plane
into the realm of irrationalism. Masks should never be used as a
decorative accessory; they must extinguish the dancer as a person
and help transcend the performer into a sphere in which vision
and reality become an entity; they can accentuate the struggle of
the individual against the forces of the universe as well as his own
struggle with himself when part of his ego becomes liberated from
his total ego and, in his dualistic fight, the dancer's creation turns
into a seemingly alien figure.

What makes Mary Wigman appear so typically "Germanic"
is her preoccupation with death and the Faustian in her personality and compositions, two factors which, often misinterpreted,
have led to misunderstanding of her intentions and, consequently,
to strict rejection of her art.

But it would be erroneous to assume that this rejection, this
bewilderment and confusion caused by her dances, was restricted
to America alone. From the very beginning of her career, every
audience has gone through a shock experience which probably was
repeated at every performance she gave. It was created by her so
definite attitude to the profound and profoundly human problems she dealt with, by her portraits of the eternal struggle of the
self with itself and the environment whose product it is. When
she came to America in the beginning of the 1930s, she had already achieved world-wide reputation. But even then the voices
of the doubters and deniers were still heard in her own country

where it had taken her years of endurance and a strong belief in herself to overcome the opposition of public and critics alike ranging from indifference to loud derision. She says in an autobiographic fragment about these formative years: "Belief, despair, belief in a constantly changing flow of back and forth. And something in the back of my mind that was a 'must' which forced its 'will.' Fatigue and exhaustion were states of transition. Climax and depression have gradually manifested themselves as a rhythm of creativeness conditioning one another. The most difficult was to learn patience and to have to wait without losing one's strength through the years; to experiment without interruption."

After each performance, after each new attempt she would call "herself to a most private trial where she had to account for every movement." And every time the result is the same—a qualified sentence: "Not yet strong enough, to begin once more from the beginning." This is the Faustian in her character: the constant conflict between the aim she strives for and the errors she succumbs to, but never to yield, since Satan dwells in the temptation to be driven like flotsam instead of striving for the higher aims. The Faustian in her work: to overcome man's instinctive cravings, the average man in us; in order to be able to exist, one has to place oneself on a higher plane of awareness, to decide for a constant struggle to secure such awareness and to decide against the peace of doubtful happiness.

Therein lies the thought of "sacrifice" which is uppermost in her mind and finds its way into her compositions time and again. Everything that is, in short, total existence is dependent on and subjected to the idea of sacrifice, knowingly or unknowingly, intentionally or unintentionally. The offer of such sacrifice has a sacerdotal connotation: to sacrifice on the altar of mankind.

In the hourly enacted drama of life and death, in the struggle with life and against death must lie man's readiness to die. In the same way as she pleads for living the day in a Dionysian manner (Dance for the Earth), her many dances on death are by no means distorted, never despairing or accusing. In them is the courage of readiness which may be full of tragic elements, but in a dramatic-heroic sense only. Mary Wigman is so deeply rooted in life that she finds in the symbol of death (which she is so often tempted to express artistically) a counter-balance to her dynamic energies of life. Death is the only point of rest, a pause, an oasis where the soul, forced into a welter of desires and demands, finds peace. The face of death has nothing frightful about it. Death is not the end, it is a suspended state.

3

Consciousness of her time and the strong link with which she is tied to her fellow-men are shown in her indomitable belief in the group dance.

"It is not the soloist's achievement which is pregnant with future," she says. "This will always remain a single and purely personal maximum achievement . . . But the young dance generation should put all emphasis on the group dance. There are all possibilities, there is future."

Mary Wigman feels that the development of every dance personality should take place in two different directions: the perfection of the performer as an individuality and, on the other hand, the adjustment of this individuality to a group.

The dancer who choreographs may bring with him a blueprint of his idea. But this, though it may be necessary, is only the smaller part of his work. He must be so convinced of, so overwhelmed by his visualization that his own experience can become the dancer's experience and that finally a single basic chord embraces the entire group. Unlike a conductor whose co-workers play from a printed score, the choreographer works with live material, he has to utilize the creative ability of each instrument and must, in fact, help form this creative ability without destroying the personality of the individual performer within the group.

In the awakening of the group to a communal rhythmic pattern there lies, to some extent, self-denial of individual expression. But this yielding of ground is not lost. It is absorbed, incorporated and brought back to life in the totality of the group's creation.

Mary Wigman as a teacher molds independent creative life, helping other talents to mature and to become an active force in the growth of her group. She watches each individual modulation to find the one forte which every personality has. She aims to transfer mere body into a sensitive dance instrument. This is a matter of patience, endurance and discipline. "Woe to the dancer who loses patience!" she said. "He will never find the way to the essence, to the resources and innermost motive of his dance. He will remain the self-centered Ego-Dancer whose language is masturbation. But never can he become a body of expression of all those things which, beyond his own ego, reaches, embraces and stirs other people."

Mary Wigman recognizes three basic stages in the development of the growing dancer, stages which may differ as to the student's abilities, that is in degree, but, nevertheless, show these common features:

(1) *The unconscious expression of the dancer's creative force*, with its instinctive groping for expression regardless of form or content; the realization of the dancer's body and the chaotic experience of its expressiveness.

(2) *The experience of artistic crystallization*, with a gradual division of expression, content, form and function; the general expression in struggle with the individual expression, lack of unity, vacillation between expression for expression's sake and form for form's sake; the body no longer exists as a body only, but is not yet instrument.

(3) *The conscious expression of the dancer's creative force*, expression and function of body have crystallized and are fusing into an entity; dance develops as a language; the body is no longer

self-willed substance, it becomes a means leading to an end: the bodily instrument and its full use by its master, the dancer.

From here on begins the hard road to artistry. The teacher has completed his work on the raw material. Now the dancer needs more hard work, self-discipline and the teacher's counsel and guidance. "The necessary corrections on the bodily instrument cannot and must not be performed according to any generally valid norm, they must stem from a human and artistic understanding of the individual and his most personal expressiveness." Her aim has never been to educate little Wigmans. Though it is only natural that her pupils grow up in the spiritual and artistic atmosphere which is hers, she sees to it that they can detach themselves from her in time. "If one wants to achieve something," I remember her saying, "one must not have oneself in view, only the work, one must not want success, but achievement. Mistaking the person for the matter, or the person for the idea leads to hidden rocks on which a great many artistic attempts have suffered shipwreck . . ."

4

1919. A war-torn Europe. The conquered people sought to overcome their physical defeat by finding new intellectual values, new forms, new expressions. Out of destruction and uproar, out of the struggle for one's existence, grew the awareness that man was inextricably entangled in political issues which reflected the economic and social revolution of modern man.

It was a time ripe for revolutionary thoughts, for otherness, for the new. Out of this maze of ruin, death and starvation, out of a world of uncertainties came Mary Wigman. She came back to Germany from Switzerland where she had lived and worked with Rudolf Laban. Hardly two decades had passed since Isadora Duncan opened up a new world of ideas, two decades in which civilization had grown rapidly, had developed according to dramatic rules and closed in on its catharsis. Modern man came of age, gave it his imprint with motor and speed on the ground and in the air—gradually leading to total mechanization. The era of a button-pressing world began to dawn. Man began to realize that no ego can exist in a vacuum. The individual discovered himself in relation to his fellow-man and the universe.

Mary Wigman gave it artistic expression through movement. "In the dance, as in other arts, we are concerned with man and his fate . . . the fate of man in the immortal and significant aspects of its endless metamorphoses shapes the ancient and yet ever-new theme of the dance form." In contrast to it, let us quickly remember Isadora's words of "the divine expression of the human spirit through the medium of the body's movements." The two worlds of before and after the first universal conflagration.

What was still lyrical romanticism in Isadora Duncan became in Mary Wigman the dramatic interpretation of the conflicts within the individual and in relation to the influence of the outside world. When man is the eternal and unchanging theme of the dance, then, consequently, these themes are constantly changing with man's conditions and his fate. They are not timeless, they are time-conditioned. Man must find his own language of expression in every epoch.

What was with Isadora Duncan "soul and beauty" became with Mary Wigman the transparency of the individual's psychological manifestations—in the Jungian rather than Freudian sense —with the subtleness of all emotional shadings. When Isadora began to dance at the turn of the century, modern psychology was in its incipient stages. When Mary Wigman toured Germany for the first time in the bitter winter of 1919–20, modern psychology had come of age.

"In the last analysis, nothing more happened than that the dancer rediscovered within himself 'the dancing human being' and confessed his acceptance of this in the dance . . ." Nothing more happened. She wrote in a new language of movements the story of the human being, the story of his life and death. Her vocabulary was full of dynamics which filled the space. Without ecstasy no dance, she said, and gave it ecstasy. Without form no dance, she said, and gave it form.

Decades have passed. Years have passed. I am left with the memory of something monumental, of something that has beginning and end and the oneness of both—like a great spheric circle that knows no end. It is like the oneness of death and life in one of her dances, *Todesruf*, of the one who calls and the one who is called. And Mary Wigman dancing both: Life and Death. And the climactic moment when Death is waiting for Life that approaches him and slowly covers its face. At that moment, Death waiting for Life is already Life itself, the coming Life.

There is so much peace in this thought and so much hope —hope for the life to come, for the new generation which will dance and build their world on the world of the past as Mary Wigman has done. And they will say the inexpressible, which delights and torments them, so clearly in a language of their own, and with every movement and with every gesture they will write their story of man and his fate.

There is nothing so necessary for men as dancing . . . Without dancing a man can do nothing . . . All the ills of mankind, all the tragic misfortunes that fill the history books, the blunders of politicians, the miscarriages of great commanders, all this comes from lack of skill in dancing . . . When a man has been guilty of a mistake, either in ordering his own affairs, or in directing those of the State, or in commanding an army, do we not always say: So and so has made a false step in this affair . . . ?

And can making a false step derive from anything but lack of skill in dancing?
— JEAN BAPTISTE MOLIÈRE

———

JOSÉ LIMON

The Virile Dance

THE MALE of the human species has always been a dancer. Whether as a savage or civilized man, whether warrior, monarch, hunter, priest, philosopher or tiller of the soil, the atavistic urge to dance was in him and he gave it full expression. He does so to this day. He will dance to the last apocalyptic hour. He dances because he is neither a vegetable nor a rock but a moving organism, and in movement finds release and expression.

Since dance and gesture were his long before the spoken word, he still has the power to reveal himself more truly in this atavistic language not only as an individual but "en masse." At some periods of his history he has danced sublimely; at others with a glittering elegance; and then again he has danced a sad

192

Carmelita Maracci is one of the most individualistic and uncompromising dancers of our time who combines classical ballet with the Spanish School in her exciting dance creations. *Photograph by Constantine. Courtesy of Dance Magazine.*

One of the most fascinating male dancers of our time, half Mexican, half American, the living anachronism of a baroque personality against the background of the twentieth century: José Limón. *Photograph by Walter Strate Studio.*

Sketch of Ruth Page by Isamu Noguchi. *Courtesy of Ruth Page.*

Costume sketch by Eugène Berman. Courtesy of Kamin Dance Gallery.

period of degeneracy, or like a clown or a fool, and his ancient
power has fallen into atrophy and decay.

King David danced before the ark of the Covenant. He
danced not only as the consecrated Pontiff, as intercessor with
God for his people, but as chief of state, as head man of the tribe,
as the man most exalted and respected, as the racial paragon.

His dance was solemn and majestic, a dance worthy of a king
and a man of God. Its cadence and measure were living symbol
and embodiment of man's high function and his noblest aspirations. It spoke of the ineffable mystery of man's one-ness with
God, for all his frailties and imperfections. The gestures and patterns must have been those of a man who was a king, who was a
priest, who was speaking to God for his people. He must have
stood tall, his powerful stride that of a man reverent and joyful,
his gestures slow with a magnificent dignity, for they must project
to the highest zenith.

This was a ritual of surpassing purity and power and showed
the man dancer at his most sublime.

King Louis danced before the court at Versailles. He danced
various "roles" in the ballets presented there for the delectation
and amusement of the court. But always he danced in pomp and
splendor as "le roi soleil," "le grand monarque." He performed
for as brilliant and corrupt an assemblage of high-born sycophants
and courtesans as ever afflicted and disgraced a nation.

The great Louis, like the biblical David, was dancing his
epoch and his aspirations. The Sun-King, between bloody and
disastrous wars, would while away his ennui with these august
spectacles. The wretched and impoverished who were made to
die for his aggrandizement and to pay for his magnificence had
no part in the festivities. Louis did not in his dance address himself to heaven and pray for enlightenment and guidance so that
his people might be blessed and prosper. He was no intermediary,

no interpreter, no dispenser of a divine and just omnipotence. These functions were left in the hands of cardinals and archbishops, and they knew their work well.

No, this was another sort of ritual. To an exquisitely formalized code of gestures and steps, the most elaborate of stylizations, dressed in the most glittering and extravagantly beautiful costumes the western world has ever seen, Louis danced this regal debauch. This arrogant, mincing, graceful figure embodied all the perfumed, cynical licentiousness of the regime. Man's highest aim was self-indulgence; the only sin was boredom; the only crime inelegance. This performance was intended to dazzle, to charm, to captivate. This was infamy executed with the flawless delicacy of a "pas de bourrée."

And a recently abdicated king danced like a clown or a buffoon until the small hours of the morning in the fetid cabarets of Paris, London and New York. And this king was not a high priest in mystic communion with heaven, nor a great leader of his tribe, nor was he a magnificent depredator, nor a brilliant luminary in the annals of iniquity.

He was a man dying from boredom, from the terrible spiritual fatigue of his time. And his dance was a ritual of futility and disbelief and unbelief. He had very little. Even the gestures and steps and patterns of his dance were not his own. They had been borrowed (for he was too tired inside to create any) from Africa. But "on him they didn't look good." As he glided and bounced and wiggled he represented the fearful spectacle of a sick world "in extremis." For a moribund society had immolated itself in a catastrophic World War I and, exhausted and spent, was gathering its forces for World War II. The little king and his anemic caricature of the primitive mating dances was symbolic of hopeless fear and despair. Yet in this Saturnalia the frenzy was hollow, the abandon synthetic. It was a dance of a man ripe for extinction, a degraded and unheroic pyrrhic dance.

The modern male as a whole has forgotten the majestic, solemn dance of King David, or the great tragic rhythms of the Greeks, and has accepted as his sole dance experience the diluted trivialities of the dance hall. Or, in the performing arts, he functions, often brilliantly, as an entertainer.

After the Sun-King the dance became more an entertainment and less a ritual. The progressive feminization of its technique, with its emphasis on coquetry and blandishment, were designed to display the charms of a ballerina. The male became superfluous. Those few men who participated were, in effect and function, effeminate adjuncts and supports of the dazzling ballerina. Later these men emerged as creatures of exquisite romantic fancy, as fauns, or the perfume of an exhausted rose, or harlequins.

It was natural that with the general surge of feminism, the female should become the dominant and creative factor in the dance, just as she has fallen heir to the wealth and power of this nation. In the environment of the serious dance the female has won indisputable stature and pre-eminence. Due to the economic factor, the male dancer tends to gravitate to more lucrative aspects of the dance, in musical comedies and the films, which certainly do not encourage serious creative efforts.

There are few men who are content to devote their time to the serious dance and to make their contribution to the regeneration of it as a virile preoccupation. It may well be that the great ritual male dance of our age is the one for which we have been in rehearsal during the last three decades and will presently culminate in an apocalyptic performance, a mighty and appalling choreography across the firmaments, a true Finale, with Viros rampant in jet-propelled, super-sonic chariots, inextricably bound to the fatal rhythm of his era. Truly a pyrrhic dance.

It is precisely because the danger of extinction is imminent that men of caliber and dedication are needed to affirm man's sanity and dance it. No other art offers such a challenge. In a society desperately in need of all its art and artists, the art of the dance offers a rare opportunity for those with the vision of its ancient grandeur to speak of it anew. The few dedicated males should take courage when they reflect that they are perhaps pointing the way. It may well be that we will be a saner world when the President of the United States, as chief magistrate, will lead the nation in solemn dance on great occasions before the dome of the Capitol.

*Nature has no Outline. But Imagi-
nation has. Nature has no Tune, but Imagination has. Nature has no
Supernatural and dissolves: Imagination is Eternity.* —WILLIAM BLAKE

JEAN ERDMAN

The Dance As Non-Verbal Poetic Image

THE DANCE, we are told by the historian, is the oldest art of
man. But we dancers today are baffled to discover that it
is treated as though it were the youngest art, the least
mature. People sophisticated in other arts retain undeveloped no-
tions about the dance. Furthermore, they are unwilling to learn,
because they would then be deprived of the last stronghold for
their suppressed sentimentality, antipode to their energetic mod-
ernism. We dancers should perhaps blame our predicament on
the wonderful development, most recently, of the human faculties of perception and understanding through the brain, which
has left our audience with poor, shriveled-up, starved infant faculties of experience through the heart. Dance, the classic art of the
childhood of the race and of our own childhood (when the body
and the heart still were able to express themselves, unintimidated,
and not yet atrophied, by the brain's requirement for mental communications), the oldest art and the youngest remains associated
with "childish" things—not as the Wisdom Child, who might
restore to us our lost connection with the mysteries of our own
spiritual (as distinct from intellectual) vitality, but as the inferior
child, the one not yet grown up, with whom adults play senti-

mentally, and without seriousness, in nostalgic recollection of
their own "dear little boy and girl land" to which they can never
return.

Many a member of the contemporary dance audience is comparable to a radio operator trying to pick up a short-wave program
on a long-wave set. When nothing is heard and the brain is left
with its own vacuum, the cry goes up: "It's beyond me! I don't get
it!" The poor man is ashamed of his brain—as though that were
the organ he should be using!—and in self-protective anger con-
demns the entire art as "too intellectual." Then if he has the ac-
cident to see a literary dance, which is not properly a dance at all
but can be picked up by the brain (some trite little love pantomime, built on cliché dance movements which he does not have
to watch very carefully; or a manifesto in illustration of the edi-
torials of his favorite newspaper, built on the same movements;
or an excursion in psychoanalysis, such as one might find in a contemporary novel, again built on the familiar movements, but in
this case, perhaps, a bit "distorted") he is reassured in his belief
that the dance should not be too "intellectual." He can lean on
his good old brain again, for it is occupied but not greatly so—
since the dance is not precisely the medium in which to present
something new and startling in sociology or science. Occupied but
relaxed, his brain can now doodle with unintense considerations
of grace, line, composition, balanced effects, etc., while his eye
regards the beautiful figures of the girls and feats of jumping such
as he used to attempt himself before his sedentary style of life set
in. If the steps and costumes are those his mother used to like,
he feels a wonderful accompaniment of sweet emotion, and the
brain turns for a moment from the terrors of the brave new world,
which it is building, to a recollection of the now historic past. The
heart is happy, almost as though one were sitting in some dim
theater of long ago, holding mother's hand.

The dance, on the other hand (as an art, that is to say, not as
cheesecake), properly speaks of potentialities and aspects of

man that are antecedent to words, antecedent even to the spheres of personal recollection, and constitute the primary heritage of the embodied human spirit. Therefore, it is at once simple (in as much as it gives manifestation to the roots or seeds out of which the complicated fabric of human life grows) and complex (since it is forced to make use of a highly inflected visual language of aesthetic devices, to give significant expression to such hidden things). An idea for a dance can be sometimes stated in words. Many dancers, indeed, work from a script. But the idea, this thing that can be talked about, must be realized in immediate physical terms. The dance itself, then, becomes a direct image of something that was formerly invisible, though denoted or suggested by words. And for senses trained to behold, words become therewith superfluous and thin—like descriptions of the taste of sugar for someone eating sugar. Usually the title is the only thing that remains of the verbal aspect of the dance when the work is complete and in performance. If it is a good title it is suggestive and does not pretend to be definitive. It is not intended as a rescue line, but rather as a catapult, to pitch the mind in the right direction, leaving it then to rest on the activity of the imagination. Pessimistic artists sometimes supply, also, a program note; but this always has the disadvantage of making the audience believe that it can know what is going on by keeping the brain ticking along with the eye, instead of letting the forms speak through the eye to the short-wave reception set that is in the heart.

And the Earth Shall Bear Again, the title of a solo by Valerie Bettis, suggests a possible drama of famine or loss, with ritualistic effort to persuade a renewal of nature's production; or the moment following a catastrophe, when the world has been desolated: the courageous human being reasserts the faith that he will not be forsaken; or perhaps the simpler tale of a fertility rite in the spring season. The actual dance depicts none of these dramas in a literal or even impressionistic way, yet speaks of any meaning that the mind might be able to invent from the title; for it is built upon the pulse and dynamics of a generating force. That seed quality within all tales of renewal is the only protagonist here. The unfolding of the path of the rhythm bringing the generating force to maturity is the only plot. The beholder experiences an archetypal *form* and is assured by that of the knowledge that the earth shall bear again and again—through the sequence of these rhythmical-spatial-movement events.

In the initial statement of this generating pulse of movement, the feet beat the floor in rapid alternation while the arms, with an explosive impulse, push out from the body center, then circle around to the sides, to curve in to center again, once more parallel to each other but with the palms turned upward and the arms curved as though to hold something. The phrase is finished by two quick scooping movements of the arms in their position—finishing forward; while one foot remains suspended forward, following its last beat on the floor—the end of the whole phrase being up, rather than down solid on the floor. The body seems to have bounded off the floor and to be soaring upward, even though the dancer is still standing firmly on one leg. Like something coming, which cannot be stopped, the dance then grows from the beginning, way back, upstage right, to its finish, downstage left; the pulse and rhythm announced at the beginning being carried through many spaces and levels. When the dance ends with an enlargement of the suspension motif—the dancer poised again, with arms scooped up and one leg lifted forward, suggesting continuous growing—one feels the appropriateness, both as a recollection of the end and of the first statement, and as a visualization of the fact that the seed impulse is powerful to grow and to infuse all things with life. Out of the very rhythm itself comes the expression of joyous celebration. The dancer has no need to supply us with extra "asides" of facial expressions or pantomimic gestures. The whole statement is made through the rhythm and movement-texture, and then the development of these.

Rhythm and movement-texture constitute the chief tools, or vehicles, of the dancer. When properly handled, they free the artist from all need to fall back on the imitation of surfaces. The moment the stage is regarded not as a mechanical area but as a magical or spiritual space (different in character from the rest of space) the meaning of stylized movement propelled by a chosen pulse becomes visible and valid. A stage can be transformed by a competent dancer into any kind of place desired—interior worlds, or extramundane worlds, or even two simultaneous worlds—without the need of any scenic signpost.

Daughters of the Lonesome Isle (a trio by Jean Erdman) takes place in such a magical area. The title itself would lead one to expect some kind of personification or emotive image, not merely a phrase of movement developed primarily for the sake of formal color or design. The curtain rises on three female dancers in a circle, facing outward, holding hands, costumed precisely alike, in stately, somewhat archaic, highly accented, very feminine costumes. They circle slowly to the right in an atmosphere of twilight. Then the central form steps forward, causing a break, a shift of places, and a new movement. The dance is slow in tempo; it seems peaceful while waiting; there is no real progression, it would seem, in time. Three aspects or qualities of woman here manifest themselves: the nourishing, creating; the youthful, brilliantly flashing; the yearning, eternally insatiate. The dance of the first draws the others into movement, but the only drama is that of the advancing and receding of the three.

The creative Mother starts things off, youthful exuberance carries all along, and at the downward curve experience is remembered, as it were, with yearning. The dancers move in three distinct styles, and these varieties of rhythm and movement-texture constitute the language of the story. The interaction of the movement themes and the way they affect each other is the "action." Three human forms enact a visual drama, and yet their movements represent no recognizable scene or sequence of event. Toward the close, when all has quieted, the maternal form again asserts her characteristic movement-of-impulse, after which the group briefly dances, only to return to the original circle, back to back, one to the eye—three aspects of womanliness, alone. The dance is an expression of that which is female without the male, rather as potential than as fulfilled, in a place invisible to the natural eye—outside of time and space—in fact nowhere at all, yet everywhere; as the very principle that invites the male to action, making vivid the answer to why the world goes on creating itself. Hence the mood of timelessness, and of archaic dignity and peace. Overtones of the Celtic tales of the "Isle of Women" as well as of the remote matriarchal past are in the air; but these are not meant to be quite perceptible, necessarily, to the mind; rather, they clothe the dance in an atmosphere. An intangible re-enforcement has thus been brought to support the rhythms and the movement-texture, but the latter still are the vehicles of the dance-communication, without which there would be no structure, no image, no rendition of idea.

The human body is the carrier of all these rhythms and movements. It is a primary condition of the dancer's art that this medium is not a plastic one like, for example, paint. Not only has the human body its classic limitations, but each individual anatomy has limitations and unique characteristics of its own, which ask to be considered. Nevertheless, if properly handled, the rigid shape of humanity can be transmuted, becoming a window into supra-human worlds.

Proper handling means, first of all, avoidance of the error (*hybris*) of supposing that, although one is composing with bodies, they need not be thought of as human beings but can be treated as sheer material and freely molded to the designs of a creative spirit. No honest audience can be expected to shut its eyes to the frequent bursting out of the human ingredient, like a polite friend avoiding the notice of some obvious fault in one's clothing. However, by depersonalizing the dancers through mass groupings, there can be achieved an immediate enlargement of meaning. The individual personality is then subsumed in the larger unit, which expresses a mood, an action, or a force, in heroic proportions. Like the Greek chorus such a group-body can become one voice; no dancer is a complete unit in himself but is only a part, like one limb of a being; individual differences in performing or technique are then out of place. Movements have to be designed that all can execute without evidence of difference.

The form of a dance composed with massings of this kind must be architectural, having the simplicity of basic structure. The movements need not refer back to anything in normal human behavior, yet they will speak of the human soul. Watching Hanya Holm's *Trend*, one experienced in non-objective form a revelation of the human social organism in its cycle of decline and recreation. "*Trend*," as we read in the program, "is a *picture of the process* [the italics are mine] of man's survival when the usages of living have lost their meaning and he has fallen into routine patterns of conformity." We were carried through the drama of the dynamic principles that shape our social being, not by their representation in any particular historical or invested allegorical plot, but by seeing the rhythms of the forces themselves in conflict. The groupings of the dancers rendered them, and carried them into play. One tended to forget that one was watching thirty-five individuals; one was caught in the drama of elemental forces pounding against each other. The formal pattern of the cycle of organic life was laid bare, without reference to specific event or individual catastrophe, for us to respond from the depths of our own organic being. One great Being of beings moved before us, in choral song, chanting the oracle of the everlasting Form. The "Mask Motions" and "Satiety," the "Cataclysm," the "Desolation," and finally the "Resurgence" out of the ordeal itself and the "Assurance" * of renewed life, was the series of spiritual conformations made

---

* These are titles of sections of the dance.

visible in movement-texture and formal, rhythmical relationships. The artist's choreography presented an image for our contemplation that, when understood, lifted us above our small egocentric horizon to a grandiose experience of a perspective from which came a deeper understanding of ourselves and our containing world.

The dance is an art wonderfully qualified to objectify the great, sustaining, inner rhythms of existence. The method of breaking our shackles through a depersonalization and amplification of human meaning, brought about by sheer movement and formal structure, is perhaps its most distinctive procedure, setting it apart from the other arts. Indeed, this is the trait that made it such an important power in primitive society, where the individual as such was of no moment except as a carrier of tribal values, and the tribe itself was thought to be without support unless linked to the perennial forces of the cycles of the natural world. The realization of anonymity in and by the individual, and therewith of an immense amplification of spiritual experience, was the sense of the Dionysian ecstatic agony of the Greek satyr-chorus. And today, when the cult of the self-defensive Ego, the self-expressive genius, the self-made man, the unique Personality, and the rational individual, has cut us all off from the unnamed immensity within us, the dance again can serve as a Mystery of transfiguration.

But the path of expression through the little world-mirror of the Personality is also available to the choreographer. Provided the specific virtues of the dancer's art are not vitiated by a lapse into face-making and naturalistic imitation; or by a willingness to exploit the effects of the performer's personality on the audience; an exquisite, quite personal art of great suggestive power can be developed, and inflected to express an endless range of poetical insights into the nature and peculiar case of contemporary man. Here the qualities of individual style and possibilities of movement have to be explored. The physical and spiritual nuances of the specific human presence on the stage cannot be made to disappear, and so must be handled consciously, as inevitable elements in the composition. The force of the dance will be proportionate to the incorporation of this specific body in an image of more than its own corporeal weight.

Marie Marchowsky's *Ebb Tide* is a dance portraying, or rather suggesting, a creature at the bottom of the sea, some submarine plant or animal. Simultaneously, however, the feminine human form of the dancer herself, distorted, lying on its side, facing the audience, with arms spread out on the stage floor and the legs bent upward to resemble someone walking upside down, creates the effect of a montage: submarine plant-animal human. The title suggests the reference of this double image. The dance is a non-verbal metaphor. The costume is made of many differing shades and cuts of fishnet material, all of cool color. The stage is dimly lit and a stillness pervades the atmosphere. A rocking, lilting pulse begins in the body and the form seems to change shape before our eyes. A rhythmic phrase of rising and falling back to the quiet of the first movement is developed. It is made to grow, in *crescendo*, until the dancer is standing—only to circle again downward. Always she is returning to the quiet of the first moment, with an ebbing of energy which at the same time is peaceful: empty yet full. A strange image is thus presented—not of the human being rendering a human emotion, but of the human body transformed by the rhythm and space into an inhuman image of its own condition. There is no need to say, "This is human," because the very fact that a human being is dancing before you makes the reference immediate. By the use of the magical shape-shifting rhythm, movement is made to express more in one eloquent moment than the naturalistic acting out of some human scene could have rendered in a considerable time.

In this dance the body is dehumanized, yet at the same time used as human. The bifocal vision is the chief vehicle of the message; but the vision is rhythmical, not static. The dimensions of the image are not three but four, the fourth being time. The composition is in space-time, and the structural forms not those of pantomimic acting but of dance.

This structural principle is illustrated, the other way round, in Sybil Shearer's *In a Vacuum*: a hilarious insight into the inanity and hopelessness of our self-inflicted machine-age prison. Starting now from the human term of the comparison, portraying through costume and posture a conscientious-looking female, eminently undeserving of torture, the dancer begins to move. She remains always within a circle of light that is cast on the floor of the stage. Starting with a sudden fury, as though someone had thrown on a switch, foot patterns, hand patterns, head and body movements, all in different rhythms, develop a phrase that is repeated again and again, as by a machine. Bang! the foot slaps down, solid, on the floor; the switch is off. No! it's on again. The fury of patterns carries the conscientious, hard-working female—as before—in slow progress around the edge of the circle of light. Halfway along there is an abrupt human revolt, a lyric movement—of trying to escape, perhaps—to change things; yet directionless, crisscrossing aimlessly through the center of the lighted area; struggling—only to return, at a moment least expected, to the "groove."

It is not a *danse mécanique*, not a direct imitation of the machine. Nor is it a pantomime of the life of a stenographer. It exposes, rather, the flavor of that spiritual brew which is life today, telling us more acutely than could any word or naturalistic story how tragically hilarious is the human machine. The audience is never allowed to forget that the object on the stage is a human being, nor that it is also a machine. The concatenation of rhythms and the melting of a human walk into the advance of a mechanism is side-splitting; but the vacuity of the life resulting is also keenly felt. Like the rippling of waves sent out by a pebble dropped into a mirror-pond, the suggestions and meanings rendered by this montage go out in all directions.

In a Garden (again a solo by Sybil Shearer) employs the

device of the montage in the form of a most subtle juxtaposition of pantomimic and sheer dance-texture movements. Here, I believe, we shall be able to bring into focus the critical touch involved in the successful employment of this visual device of the dancer's art. In this composition, Miss Shearer frankly uses movements of naturalistic imitation, but they serve as a base for movements of a very different kind, which make visible an intangible textural experience of the feeling of space. The dancer portrays a girl, first seated in a garden chair, then strolling and returning. The feeling of a cool garden is vividly experienced. By means of an intense focus of her gaze as it moves slowly about, and the simultaneous vibration of her hands, closing and opening, like the flapping wings of insects, her arms moving around her body like an atmosphere, the dancer creates for her audience a sensuous experience of the feeling of air, as if it had the substance and visibility of the dancer herself. One could not say that the vibratory movements of the hands meant "air," or that they were the cause of the experience of air. Nor could any other single element of the dance be indicated as the symbol of any aspect of the total effect. The putting together and the timing of the sequences is what creates the curiously spiritual atmosphere; and, furthermore, something more is said about the relation of human beings to air than one can quite locate in words.

Martha Graham's *Lamentation* introduces another method of rendering visual a poetic image, namely that of selecting and modifying natural human gestures in such a way that they become textural movements carried on the pulse of an emotive rhythm. The lights go up on a shrouded woman, seated in a posture of sorrow on a bench. Gestures of lament begin. Perhaps it is the use of the costume as the sign of both the woman's spiritual state and the very fate or tragedy against which she is writhing that immediately makes for the monumental stature and concise impact of the image. Without moving from the bench, hardly even standing, she communicates the impression of a titanic struggle

of the individual in her sorrow—as though she had ranged over
the face of the earth. The single white bench is invisibly transformed, by her relationships to it, into the side of a well, the edge
of the world, a tombstone, any number of fleetingly present suggestions traditionally associated with the Mother of Sorrows; and
withal, the dance is no more than a few minutes long. One never
loses touch with the identity of a woman lamenting, and yet the
dance is an expansion, a generalization, of that particular woman's
sorrow to heroic proportions. The individual sorrow becomes uni-
versalized without forfeiting for an instant its immediate, specific,
human focus. The woman becomes a monument; but the monument, at the same time, is a woman—just as the gestures are at the
same time dance; texture-movements but at the same time imi-
tative. By means of the rhythmical structure, which modifies the
gestures and informs them with the principle of music, as well as
by a telling limitation and usage of the space, an eloquent costume,
and extremely simple décor, something that might have been regarded—and personally sympathized with—as the personal sorrow
of another, becomes the sorrow that sustains the world, and which
lives in every heart. The device by which this amplifying effect is
achieved may be termed "dance abstraction," or "rhythmic distortion." The forms of life are opened, magnified by the breath
of music, so that the eye beholds in the individual enactment the
manifestation, simultaneously, of impersonal, almost mathematical forms. The effect is a resolution of the sense of agony in a state
of almost cosmic, basic repose.

The introduction of a narrative, or thread of story, is the final
theme that I wish to consider in this brief review of some of the
main problems and devices represented in the dance as a non-
verbal poetic image. The danger of narrative is that its fascination
for the mind tends to throw into abeyance all the faculties of
sensuous experience while the tense intellect awaits the resolution
of the narrative suspense. *Sea Deep: a dreamy drama* (composition Jean Erdman) introduces characters and a plot, scenes and

theatrical props. The theme is that well-known problem of adolescence, of the young maiden's conversion from the *farouche* estate of "Daddy's little girl" (or the tomboy imitator of her brothers) to the romantic readiness of the young woman aware of what she is. The narrative is rendered in a context of dream, illustrating the process from the point of view of the young woman's own Unconscious, not that of external event; but in a mood of gentle banter, burlesquing, by the way, both the romantic cheesecake of the ballet and the pious attitude toward the treatment of psychological themes characteristic of the present fad. The dance is thus embellished by a multitude of overtones, while the tried and true, classic little plot unwinds its thread. The choreographic devices are, again, rhythm, montage, movement-texture and the "dance abstraction" just described. The setting is the world under sea, and the characters, except for the protagonist herself, are of the stuff of dream.

Briefly: The curtain rises on a dark stage with a glare of light across the foreground, through which runs a blood-red ribbon, from close to the floor, stage right, at a fifteen-degree angle of rise, out into the opposite wing. The ribbon moves, and with a rush "The Dreamer" bursts from the wing, fishing with a pole: the red ribbon being her line. This is "Daddy's little girl," clad in shorts and trying with all her might to be a boy. But she has an abrupt fall—and the lights go up on a wondrously luminous, strangely peopled stage.

The Dreamer finds herself lying beside an immense Alice-in-Wonderland shell. Her long red line she perceives entangled about the arms and persons of three feminine underwater beings —mermaids?—who display to her the various movement themes of feminine charm. These are "The Graces"; a montage of the human being and the mysteries of the deep, the outer and inner realms. The red fishline, thread of adventure, the simple thread of desire leading the unknowing little victim into spheres of new experience, gets her mightily entangled. A merman appears—

"The Dream Man." The Graces show what feminine powers they control. Then, in a series of dance episodes, the heroine loses gradually her extreme fear, gets over the opposite of fear, excessive eagerness, and finally learns, in imitation of The Graces, precisely the attitude that brings about the true waltz; whereupon flowers descend from every side, and all celebrate in roundelay her admittance into the club. The dream fades, and the stage is bathed in common daylight. But the tomboy's sash has descended and become a skirt, the ground is scattered with the flowers, and the couch of the mermaids still is where it was. The Awakened One, a little joyous, gathers the flowers into her skirt, finds again the red line, and now, with a knowing tilt of the head, begins to thread herself a garland. Finis.

The plot is smothered here in dancing episodes, so that the line of story is rather static than dynamic. The piece yields its full secret only in retrospect; meanwhile the experience has been primarily of dance, not of storytelling. This is a common device for the manipulators of images, who wish the eye, and the mind's eye, to search their forms for meaning.

The ultimate distance dance can go in the direction of drama, while remaining true to the formal principles of four-dimensional, non-verbal poetical imagery, is to be found in the latest works of Martha Graham. *Letter to the World* will serve to illustrate; and it is particularly instructive, since it employs, and actually absorbs into the image, a text of rhythmically spoken words. The work both does and does not render a story. Every dancer has a specific identity. No use is made of an anonymous chorus; rather, each character is symbolic and meaningful in itself, like a figure appearing to the mind in a visionary moment of self-recollection. The story of a life, through the story of a soul's recollection of its own destiny, reveals the story of the Artist's fate; and this the audience experiences as not different from the story of any soul's life-realization, only greater in intensity than most. The very opening phrase of rhythmic movement delineates an image that casts over all the magic of a moment within the heart. Without a sound of explanation the path of the duet between the "One Who Moves" (Martha Graham) and the "One Who Speaks" (Jean Erdman; after 1946, Angela Kennedy) reveals the relationship as two aspects of a single individual, and asks for a tale of elucidation. Later, when the words are uttered (fragments from the poetry of Emily Dickinson, whose biography is the inspiration of the dance) they pass not as from one person to another but as from a soul to the universe, expecting in reply only some new phase of vision; or as from the vocal aspect of the individual to the universe inside, with the answers from that depth then appearing in the form of the scenes of the dance. A sequence of ephemeral movement-images is brought before the onlooker, not in naturalistic sequence, but as though painted one over another, each melting into what has gone before, enriching meaningfully an ever-present static, total image of all-inclusive proportions, which is the vision of the dance itself. The poems add word-images which spread their forms invisibly, in re-enforcement of, or in contrast to, those of the eye. They are words midway between music and dance, not the least help as narrative. Music by its sound and rhythm spreads out its spell; the words resound in that, and the dances move. All builds into a unified, ever-changing yet fundamentally still and static, visual and auditory, lyric revelation.

In the final scene, when the two-in-One are beheld again precisely as they were at the opening, standing in the entrance-way, about to walk down into the garden, the stage is flooded one more time with the figures of the life dream and again is emptied. The "One Who Speaks" walks down then and across the garden, past the garden bench, and off, disappearing as antagonist to the unity and resolution, melting back into the One, out of sight as a separate entity, with the utterance: "This is my letter to the World." Then the "One Who Moves" follows to sit upon the bench. And there dawns upon the mind, with a certain flash, like a vision, the revelation that the drama just experienced took place during the little span of time it takes a lady to walk from her doorway to her garden bench: a glimpse of eternity in an hour.

As we have said, the "childlike," the early memories and "seed-forms" of the personality (and of the race as well) lie waiting to be touched and brought to life again by the magic of the rhythmic element of the dance, which is the fundamental principle of the dance. All else rides upon that, like fleets upon an ocean. But the other essential term is the human form. Associations of history, poetry, biography, love, war, adventure and banality cluster to this wondrous image. The dance controls in its own terms, therefore, the whole range of human experience from the primeval, germinal, first pulse to the most complex tapestry of civilized neurotic tension. Its power as poetic image lies in its capacity to inform whatever aspect of humanity it presents with the secret rhythm of some other, hidden, forgotten, yet essential portion. It breaks the shackles, thus, of the rigid human form and expresses for our benefit the things that we require to make us know wholeness. This is the wholeness of the *puer aeternis*, the Wisdom Child, whom we associate instinctively with the very idea of dance. But we cannot wake the child in his strength by simply relaxing to childishness. Rather, a work is required from us of active cooperation. If we only will listen to the pulse of the dance and let it be free to be itself, it will conjure the new, whole being that lies within us. The magic of its rhythm is the force by which the human body is transfigured, so that it renders visible a truth, an existence, or a new understanding of some relationship of existences, such as the mind has no word to describe.

The finest satire is the one in which ridicule is combined with so little malice and so much conviction that it forces a laugh even from those it hits. —G. C. LICHTENBERG

The satirist, like the critic, is not someone who hates happiness and beauty, and tries to spoil them for you by finding fault when you have been enjoying yourself . . . He may love them, and want to free us from a degrading conception of happiness or a cheap counterfeit of beauty . . . He may aid us in seeing the things that should be there as well as in rejecting the things that shouldn't. To destroy falsehood is not the least of the ways of praising and loving truth. —EDGAR JOHNSON

IVA KITCHELL

The Dance and Satire

SATIRE HAS but lightly touched the art of dance in the past, and it is only in recent years that it has invaded this realm in a big way. Such contemporary masters of choreography as George Balanchine, Anthony Tudor, Martha Graham and Charles Weidman have so digressed from their usual serious vein to contribute such delightful and amusing commentaries as *Bourrée Fantasque*, *Gala Performance*, *Every Soul is a Circus*, and *Flickers*. Satiric compositions comprise a large portion of the repertoire of Angna Enters, the great mime of dance. The satiric approach is also employed by the team of Mata and Hari, Trudi

Schoop, and this writer, who has based her entire career on this medium.

The dance satirist is one who reveals to the public the short-comings and weaknesses of the art of the dance, and comments on the manners of individuals and society. The satirist calls attention to comic situations which have been hidden or concealed. Man's foibles easily lend themselves to indignant attacks or humorous expositions.

Satire can, with a gesture of bitter accusation, point to man's sore wounds, as Kurt Jooss did in *The Green Table,* or it can, with affectionate good humor, point out the exhibitionism of ballet as Ruthanna Boris did in *Cirque de Deux.*

There is no school of dance satire and it is hard to imagine how there ever can be one. Satire is a point of view about a subject and is essentially an individual matter. Dryden defines satire as "a sharp well-mannered way of laughing a folly out of countenance." It is this kind of satirical humor which is most adaptable to the dance.

Trudi Schoop showed the inanities of social behavior, in a danced theater piece called *Blond Marie.* It proved to be more than excellent entertainment, it fulfilled the task of dance satire by exposing some of the ludicrous customs of civilized man. In other words, it made the public laugh at itself in full awareness of its own deficiencies.

The satirist is a sort of self-appointed critic of manners and a multitude of things. He is aware of the humbug, and the charlatan, and he feels impelled to deflate these phenomena. Aesthetic sham is his pet peeve. He does not despise the light and playful touch for it adds spice to his declaration. There is much sense in nonsense. If you use satire as a weapon, its point is sharpened by the laughter it attracts. Laughter can sometimes be close to tears.

Charlie Chaplin is well aware of pathos. Anyone who has seen Charlie eating the sole of an old shoe in *Gold Rush* will remember the audience's reaction—it roared with laughter. What sympathetic laughter it was though, for Charlie looked so pathetic and he was so brave about it all. Everyone felt very sorry for the hungry little man. The essence of his humor contains the tragic element of the human comedy.

The dance satirist on the stage and the audience on the other side of the footlights acquire a feeling of "camaraderie" at the jests that they share with each other. The performer must be aware that he does not stray from the point of his satire into a blind alley of mere ludicrous action for the purpose of creating laughter. He may be easily carried away by the response of his audience, which is inclined to accept more readily an outer gesture than the message behind it. By losing sight of his aim, he defeats satire and yields to mere clownery.

On the other hand, the sensitive artist may be inclined to underplay; to handle a situation so subtly that the audience is in doubt whether the spirit of fun is still there. The satirical point must be stated clearly and forcefully. The degree of exaggeration necessary for putting a point across is a subtle thing and the comedian's success or failure hinges on it.

Lichtenberg says, "It is almost impossible to carry the torch of truth through a crowd without singeing someone's beard." In our present state of civilization, truth is often submerged beneath a surface of artificiality. To see people stripped of their masks and disguises amuses us. The truth surprises us when we see it out in the open. The impact of surprise is a fundamental component of what makes us laugh; it is a vital element of satirical humor.

No rule can be set for what evokes laughter. People laugh when they anticipate a certain action and are presented with something completely different. They also laugh when you reverse the situation by leading them to expect something and then give it to them.

Eglevsky, who is famous for his sensational pirouettes, uses the former method when satirizing himself in Robbins' *Pas de*

Trois. At one point in this work, Eglevsky takes a great deal of time to adjust himself in preparation for a pirouette. He meticulously places his feet in the correct position, bending his knees to the exact degree, arranges his arms and is ready to take off, and then he surprises the audience by merely pantomiming the turn with a few circling motions of the index finger. The audience thinks this is a great joke and there is much hilarious laughter.

It is very amusing to see Mr. Eglevsky not do something that he can do so well. This bit of fun will always be more amusing to the dancers and the balletomanes in the audience than it will to the general public.

If satire is your business, you have to consider the universal knowledge of the public and take care not to over-indulge in ideas known only to the initiated.

It is wise to steer clear of the esoteric. A person can seldom appreciate a joke about a subject altogether unfamiliar to him. There can be exceptions. The unusual in movement may be laughed at, because the unusual in anything is apt to appear ludicrous.

One of the funniest dances which has been conceived recently out of pure movement, with no pantomimic association, was called *In a Vacuum* and was the work of Sybil Shearer. It is difficult to do a comic dance of any length on a basis of movement alone, and there is doubt that even the articulate Miss Shearer could make an entire program of comic dances using abstract movement.

Many people, who have never seen the modern dance, find satires of this style of dance amusing. One may conclude that the oddness of the movement, the unfamiliarity, the lack of prettiness so long associated with the dance causes this reaction. No doubt people were once amused by the fact that a dancer did such an unnatural thing as toe-dancing. Familiarity brings acceptance of almost anything.

The dancer who satirizes a dance style profits from the audi-

ence's opinion of former dance events. If the audience on previous occasions has felt an impulse to smile, chuckle or to laugh
heartily when attending a serious dance spectacle and has restrained itself, it will, of course, relish the opportunity to behave
naturally when the occasion permits.

A satirist recalls these incidents to mind. The audience
laughs a laugh of agreement—an "I think so, too" laugh. The audience becomes almost a partner in the performance and gets a
vicarious pleasure out of the satirist's skill.

Most dance satirists sprinkle their work liberally with humor;
without humor satire is invective. A humorous dance, however,
is not always satirical. Ray Bolger often does comic dances with
no particular target in mind, and they can be very funny. What
makes a satirist is the purpose behind the fun. He exposes human
foibles for the sake of their remedy. He is apt to attack anything
that is too rigid, too serious, too sweet, too coy, too artificial, too
pompous or anything that is overdone. Everything that is "slightly
off" is a source of gleeful pleasure to the comic dancer. If given
time, a humorous dance can be built around anything condemned
as less than perfect by serious analysis.

Too much of any one thing can become absurd. Holding an
arabesque on "pointe" is fine, but if you make a point of holding
arabesques indefinitely as some singers hold high notes, the artistic quality is lost and it becomes comic. Technical dexterity can
let one down as well as hold one up.

It should never be the object of a satirist to make a travesty
of a genuine work of art. He must use his critical judgment to
build up and correct through the medium of the dance. For instance, the comedian who dons a ballet skirt and minces across
the stage may be laughed at for his ludicrous behavior. Such farce
may appeal to some, but it can make no serious comment on the
dance. The satirist has the ability to make people laugh with him,
whereas the clowning comedian is merely presenting himself as
a target to be laughed at. By pointing out the weak spots, such

as the style that has become static, the overbearing seriousness, the simulated sentimental extravagances, the satirist does his bit toward keeping the dance in good shape. The satirist loves the dance even though he finds innumerable targets in choreographic work, or in various dancers' personal idiosyncrasies.

Parody is one of the tools of the satirist. When a dancer parodies a work, he imitates the form and style. While imitating the original work, there is in parody an element of criticism. Though aiming at a certain work, the parodist does not always ridicule the choreographer. His target is apt to be the manners and form of a particular dance style of a certain period. In a sense, the choreographer is being flattered for his acclaim and distinction. No one makes a parody of an unknown composition.

The person who is both a dancer and a humorist has an enormous field to encompass. There is so much to be learned that only a lack of vitality can limit his accomplishment.

In order to say what he wants to, the dance satirist is apt to embrace not only several styles of dance technique but utilize pantomime as well. He should develop a range of facility comparable to the character actor. The stylistic qualities of his various dances must always be kept distant when giving an entire program, to prevent it from becoming a monotone. The dancer has to be careful to avoid repetition in gestures, ideas and movements. This is important for the comedian because of his natural aptitude for adopting mannerisms.

The physical part of dancing must be mastered to such a degree that the technique is adequate to carry one along without taking any of the attention from the characterization. Learning the various techniques and perfecting them to a point where they no longer retard the creative side of the work is the goal. No dancer ever thinks he has reached this goal, but it is a fascinating pursuit.

Nothing hinders the dancer so much as overstraining in order to put a point across. When the dance satirist is the least bit apprehensive he loses control and the freedom of motion is restricted. In order to get the most out of a subject, the satirist must be free enough from technical worries to completely enjoy what he is doing.

Expression of ideas and emotions in dance form start by allowing the idea to motivate the action of the body. The entire body changes with the emotional state. The fact that every part of the body is expressive led some dancers to scorn the use of facial expression. They felt their ideas and feelings could be expressed without pantomime. They wanted the dance to be a pure art form.

Why eliminate the face when attempting to express an emotion or thought through dance? It seems an arbitrary choice. One might just as well eliminate an arm. Perhaps the decision to dispense with the face grew from the fact that few dancers are good actors. In wishing to avoid the pitfall of overacting, it was easiest to make a mask of the face. A person's face reflects every thought and feeling and is often a more honest indicator of his mental processes than his speech is. By deleting such an effective means of communication the full expression of the dancer's body is partially handicapped.

It is not easy to coordinate characterization with dance movement. To portray a part, the dancer must not only play the character, he must become the character. If he has difficult steps, they should be done by the particular character that he is portraying. The dancer should guard against the inconsistency of pantomiming a part for a moment and then dancing with only the technical tour de force in mind. The trick is to do these things simultaneously.

A comic dancer—as any other dancer—must know how to communicate what he wants to say to his audience. The dancer may have thought for a long time about the subject matter of a dance and be surprised when some members of an audience do not understand what they are looking at. The audience only sees what is presented to it, and unfortunately there is sometimes a wide gap between the dancer's intention and the audience's perception. Clarity is not the obvious thing it seems. Projecting a thought takes a good deal of study in the art of communication. The audience should not need a course in dance appreciation to know what it is looking at if the dancer is very sure that he knows himself what he is doing. For every member of an audience is conscious of movement. Each person has expressed an idea through pantomime many times, though perhaps unconsciously. Therefore, since everyone possesses the instrument for dancing in his own person, this art should remain a mystery to no one.

The dance has rid itself of much convention by the thinking of such great individuals as Duncan, St. Denis and Graham. Imagination and improvisation still lie dormant behind the barriers of various accredited techniques. Dancers should be as different as men who pass in the street. Someday, the essential technique of dancing will undoubtedly be based on a few fundamental principles. The dancer's personal technique and emotional feelings can then be more easily synthesized into a personal expression. Many dancers are malleable enough to conform to the most exacting standards, yet they have little imagination. More dancers might produce interesting individual dance styles, if they used their imaginations as diligently as they practice technique. It is regrettable that the inventive phase of the dance is seldom stressed in ballet schools.

A dance satirist should take one good, long look in the mirror early in his career to find out how expressive he is. Sadness, joy, eagerness, distress or embarrassment, the entire scale of human emotions, the entire range of human thoughts, must be reflected in the expression of his body and face. If he is capable of expressing these thoughts, he need not use the mirror again. He will be free to work from the inside out. His expression and movement will mirror his thoughts.

Timing is a must. Not what you do but when you do it is the crux of the matter. The comedian knows this intuitively. Ask him what is funny, and he may not be able to tell you, but he probably will be able to demonstrate. It takes merely a twist of the wrist, or a lift of an eyebrow at the right moment to set off the fuse of laughter.

If a satirist does not feel in the mood for being funny, he is in a dire spot, since the audience expects to be amused. No dancer can maintain his top quality for every performance, physically, mentally and emotionally. He is subject to the same ups and downs of mood and health as other mortals who are less in the limelight. However, every performer can so discipline himself in every facet of his medium that when one falls below par, the others work overtime to help bring about a successful performance.

Everything that takes place on the stage must have a "nowness" about it, an irreplaceable "I've just thought this up" quality. A spirit of playfulness and freshness must carry each presentation and the entire program.

Something that is funny at one moment may not be at the next. There is a point at which one must leave off—change the tempo, turn the tide. A point is only funny when it seems to be tossed off impetuously, on the spur of the moment, and has the quality of improvisation. That elfish, indefinable, bubbling quality is volatile. The glass must never be offered when the champagne has gone flat. Last night's performance will not do for tonight. Each performance must be created anew. It is not enough for the dancer to feel the emotion while creating the part; he must feel the same thing every time he performs the piece.

The more the dance satirist knows of human nature, the more accurate and profound will be his expression. The greater his interest in things outside the dance, the wider will be the range of his subject matter. The better his body is trained, the more fluent and expressive will be his vocabulary. It may suffice to be talented, to acquire technical skill and to love to dance in order to become a good dancer. The dance satirist must, moreover, love man. His art will grow with the continual shifting of the center of his interest more and more from his own ego to that of mankind.

Dancing needs only a fine model, a man of genius, and ballets will change their character. Let this restorer of the true dance appear, this reformer of bad taste and of the vicious customs that have impoverished the art; but he must appear in the capital. If he would persuade, let him open the eyes of our young dancers and say to them:—"Children of Terpischore, renounce cabrioles, entrechats and over-complicated steps; abandon grimaces to study sentiments, artless graces and expression; study how to make your gestures noble, never forget that is the life-blood of dancing; put judgment and sense into your pas de deux; let willpower order their course and good taste preside over all situations; away with those lifeless masks but feeble copies of nature; they hide your features, they stifle, so to speak, your emotions and thus deprive you of your most important means of expression; take off those enormous wigs and these gigantic head-dresses which destroy the true proportions of the head with the body; discard the use of those stiff and cumbersome hoops which detract from the beauties of execution, which disfigure the elegance of your attitudes and mar the beauties of contour which the bust should exhibit in its different positions."

—JEAN GEORGES NOVERRE

RUTH PAGE

Some Trends in American Choreography

THE "WAR" between the "classicists" and the "moderns" is always with us. The first are conservative, accepting the wisdom and the working principles of the past as they have been evolved from period to period, building squarely upon them and abandoning only what by common consent has become too obsolete or outmoded to have any further present usefulness. The others are more radical. Impatient with what they feel are the outworn traditions and restrictions of the past, they seek to create wholly new and spontaneous forms, drawn from the direct, first-hand and personal experiences of the individual creators themselves.

"Revolutionary" versus "Reactionary"! Who has not heard their champions extol their respective virtues, not without dwelling upon the vices of their opponents? The fact that the one tends to absorb and be influenced by the other is forgotten in the heat of present controversy. Asked to play the part of final arbiter, the public favors first one side and then the other, usually depending upon which is more in tune with the basic economic, social and political trends of the time.

Probably at no time in the present century have these two forces been more equally in balance in the art of dance than they are today. At one extreme we have the European tradition of strict "theater dance," embodied in America in the "classicism" of Massine, Balanchine and their followers; at the other, the extremely personal and subjective "kinesthetic" communicativeness exemplified by Martha Graham, Doris Humphrey and their imitators. Midway between them is rapidly evolving a truly theatrical and dramatic dance form which borrows from the stylized movement of the one and motivates it by the psychological and emotional drive of the other.

We are thus at the threshold of a new cycle in the history of dance. In one sense, of course, it represents merely a return to the "synthetic theater" of the Greeks in which all of the theatrical arts—pantomime and dance; costumes, properties and décor; spoken and chanted words and song; instrumental, choral and other musical accompaniments—were freely and interchangeably united to heighten the intensity of the drama. But it also makes use of our present knowledge of theatrical means, and of our modern understanding of human psychology and motivation. Like every new cycle, it obviously has both ancient and modern origins.

In order to evaluate the contending forces which are bringing about this change, it is necessary to review the work of the present-day American choreographers and to recall the extraordinary changes which have already taken place in dance as a recognized art form during the lifetime of the same choreographers whose contributions are bringing about these changes.

When the comparative calm of the Victorian era had come to an end with the iconoclastic violence of the cubists and futurists, who owed so much to the Diaghileff Ballet Russe without acknowledging it, the ballet had not yet become an art with a widespread public as we know it today. Diaghileff's annual tournées—from Monte Carlo to Barcelona, Paris and London, with side excursions to less important European capitals—did not prevent his single visit to the United States terminating in dismal failure for want of an audience in every American city he visited. Meanwhile, Anna Pavlova, aided by her indomitable husband, Victor d'André, was touring all over the globe, giving performances which were notable for the extraordinary combination of her ethereal charm and the passionate intensity of her unique theatrical personality, rather than for the artistic merits of her ballets. In her case, the largest American cities offered her enthusiastic audiences, but in only a limited number of performances.

During the twenties the prolonged strain of the First World War began to make itself felt in Western Europe, and particularly in France, by a sort of delayed action, after a brief period of intellectual experimentation somewhat similar to the emergence of existentialism immediately after the Second World War. The artistic chaos exemplified by surrealism, dadaism, fauvism and so on, and the growing craze for novelty at any price, were well illustrated in the productions of the late Diaghileff period. The same decade marked the advent of the new German "physical culture" dancing. Thus, by the time the Diaghileff period had ended in 1929, the forces which were bringing about the social, economic and artistic break-up were already well advanced in Europe. Massine, Balanchine and their European contemporaries began looking to the New World in which to transplant the European tradition. This tradition is still very much alive today, especially in the work of George Balanchine.

Balanchine is the true classicist or rather "neo-classicist," as we are fond of saying where the spirit is classical but the manner of expression consists of modern variations and adaptations of the old stylized classical vocabulary. Although he does not believe that any dance can be called "abstract," Balanchine's ballets of the type of *Concerto Barocco, Theme and Variations* and Bizet's *First Symphony* come as close to being "abstract" as is possible with the living human body. Almost all his latest ballets might be termed "musical visualizations," in the sense that his individual steps fit the music almost note by note, and his choreography as a whole is a nearly perfect reflection of the structure of the music upon which it is based. Balanchine himself has said of his own work, in speaking of *The Four Temperaments* to music by Paul Hindemith: "I have attempted to design a kind of stereoscopic choreography for Hindemith's strong score. My dances form a negative to his positive plate." What is true of Balanchine is almost equally true of his followers from the American Ballet School, in this deep respect for, and almost photographic reproduction of, the music with which he is working and which forms the stimulus for his best choreography.

In truth, it seems that Balanchine is becoming more and more classical as time goes on. But as indicated before, it is classicism of a new sort, and in no sense a slavish adherence to the past. His ballerinas do not try to charm their audiences. In the old days Maestro Cecchetti, the greatest teacher of classical ballet in history, used to say to his pupils: "When you are on the stage you must try to make every man in the audience fall in love with you." Those were the champagne-in-the-slipper days of dancing.

Balanchine's dancers make no such concessions to the public. Their bodies are simply wonderful instruments of precision, going through their severely stylized movements like the high priestesses of some religious cult. Their faces are like masks, and all their patterns are formal. Flinging their legs higher than is necessary and being very athletic about it, they do scores of pirouettes, seeming not to care one bit about the audience. These Balanchine ballets are absolute and pure dance. But in spite of their seeming coldness, his poetic designs do not fail to draw an emotional response from the audience. Like the best of contemporary abstract music and painting, Balanchine's clear though often intricate patterns of movement have their own emotional excitement for the spectator.

This is not to say that Balanchine has not also created unusual and interesting ballets of the romantic type, such as Ravel's *La Valse*, and others with a strong dramatic or story element. In the light of the present trend toward theatricalism, it is interesting to note the critical acclaim which greeted his creation of *Orpheus*, to which some of the critics have applied the words "masterpiece" and "genius." Almost self-consciously, since he insists that words are always literary and therefore unnecessary, he at first refused to aid the uninitiated with a program note describing the action. As if to prove his point, the essential details of the story are so clearly and simply set forth, and the collaboration between the various arts of music, décor and choreography is so perfect, that the spectator is never in doubt as to the plot and its development.

Here we have one type of lyric theater which is the perfect illustration of the classicist's approach towards the dramatic dance. In its essence, it is at the same time both stylized and human. Unlike his earlier failure to combine the music of Gluck and the neurotic and surrealistic décor of Tchelitchew with his own classical dance modernizations, Balanchine's re-creation of *Orpheus*, to the profound music of Stravinsky and the functional setting by Noguchi, is a nearly perfect synthesis of the theater arts.

But no matter how far Balanchine may go in this direction, it seems most likely that his purely abstract choreography will be his greatest contribution. More than the other inheritors of the European tradition, he is creative enough to rise above the limitations inherent in the classical style. In this he stands unique and unrivaled, and it is fortunate that we have an artist of his caliber working so strictly within the limits of the classical spirit, as a contrast to the more theatrical and psychological approach of most of the other American choreographers.

Looking backward, the limitations and difficulties which faced the American choreographers in the not very distant past now seem so great that it is a wonder that they have had a chance to develop at all. Throughout the twenties there were no ballet groups available for experimentation. The only performing companies in this country, excluding the European ballet troupes, were Ted Shawn's pioneering Denishawn company, from which most of the modern dancers came, and the small traveling group of Adolph Bolm, originally called the Ballet Intime, which later grew into the Chicago Allied Arts, the first ballet company in this country which regularly commissioned and performed new ballets. In those days, there was no Choreographers' Workshop for young choreographers to try out their ideas. All of the dancers creating in this country were soloists who attempted to give solo dance recitals at large expense and against great difficulties in some New York theater on Sunday nights. Neither audience nor performer could ever be quite sure that the performance would take place, for if it was classified as a theatrical show rather than a recital, the performer would be chased out of the theater for violating the Sunday Blue Laws. And yet it was from these solo dancers that the group of present-day American choreographers has largely been drawn.

Martha Graham is typical of this development of the American choreographer of today. Many people seem to think that her highly individualized technique is based upon the Laban, Wigman and Central European schools of modern dance. Actually, the Graham technique was well formed by the time she first saw Wigman, and it is doubtful if she was much influenced by these schools, except by a few photographs which may have encouraged her.

Starting with solo dances, Graham has invented a whole new system of movement, first for herself and later for her dance group. Her work is highly original and personal. It is not at all based on the tension and relaxation principles of Wigman. In fact, in the Graham technique, the dancer never seems to relax. Hers is a strident, virile type of movement, admirably suited to the dramas of inner conflict which have been the subject of so many of her later compositions.

At the beginning of her career, Graham broke away from the eclecticism of the Denishawns and showed a strong tendency toward pure abstract movement. But gradually, from year to year, her work has become more and more dramatic, and more and more theatrical, until today it has achieved psychological depths and powers of symbolism which are not available to any other choreographer, except perhaps Anthony Tudor.

Graham has always used lots of properties. In fact, her scenery and props are as much a part of the choreography of her dances as her own arms and legs. Even in her early solo dances, she used the materials of her costumes as a part of her choreography. More recently, she has gotten away from the use of materials, but she still wears a long skirt and builds much of her movement upon and about the properties and set-pieces created for her by Isamu Noguchi. Almost all of the American dancers tend to follow her in this respect, in contrast to the usual type of painted backdrop and unimpeded open stage, which are typical of the classical ballet companies.

Graham has never been dependent upon her musical accompaniment. In fact, she is so independent of it that she would prefer to create the movement first and then have the music written as a mere accompaniment and background to it, although for most of her latest ballets the music was written first. She has used words with dance most successfully in her *Letter to the World*. But instead of speaking them herself, the beautiful words of Emily Dickinson are spoken by a dancer-actress.

Graham is typical of the American choreographers in the sense that she has consistently used American folk material throughout most of her career. In the twenties and thirties she was working with American Indian rituals, and it is typical of her development that she has passed from them through the New England heritage of Emily Dickinson to the point where today she, like her contemporaries, is at last ready to abandon what we like to call our "Americana," in favor of a wholly universal form of human symbolism.

In Graham's individual case, it is too soon to tell whether her technique will die with her, as Isadora Duncan's did when she had gone. No doubt sensing this, Graham is gradually giving some of her best roles to her younger dancers, and it is to be hoped that she will continue to do this. One of the best tests of good choreography is whether it is still successful if more than one person performs it. Judged by this standard, and considering Graham's extraordinary theatrical personality in her own roles, it cannot yet be said to what extent her dances will survive her. One can say with certainty, however, that her contribution to the dance art of her times will be both great and lasting.

Although he is not an American by inheritance, Anthony Tudor's contributions to the classic ballet have been comparable in their originality to Graham's innovations in modern dance. Like Graham, he deals with psychological conflicts and symbolisms, using the more conventional theatrical and musical approach of the classic ballet. Typically English in the romanticism and sentimentality which floods all of his ballets, both comic and tragic, Tudor is one of the great creators of our time because he has added to the classic ballet a completely new dimension. Tudor is the great psychologist of the dance world. He has revitalized the old classical steps through the expressive use of the upper-body, thus giving every movement a dramatic quality which shows in no uncertain terms the inner mood of the dancer's state of mind. Although his movements are completely balletic and make great technical demands of his dancers, he never uses virtuosity per se. His dancers do not act or pantomime as Agnes de Mille's dancers do. For with Tudor, the movement of the body as a whole says what he has to say, usually on the toes and in intricate choreographic patterns. Like Balanchine, he is extremely dependent on the music and is at his best when he chooses music already written. Unlike Balanchine, he does not take the music so literally. Sometimes his climaxes come before the climax in the music and sometimes after, but always there is an interesting counterpoint.

Agnes de Mille is another American choreographer who started as a concert soloist. In her early solo dances could be seen the germ for almost all her future work. Much of her success depends upon her dramatic skill at pantomime. Her dancers are real people and real characters, in contrast to the mythological characters so dear to the *Swan Lake* school. De Mille will borrow movement from any school whatever, if she thinks it will probably point up the essential meaning of a situation. Not only has her greatest success come when using American folk material, but her greatest talent is in making such folk material truly theatrical. It is this which causes her dances always to seem so fresh, healthy and amusing; and it is not surprising that these qualities have endeared her to her Broadway audiences. Her most recent ballet *Fall River Legend* is definitely in the Tudor psychological trend. It is too soon, however, to tell whether this work represents a new departure or is merely a side excursion.

Jerome Robbins started his career as choreographer brilliantly with *Fancy Free*, a work logically stemming from early American "genre" ballets, but displayed more originality in *Interplay*, which makes such free use of classical movement that he seemed to have invented a new kind of Americanism. Both of these works are light, witty and amusing, and have made him in great demand for Broadway shows. However, *The Guests* and *Age of Anxiety* show him branching out into significant new channels far removed from Broadway.

Another typical American dancer who started her career as a soloist, and whose work has been founded almost entirely on the folk material of North and Central America, is Katherine Dunham. Her best ballet, *L'Ag'ya*, illustrates clearly the exotic style which she has created for herself and her Negro dancers. Josephine Baker was the original Negro exotic. With her nude body clad only in a short skirt of bananas and dancing in the loose, shimmying manner of the Negro, she took Europe by storm. Dunham's choreography also consists largely of shimmies and bumps, and shaking of the shoulders and pelvic region. She is greatly aided by John Pratt's costumes, so perfect for Negro dancers that they sometimes seem as important as the choreography.

Reviewing Dunham's career, though no truly great ballets have been created, her work adds up to beautiful and stimulating theater. In an effort to keep her group together, and before her conquest of Europe, she was driven into the commercial theater and the night clubs. But she started out as a student of classical ballet, working with the poet, Mark Turbyfill, in Chicago. Later she became a graduate of the Sunday night concert and the WPA. Her first important introduction to the West Indian material, which she has since made so famous, was in a ballet called *La Guiablesse*, based on a Martinique folk tale, with music by the Negro composer, William Grant Still, which I choreographed for Dunham and a company of fifty Negroes. It was performed with the Chicago Symphony Orchestra at the Chicago World's Fair in 1933, and later was repeated with the Chicago Grand Opera Company, with the same Negro group and with Dunham in the leading role. From then on she has developed this type of material almost exclusively. She has never used the Negro tap dance, although she was successful in a comic ballet of the twenties, and in various types of Negro "blues" which employed jazz "plastique." Her work has inspired the younger generation of Negro dancers upon whom her influence is both permanent and important.

One of the earliest of our American choreographers to use American material is Eugene Loring. The recent revival of his original production of *Billy the Kid*, which he choreographed for Ballet Caravan in 1938, confirms both the originality and the high quality of his work. His use of the Western cowboy material has been so often copied since that it now seems to be part of the American vocabulary. His *Great American Goof* was another interesting and daring experiment with words and dance. Unfortunately, the words used by the dancers were not clearly audible, nor did they seem to add anything to the movement, and the ballet in its original form was not a success. Loring is himself a fine actor, and it is possible that the present trend towards the use of words in ballets will stimulate him to new experiments in this field.

Helen Tamiris started out as a Sunday night recitalist. Her realm is completely in the so-called "modern dance," in which she did several excellent and memorable works for the WPA, before going on to devote herself almost entirely to Broadway musicals. Her first successful collaboration with Valerie Bettis, an exciting dance talent, reveals the extent to which "modern dance" has become accepted by Broadway audiences, especially when presented by a strong theater personality in a form which is easily comprehensible to the general public.

José Limon is better known as a magnificent dancer interpreting Doris Humphrey's works than as a choreographer, but his own two ballets, *La Malinche* and *Moor's Pavane* are masterpieces of the modern repertoire. They do not blaze new trails as Martha Graham did, or open up new vistas, but they are both touching works of art in their "rightness" of movement for their ideas.

Doris Humphrey's *Inquest* is another important ballet which is definitely a part of the present trend towards theatricality and dramatic effectiveness. Here she has used her material with such inspiration that a theme of sordid poverty soars to heights of great dignity and nobility. Charles Weidman's gift of satiric comedy is part of the same movement. In his *Fables for Our Time*, he has skillfully expressed the profound nonsense of James Thurber in pantomimic dance in a manner which is frankly entertaining. Both he and Humphrey have used words spoken by narrators in many of their ballets. Hanya Holm's work in *Ballet Ballads* and *The Insect Comedy* also shows her great ability in combining movement, words and song.

This strong present-day trend towards the use of words with dance is merely another aspect of the choreographer's effort to achieve greater dramatic clarity. The success of *Ballet Ballads* is important, not so much for the use of words sung by the singing dancers as for the intensified theatrical effectiveness of the dancing when supplemented by words. In a memorable "American Choreographer's Evening," given by Ballet Theatre, all four of the ballets presented used spoken words in some way; and in *Billy Sunday*, introduced by the Ballet Russe de Monte Carlo, all three of the principal characters, performed by Franklin, Danilova and Talin, spoke their lines while dancing. Roland Petit's delicious *La Croquése de Diamants*, in which he has his dancers successfully singing, may well influence American choreographers in the same direction.

Perhaps it is not surprising that the classical balletomanes, with a more conservative and conventional viewpoint than the general public, have been shocked, if not horrified, by this strong modern trend toward theatricality in ballet. Some of the critics who share their views deny the propriety of the use of the term "ballet" in this connection. One recalls, however, that when César Franck used an English horn in his first and only symphony, some of the critics claimed that it was not a symphony at all because neither Brahms nor Beethoven had ever used an English horn.

Other critics maintain that the voice is a mere prop on which to lean, claiming that the choreographer should be able to express whatever he has to say in dance movement alone. But in the last analysis, music and costumes are props also. Theatrical dancing is not an art that can stand alone. It needs every possible aid in the form of music, lights, scenery (which moves if necessary), costumes, properties and, finally, words, if they enhance the dramatic effect. No ballets have ever existed without music; and those which have survived longest are the very ones in which the musical score is most enduring, both as music and as accompaniment to the movement. As our knowledge of theatrical means improves, it seems likely that all of the theater arts, dancing included, will be combined to a common end.

All art is invariably a reflection of the times which create it. If art so often seems prophetic, it is due to the greater sensitivity of artists to their environment, rather than to any special powers of prophecy peculiar to artists. Possibly we are indebted for the extraordinary changes which have occurred in the dance art in the last quarter century to the general chaos and unrest of that period. But whatever may be the cause, it is possible to view the new synthesis of the theater arts as a bright portent for the future, in which dance will have the major role.

Certainly there has never been a time in the history of the dance when the choreographer has been freer to work in so many media as he is now. There was a period during the late twenties, when Wigman and Kreutzberg were at the height of their successes, that the classical ballet was considered dead or dying. If a dancer wore a tutu and danced on her toes to a Chopin waltz, she was regarded as outmoded. Today both the classical ballets and Martha Graham play to crowded houses, and the New York critics recognize equally the merits of both classic and modern dance.

The variety of choreography today is almost endless. There are classical ballets (Balanchine-Tchaikovsky's *Theme and Variations* and Bizet's *First Symphony*); modern ballets (Graham's *Errand into the Maze* and *Cave of the Heart*); psychological ballets (Tudor's *Pillar of Fire* and De Mille's *Fall River Legend*); ethnological ballets (La Meri's *Swan Lake*); exotic ballets (Dunham's *L'Ag'ya*); folk ballets (Maslow's *Folksay*); ballets combined with singing (LaTouche-Moross' *Ballet Ballads*); ballets in which the dancers themselves speak (Humphrey's *Lament for the Death of a Spanish Bullfighter* and Page's *Billy Sunday*). Sometimes there is no scenario, as in most of Balanchine's ballets; sometimes the stories are so complex that they have to be explained by a narrator on the stage (Humphrey's *Inquest* and De Mille's *Fall River Legend*). Or we have ballet operas (*Ballet Ballads*) or ballet plays (Stravinsky's *Story of the Soldier*), in which the words are not spoken just to explain what can't be danced, but are used because words, with the dancers themselves speaking, add arresting new dimensions to dance and open up fresh fields of experimentation.

The American choreographers have, in a sense, brought ballet down to earth (*Rodeo, Fancy Free, Frankie and Johnny*). Even a scenario on the order of *Hear Ye! Hear Ye!* (Chicago Grand Opera Company, 1934) using a murder trial with judge, jury, prosecuting and defense attorneys, became the plot of the "hit" ballet in a Broadway musical (*Tiger Lily* in *Inside U.S.A.*). An old-fashioned fairy tale done "straight" (*Beauty and the Beast* in *Music in My Heart*) was also a success. What will it be next?

Obviously this is a free country.

There never was in the world two opinions alike, no more than two hairs or two grains; the most universal quality is diversity.   —MICHEL DE MONTAIGNE

The Dance Has Many Faces

WALDEEN

SOCIAL INFLUENCES AND EMOTIONAL MOTIVATION

Is THE artist a world unto himself, a world "free" of the disturbances of society? Is the dancer inseparable from people and their lives, or is he mysteriously uninfluenced by them in his creative work? Is there such a thing as "pure" dance?

For some dance artists the answers to these basic questions are complex. They are simple, for those who have been conditioned to accept the traditional idealist approach to the dance as the only theory suitable for explaining such a "subjective" art. Dance critics have based their books upon the idealist system, which they consider to be the only measure for determination of the aesthetic emotionism of the dance. Defenses for "pure" dance have been many and extend far back into the literature. But the theory that dance is inseparable from reality has been relatively unexplored. It is a challenging theme, plunging us deep into the dynamics of the historical growth of all art forms. It holds before us the irrevocable interrelation of the dance with other arts and reminds us that dancers are not isolated inferior inhabitants of the great world of art.

In primitive stages of society, dance was an instrument for collective activity. The relationship between imagination (fantasy) and reality was simple, because primitive society was simple. But as it divided, society grew more complex, and its stratification ensued. In addition to the conflict between society and nature, a new factor developed—the conflict between the individual and society. If we keep this process in mind, it will throw light upon all succeeding developments in the dance: from rehearsals for collective action, to magic (ritual dance), to a highly developed art form.

The earlier stages of the dance, as in the Greek period, were entirely social in character. If any soul states were communicated they were not of an individual nature but expressed group feelings; whether of worship, fear or conflict. In other words, the dance was a reflection of a people undergoing sharp struggle, part of which, it is well to remember, was political, there having been a democratic revolution in Greece in the sixth century against the tyrants of Athens.

The dancer as independent creator is still nonexistent at this period; his function is still of a collective improvisational character; his power is magical, demonic; he is possessed, ecstatic. In one of Plato's dialogues, a Homeric minstrel speaks of the reaction he has on his audience: "When I am narrating something pitiful, my eyes fill with tears; when something terrible or strange, my hair stands on end and my heart throbs . . . And whenever I glance down from the platform at the audience, I see them weeping, with a wild look in their eyes, lost in rapture . . ." This might equally describe the state of the Greek dancers' audiences. How many present-day American dancers, looking down at their public, would encounter the same inspiring sight? This is true communication, the reward that awaits only the dance creator who marries his art to the realities of human existence.

History's procession carries the dance through the growth of nations during the Middle Ages when it found its social expression in mass dances of religious frenzy and identification with death like the "danse macabre." Such manifestations of a people's suffering were products of the feudal system and provided release for mystic ecstasy, and fury against the oppression of their rulers.

The procession sweeps into the fifteenth century, into Italy of the Renaissance with its reawakening of philosophy and commercial expansion of the middle class. At this point the dance begins to evolve into an art form; it acquires teachers and rules, which, however, primarily served the aristocracy. But the dance works then created are still related to social use: dancing masters designed wedding dances and court ballets.

But in the sixteenth century mythological and allegorical content entered into the spectacular dance. With this step the dance began to recede from the people and to restrict itself to remote themes, revolving around classical gods and heroes but without any religious or magical implications. "The European ballet is no longer in the service of God and Nature, but in that of the ruling princes . . . Magnificent images have become petty caricatures, spiritual symbols have become empty allegories," says Curt Sachs in his World History of the Dance.

It is striking to note the close relationship, the interpretation of dance with social phenomena in the early history of the dance. An undeviating mirror, for centuries the dance presented the image of humanity's upheavals, and its consequent inner life. But in the seventeenth century the dance underwent a revolution. From exclusive possession by royalty, it became a medium for professionals performing for paying audiences. Nevertheless, it still remained a subject art, the property of rulers, whether aristocratic or bourgeois. Throughout the eighteenth century it perpetuated the elegant court dance forms until the great ballet master Noverre, "the Shakespeare of the dance," transformed the pedantic divertissement into vivid dance drama. His reforms influenced

ballet until the first part of the nineteenth century when it de-
clined once more into mere mechanical excellence.

During the romantic period which followed, the other arts,
especially poetry, grew disillusioned with the encroaching bourgeois world and flowered into a passionate rebellion against the
pressures of a philistine society. Oddly enough, the dance remained relatively untouched by an historical movement which
produced poets of the magnitude of Shelley, Keats and Heine.
One of the main reasons for this phenomenon was the direct economic dependence of the dance upon the whims of a leisure-class
audience. To gratify its taste for gauzy escapes from the increasing stolidity of an expanding industrial environment, theater
dance was compelled to produce sentimental fairy tales of love,
gallantry and death. Wings sprouted on wasp-waisted ballerinas
and the "ethereal" was the highest aesthetic aim.

This artistic anemia flowered with pale phosphorescence in
such famous dancers as Fanny Elssler or Taglioni, who gave
"dance interpretations" of Goethe. As the social character of art,
the dance in particular, began to disappear and be eventually
transformed into a commodity purchased by "the public," the
artist no longer felt at one with society, no longer the supreme
expression of its emotions and purposes. On the contrary, he grew
pessimistic, aloof and hostile to society. The dance, until this
time, along with music, song, and commedia dell'arte had been
one of the arts most dependent upon collective mass audiences
for its realization. In the late nineteenth century it became individualistic and antisocial, and its power and variety of expression
dwindled pitifully. The social influences of the Victorian era com-
pressed the dance into the tight corset of effete aestheticism, narrow ideas and insipid nationalism. These sterile trends persisted
until Isadora Duncan appeared wielding her liberating sword of
Rousseau humanism, classical naturalism, free and untraditional
use of the body. She defied the decadent romanticism of *fin de*

siècle dance, although Isadora herself was one of the last great romantics, and the first given us by the dance.

After the wide swath she cut, others followed in her path. From the Russian Ballet, through postwar expressionism, into America and the "modern" school, the dance has steadily deepened its course, enlarged its techniques and experimented in form and content.

Inherent in this fundamental change of direction and outlook is the development of dance philosophy, the concepts that determine the artist's consciousness, his aesthetic and creative attitudes. This implies that the artist is no "unconscious" creator; that an asocial artist is an impossibility. This does not mean that he is always aware of his direction or point of view, but it will always be implicit in his work. After all, there are many levels of consciousness through which filter the reflected rays of social influences, but their impact upon the artist's creative mechanism is inescapable.

The great Renaissance humanist philosopher, Pico della Mirandola, has stated this basic truth very clearly and beautifully. In his *Treatise on the Greatness of Man*, he conceives of Nature addressing Man. Let us transpose this into the World addressing the Artist and in particular the Dancer.

"We have given you, Adam, neither a definite dwelling, nor a specific face, nor a special function, so that you may choose the dwelling, face, and function that you wish. We have placed you in the center of the world, in order that you may more easily look all around you in the world; we have made of you neither a celestial being nor an earthbound being, neither an immortal nor a mortal, so that you yourself may mold and shape like a sculptor the form you prefer to give yourself. You can plunge into the lower ranks of brutes or lift yourself into the higher ranks of divine beings."

How undeniably true that the dancer can "mold and shape" the form he prefers to give himself or his work. How narrow and untrue that he is a helpless victim of his own unconscious. Emotional motivation in a work of art derives from the artist's relation to life, from his awareness of reality. The unconscious mind as well as the conscious should be utilized to extend his understanding of reality, not to turn away from it. The artist should be concerned above all with truth: artistic and human truth. How then ascertain and express these truths without a profound investigation of life's movement in all its aspects, emotional, intellectual and social? To the dancer this need should be self-evident because the dance more than any other art is the exponent of movement, of the human being in its living totality of mind, spirit and senses. Use of the body as an artistic medium is the dancer's exclusively, although other art elements, especially music and design, are organically part of the dance. Paradoxically, the physical limitations of the medium constitute its illimitable scope. For, through the body as symbol, the dancer may reflect, perceive and encompass the whole of man's experience and potential. Because of this powerful capacity, the dance is a profoundly moral art capable of wielding a deep influence on people and their thought, and consequently on their actions. This is true despite many bleak and vapid epochs when, as a subservient art, it was debased into a means solely for titillating the senses.

When the word "moral" appears, derisive protests may arise. However, in this context it is used not in the Platonic but in the Epicurean sense: thought derives from sensations; body and soul are one, not separate, not "eternal realities" disassociated from our individual experiences both in sense and spirit. For the root of individual experience, both sensuous and spiritual, is also the root of artistic creativity. Did not Milton demand three things of poetry—that it be "simple, sensuous and passionate"? Could not this demand apply equally to the dance? Any dance creation that lacks these elements lacks comprehension of the real world, and consequently lacks the power to communicate with its audience. Thereby it fails its own essential and special function as an art.

But why call it a *moral* art? Why insist upon it being a social influence? Why not leave the dance creator "free" to do anything he wants? If to be free means to be cut off from life in the world, to create in one's own private world of unreality, to compose and to perform in a void, uprooted from our history in the making, isolated from mankind, then certainly any dancer or choreographer should be free to choose this sinister and lonely path. But will not this "freedom" once it is analyzed stand disclosed as an illness, a tragic malaise, a failure to fuse with reality? This failure has assumed many guises: Dadaism and surrealism among others, and now existentialism, the end-product of absolute world-despair.

These despair-movements in painting, literature and music have their equivalents in the dance. Now, in New York City, it is difficult to find a dance repertoire, modern or ballet, that has not been contaminated by this decadent tendency, this retreat from all that is healthy, hopeful and inspiring in life. The leading choreographers in both fields are absorbed in exploring the penumbras of their own subconscious lives rather than in penetrating into the lives of their spectators, who are as urgently in need of spiritual and emotional sustenance in these violent times of conflict as the dancers to whom they turn and who too often fail them. Recognizing this tragic cul-de-sac down which the contemporary dance has fled, we can understand better how the dance artist, who is "free" to create for himself alone and imperiously expects his audience to love him for it, is simultaneously betraying his function as a dancer and his moral responsibility towards his audience. What is this responsibility? Does it really exist? isn't it a matter of choice for the artist whether he assume it or not?

Roger Fry, eminent art critic and founder of British post-impressionism, has this to say:

Art, then, is an expression and a stimulus of the imaginative life, which is separated from actual life by the absence of responsive action. Now this responsive action implies in actual life moral responsibility. In art we have no such moral responsibility—it presents a life freed from the binding necessities of our actual existence . . . Morality appreciates emotion by the standard of resultant action, art appreciates emotion in and for itself.

How is it possible for the artist to separate his interpretation of reality from his communication with his audience? Does not this very communication establish a bond with his public? Another English art critic, Klingender, replies to Fry:

> In so far as the artist communicates the image of his perception to his fellow-men he is morally responsible for it . . . Society cannot be indifferent whether a given work of art inspires by its profound insight, whether it stirs to action, whether it soothes and refreshes, or whether, on the other hand, it opiates and disrupts. The *aesthetic* value of a work of art must in some way be related to the effect it produces . . .

The effect a dance produces upon an audience is direct, instantaneous and organically related to the spectator; it reaches all his senses, and these, as Blake says, are the "windows to the soul." It follows, then, that the dance as an art has a deep and inevitable moral responsibility, for it reflects, shapes and indicates states of the human body, heart and mind through an artistic medium with which people can most closely identify themselves: it *is* the human being in action and therefore can arouse responsive action as well as emotional response. To divorce the dance art from life in its physical aspects (technique of movement) and its emotional experiences (form and content) is to mutilate its beauty and effectiveness and reduce its scope to mere abstract manipulations of the body in space. This mutilation serves only to stunt the growth of the dance which, since the close of the nineteenth century, has slowly been gathering force as a dignified creative art. Now in twentieth-century America, dancers have attained a peak of technical skill far surpassing that of any previous period in dance history. The modern dance has gained an enormous amount of converts and enjoys representation on the curriculum of a large proportion of the universities throughout the nation. Dance schools abound and thousands of pupils pass through them annually. In New York City, the dance capital of the country, the number of accomplished experienced dancers is staggering, as is also their record of unemployment. Merciless competition prevails among them for every casting of a Broadway musical or ballet company.

This teeming abundance of youthful energy, expertness and talent strangely enough produces a distressing spectacle. The individual frustrations, the blind plodding in the footprints of famous predecessors saps the creative vitality and originality of the present generation of choreographers. Picasso has spoken very clearly about this imitation of models:

> No doubt, it is useful for an artist to know all the forms of art which have preceded or which accompany his. That is a sign of strength if it is a question of looking for stimulus or recognizing mistakes he must avoid. But he must be very careful not to look for models. As soon as one artist takes another as model, he is lost. There is no other model, or rather no other point of departure than reality.

Today, ironically enough, the modern dance has become a neurotic stepchild of Isadora and her humanist concepts. It has run an exhaustive circle and returned to esoteric forms clothing egoistic ideas divided from humanity. Appropriately, its audience is again a limited aesthetically incestuous group of dance devotees.

What must the young American dance artist do to prevent his art from entering another of its phases of eclipse, as in the nineteenth century, when survival meant a sterile individualistic expression servile to the demands of a decadent public? What hopes are there of becoming artists with a vaster significance, a wider audience? When will we follow the great humanist tradition of our country and grow into true creative citizens of our time?

Not by reflecting inner despair and nihilism; not by worshipping our own subjective struggles and complexities, but by finding the courage to believe in mankind's vigor and future, and by creating the dance medium which will portray this conviction. A huge untried audience awaits us; wanting to see this in dance, in a form directly identifiable with their own lives and hopes, wanting to be inspired, not shocked into a stupor of hopelessness by morbid, pseudo-psychological outpourings.

There is no question that technical skill, however brilliant, is an important asset only when placed in the service of deeply human content and beauty of form. "If I were to insist," says André Gide, "upon the gentle truth (gentle and so simple that I blush to repeat it) that in any art technical skill should never be more than a well-disciplined instrument, I would be treated as a vandal, so little is this truth appreciated nowadays, so much, in our time, has this handmaiden been turned by us into the mistress, so much is all the rest reduced to silence in her despotic presence."

Inspiration, humanity, beauty—do not these ancient priceless words produce an antique harmony in the avant-garde ears of the present dance generation? Before hurrying to scoff, let them realize that these essentials are vital organs in the anatomy of art—any art, in any period of history—and that to deride and overthrow them, even temporarily, is a dangerous formalistic error. They belong to the indestructible heritage of man's culture, and whatever forms they may assume, in accordance with historical change, they must never be discarded, for then art becomes dehumanized, and thereby forfeits all rights to love and appreciation by a wide audience.

Let the young American dance creator turn away from the wish for quick "success," obtainable by imitating famous dancers in every turning of their careers. Let them develop their own voices, speak with their own bodies, hands and faces, tell of the

artistic and human truths they have discovered, through the sources of their own experience and inventiveness. Then they will achieve an honest success, the slowly constructed, soundly complex, aesthetically fresh art form, capable of arousing enthusiasm in universal audiences through its inspiration, beauty and humanity.

FREDERICK ASHTON

NOTES ON CHOREOGRAPHY

With every new ballet that I produce I seek to empty myself of some plastic obsession and every ballet I do is, for me, the solving of a balletic problem.

But let me begin by explaining what I understand the function of the choreographer to be. First of all, he is to the ballet what a playwright is to a play; but whereas the playwright writes his play and generally hands it on to a producer who animates it for him and puts it on the stage, a choreographer does all this himself. Usually he is his own librettist also, so that in a sense the whole fount of the creation comes from him.

When I was younger I created ballets freely, spontaneously and without much thought; the steps just flowed out of me and if they had any shape or form at all, generally it was because the music already had it, and not because I had consciously placed it there. Also, as befits the young, I wanted very much to please my audience and I thought it of great importance that I should entertain, amuse and charm them. Now I don't think that way. Up to a point I don't care what the audience thinks, I work purely and selfishly for myself and only do ballets which please me and which I feel will both develop me as an artist and extend the idiom of the dance.

There are many different sources from which a ballet may spring to life. One can be affected by the paintings of a great master and wish to animate them; one may read a story which calls to be brought to life in movement; or one can hear a piece of music which somehow dances itself. And one can have strange ideas of one's own, or a theme may be suggested by some outside influence. In the course of my career I have responded to all these different forms of impetus.

As I said, one can be moved by the paintings of a great master and wish to animate them. This I have done in two or three of my own ballets, such as my very first which was *Leda and the Swan*. In this I was stirred by the paintings of Botticelli; I copied the postures and generally created, I think, the fresh springlike morning of the world atmosphere of his paintings. I think this is a very good way for young choreographers to begin. Now that I am older I rather despise this form of creation, but it is certainly an absorbing way of working, for it necessitates the study of a whole period of painting and of manners, and this gives plastic richness and diversity to the pattern of the dance.

In my ballet *The Wise and Foolish Virgins*, which was arranged to the music of Bach, I went to eighteenth-century baroque but whereas previously in *Leda and the Swan* I had studied the paintings, in this ballet I not only studied baroque painting in general but also sculpture and architecture, and I tried to convey, with the bodies of the dancers, the swirling, rich, elaborate contortions of the baroque period. In this ballet no lines were spiral, everything was curved and interlacing, and the line of the dancers was broken and tormented, so to speak. That was a fascinating exercise for me.

As in the two ballets I have just described I studied the visual arts of painting, sculpture and architecture, I would like now to tell you of another ballet I did, which was taken from a literary theme. This was called *The Quest*, and came out of the first book of Spenser's *Faerie Queen*, about the legend of Saint George, Una and the Dragon. It was an enormous canvas and I must say that I found it a struggle to give any idea in the ballet of the richness of Spenser's imagery, and quite frankly I don't think I really succeeded. The danger, in this kind of ballet, is that one comes upon situations which are purely literary and unballetic and are thus impossible to convey clearly to an audience without the use of words; for I personally do not like a ballet in which the audience has to spend three-quarters of the time with their noses in the program to try and find out what is happening on the stage. And I found it difficult, with allegorical characters, to convey clearly their humanity and to bring them to life on the stage as Spenser has brought them to life in his great poem. I personally am not fond of the literary ballet, because it seems to me that there comes a hiatus always in which one longs for the spoken word to clarify the subject. And these ballets seem to lead always more to miming than to dancing, thereby invading the functions of the drama or the cinema. In my balletic ideology it is the dancing which must be the foremost factor, for ballet is an expression of emotions and ideas through dancing, and not through words or too much gesture, though naturally these can play their part. But I am against the overlapping of one into the other, except in the case of intentional music dramas, when all the arts are welded into a whole.

This brings me to my third heading, which is taking one's lead directly from the music, and this is the method which I now prefer. Through it one gets the purity of the dance expressing nothing but itself, and thereby expressing a thousand degrees and facets of emotion, and the mystery of poetry of movement; leaving the audience to respond at will and to bring their own poetic reactions to the work before them. Just as the greatest music has no program, so I really believe the greatest ballets are the same, or at any rate have the merest thread of an idea which can be ignored, and on which the choreographer may weave his imagination for the combination of steps and patterns.

I consider that my own most successful ballets come under this category. The first ballet that I tried in this style was *Les Rendezvous* to the music of Auber. To this gay and sparkling music, and to the merest thread of an idea—it consists only of young people meeting and parting and meeting again—I wove, I think, a rich pattern of dancing which worked up to a climax, as did the music itself. And consciously, all through my career, I have been working to make the ballet independent of literary and pictorial motives, and to make it draw from the rich fount of classical ballet; for, to my way of thinking, all ballets that are not based on the classical ballet and do not create new dancing patterns and steps within its idiom, are, as it were, only tributaries of the main stream.

Please don't misunderstand me and think that, by saying this, I mean there are not great ballets which are literary and pictorial. What I do mean to say is that they are isolated examples, and that if this line is pursued too strongly it will bring about the decadence of the dance. If the ballet is to survive, it must survive through its dancing qualities, just as drama must survive through the richness of the spoken word. In a Shakespearean play it is the richness of the language and the poetry that are paramount; the story is unimportant. And it is the same with all the greatest music, and dancing and ballets. In a ballet it is the dance that *must* be paramount.

MERCE CUNNINGHAM

THE FUNCTION OF A TECHNIQUE FOR DANCE

Since he works with the body—the strongest and, at the same instant, the most fragile of instruments—the necessity to organize and understand its way of moving is of great urgency for the dancer.

Technique is the disciplining of one's energies through physical action in order to free that energy at any desired instant in its highest possible physical and spiritual form. For the disciplined energy of a dancer is the life-energy magnified and focused for whatever brief fraction of time it lasts.

In other words, the technical equipment of a dancer is only a means, a way to the spirit. The muscles used in exercises every day are validly used only if it is understod that they lead the way, sustain the action. But it is upon the length and breadth and span of a body sustained in muscular action (and *sustaining* immobility is an action), that dance evokes its image.

The most essential thing in dance discipline is devotion, the steadfast and willing devotion to the labor that makes the class-work not a gymnastic hour and a half, or at the lowest level, a daily drudgery, but a devotion that allows the classroom discipline to be moments of dancing too. And not in any sense the feeling that each class gives an eager opportunity for willful and rhapsodic self-expression, but that each class allows in itself, and furthers the dancer towards, the synthesis of the physical and spiritual energies.

The final and wished-for transparency of the body as an instrument and as a channel to the source of energy becomes possible under the discipline the dancer sets for himself—the rigid limitations he works within, in order to arrive at freedom.

An art process is not essentially a natural process; it is an invented one. It can take actions of organization from the way nature functions, but essentially man invents the process. And from or for that process he derives a discipline to make and keep the process functioning. That discipline too is not a natural process. The daily discipline, the continued keeping of the elasticity of the muscles, the continued control of the mind over the body's actions, the constant hoped-for flow of the spirit into physical movement, both new and renewed, is not a natural way. It is unnatural in its demands on all the sources of energy. But the final synthesis can be a natural result, natural in the sense that the mind, body and spirit function as one. The technical aim is not to do a few or many things spectacularly, but to do whatever is done well, whether a smaller or greater amount of actual physical skill is required, and approaching as a goal, the flawless. To walk

magnificently and thereby evoke the spirit of a god seems surpass-
ingly more marvelous than to leap and squirm in the air in some
incredible fashion, and leave only the image of oneself. And for
that very reason, the dancer strives for complete and tempered
body-skill, for complete identification with the movement in as
devastatingly impersonal a fashion as possible. Not to show off,
but to show; not to exhibit, but to transmit the tenderness of the
human spirit through the disciplined action of a human body.

The dancer spends his life learning, because he finds the
process of dance to be, like life, continually in process. That is,
the effort of controlling the body is not learned and then ignored
as something safely learned, but must and does go on, as breathing does, renewing daily the old experiences, and daily finding
new ones. Each new movement experience, engendered by a previous one, or an initial impress of the action of the body upon
time, must be discovered, felt and made meaningful to its fullest
in order to enrich the dance memory.

The possibilities of movement are enormous and limitless,
obviously, but the understanding of organization of movement
is the high point of the dancer's craft. If the spine is taken as the
center of radius, much as the animal makes it his physical conscience, then the action proceeds from that center outwards, and
also can reverse the process and proceed from outward back to
the center. The legs and arms are only a revelation of the back,
the spine's extensions. Sitting, standing, extending a leg or arm,
or leaping through air, one is conscious that it is to and from the
spine that the appendages relate and that they manifest themselves
only so far as the spine manifests itself. Speed, for instance, is not
a case of the feet or arms twiddling at some fantastic tempo, but
speed comes from the diligence with which the spine allows the
legs and arms to go. At the same time, the spine can allow rapid
action in the legs and feet, and by the control centered in it, allow
serenity in the arms—seemingly still and suspended in the air.
The reverse too is possible.

The spine, moreover, acts not just as a source for the arms and legs, but in itself can coil and explode like a spring, can grow taut or loose, can turn on its own axis or project into space directions. It is interesting, and even extraordinary, to see the improvised physical reaction to most of the music of the nineteenth century, and then that to the folk form we know as jazz. The first is usually immediately apparent in the arms and legs, the second happens in the torso, or there is a definite visual indication that the movement impetus, however small or large in circumference, starts from an action in the torso. It is not really extraordinary, because of what lies at the root, but it is interesting to see.

Certainly everybody including dancers can leap, sit down and get up again, but the dancer makes it apparent that the going into the air is what establishes the relationship to the air, the process of sitting down, not the position upon being down, is what gives the iridescent and life-quality to dancing.

The technical equipment for a dancer involves many things. There must be an understanding of the correct vertical position of the body, and how it is obtained and held. This involves the problem of balance of the body, and the sustaining of one part against another part. If one uses the torso as the center of balance and as the vertical axis at all times, then the question of balance is always related to that central part, the arms and legs balancing each other on either side and in various ways, and moving against each other. If one uses the torso as the moving force itself, allowing the spine to be the motivating force in a visual shift of balance, the problem is to sense how far the shift of balance can go in any direction and in any time arrangement, and then move instantaneously towards any other direction and in other time arrangements, without having to break the flow of movement by a catching of the weight whether by an actual shift of weight, or a break in the time, or other means. The dynamics of the torso are thus sustained, and distilled and not lost in moving from one direction to another.

Paul Weiss says in *Nature and Man*, "the will is employed to discipline the body by making it the locus of techniques—means for acting well habitually so as to reach objectives mentally envisaged. There is little pleasure in setting about to master a technique. One must first concentrate on its different component movements and steps. Then one must firmly relate them by going over them in sequence again and again. But there are compensations. While the technique is being willingly mastered, the body and the mind are in accord, for a willing mastery of a technique requires that one keep in mind what one is doing and keep one's body from disturbing the intent of the mind. And so far as nothing arises which provokes the mind or body to work in opposition to the acquired technique, the technique promises a fairly enduring resolution of the conflict of mind and body. Though techniques enable a mind and body to work together for a considerable time, they tend to force the one or the other into a groove. The more a technique is mastered, the greater the risk that one will be too inflexible to overcome those oppositions between the mind and the body which are inevitable when the differently structured mind and body confront a novel situation."

One of the things that Western dance, and principally here in America, has not explored in any formal or technical sense, is the disciplined use of the face. The place we know of primarily that has made a continuous disciplined use of the face for definite expressive purpose—that is, a particular facial image for wrath, another for the hero, etc.—is the Hindu classical dance. But here in the United States where there has been an extraordinary amount of technical exploration into kinds of expressive movement, there has been little or no formal cognizance taken of the face. Every other part of the body has been subjected to many kinds of motion, the face left to its own devices.

The element that underlies both music and dance is time, which, when present in component parts, is rhythm. As an ele-

ment coordinating the two arts, it is more useful when the phrase and parts longer than the phrase are considered, rather than the small particularities of accent and even of individual quantity. The concentration on the minutiae of rhythm in the music-dance relationship leads to the "boom-with-boom" device, giving nothing to either and robbing both of freedom. Working, however, from the phrase leads to a related independence, or to an interdependence of the two time arts. Accents, even and uneven beats, then appear, if they do, where the music continuity or the dance continuity allows them to. (That is, an accent in the music is an incident in the music continuity which does not necessarily appear in the dance, and vice versa.)

In coordinating dance and music the one should not be submerged into the other, as that would tend to make one dependent upon the other, and not independent as they naturally are. The dance and music can be brought together by time, by a particular rhythmic structure of time involving phrases, which indicate the meeting points convenient for use, thereby giving to each a freedom to expressively play with and against a common structural idea.

Plato, in the *Timaeus*, says, "Time is the moving image of eternity." Time, the very essence of our daily lives, can give to dancing one of the qualities that make it, at its most beautiful, a moving image of life at its highest.

PEARL PRIMUS

OUT OF AFRICA

Baba stands six feet seven inches tall and his voice is like a river roaring to the sea. One day last year I met him and, learning that he was an African witch doctor, I plied him with questions.

"Tell me," I said, "tell me about life in Africa . . . about dance . . ."

"They are the same thing," he answered.

Africans used their bodies as instruments through which every conceivable emotion or event was projected. The result was a strange but hypnotic marriage between life and dance. The two were inseparable. No child could be born, no man buried without dance. They danced the sowing of the seed and the harvest, puberty rites, hunting, warfare. They danced for rain, sun, strong and numerous children, marriages, play. Love, hatred, fear, joy, sorrow, disgust, amazement: all these, all others, were expressed through rhythmic movement.

As if their bodies, developed through centuries of dance, sunshine and struggle, were not enough to portray their emotions, they created powerful rhythms and songs to accompany them, their artists carved fantastic masks, their designers created strange costumes. Priests, warriors, hunters, doctors were primarily dancers. Baba belonged to this group. When he moved he seemed like liquid steel plunging with terrifying control into space. When he was in Africa he would wrap himself around the trunk of a tree and, using his long arms and neck, he would become a serpent. Then, filled with the healing power of the God he invoked he would unwind himself and encircle the victim. (The snake is the symbol for many things, among them the healing power.)

Baba would dance until the spirit crept from him.

The role of the professional dancer was of tremendous importance in Africa. He was necessary to all ceremonies, all feasts, all occasions which involved the health and well-being of the tribe. In return for his services the tribe fed and clothed him and provided for him in his every need. He was left free to dance . . . Is it any wonder then that dance stands with music and art at the very top of the list of cultural contributions of the African to the world? Is it any wonder that the dancer developed to such an extent that he could spin his head on his neck so rapidly that the onlooker saw nothing but blur . . . or that he could leap from the ground with feet outstretched in a wide sitting position and land on his buttocks only to spring into the air again unhurt? Is it any wonder that a group of fifty warriors could dance their spear dances and not one finger be out of place? Is it surprising, with bodies so developed through dance, that these people became the choice prey for slave traders?

Today we are again recognizing the power of the dance. But in Africa the dance was not only social, but ethnic, therapeutic and educational. It was a way of getting tribes together and of exhibiting the cultural development of the people. One group of dancers competed with the other. The people judged the contest and awarded the honors to the winners. In this way the entire tribal drive was expressed through the dancer. This was very important. The dancer outside of his own immediate community was known not by his name but by that of his tribe. He was the representative of a specific group and as such was highly responsible for the prestige of that group.

The non-professional or amateur dancers included everyone else: the man who, filled with the knowledge that his wife has given birth to a new son, leaps down the street singing, or the one who rolls in dirt rending his clothing because of some personal disaster, or the woman turning round and round in the river embracing it as the symbol of fertility.

African dance forms are strong, virile and vital with a feeling of dynamic thrust and resistance. They are exceedingly controlled, having the power to project the subtle as dynamically as the obvious. To adequately study the African dance one must have excellent knowledge of African religions. In the ecstasy of a religious experience the dancer becomes a god and the body frees itself of its structural limitations. Legs, bodies, arms, heads may move in seemingly impossible counterpoint.

The dancer is very conscious of what his dance expresses. His movements are disciplined freedom. This ability to seem completely without control has erroneously labeled African dancing as wild, loose, formless. Were it so, the dancer would break every bone in his body. This then is an art, for within himself he has mastered subtle tension to such a degree that his body is freed to express whatever he desires. An African lawyer was once losing his case. It is said that he suddenly stopped speaking and began dancing. The result: he won!

This strength is something rapidly moving into the past. The African danced about everything . . . Today his struggle is not so much in the understanding of thunder, floods, or fighting against wild animals, or preparing young people for their passage into the adult life of the tribe. He is vitally concerned with understanding this new European life which is gradually displacing his own. He feels sharply the conflict between the new religion and his own out of which his art forms had developed. The artist is confused and is searching for an avenue to express himself. Clan life is no longer important; the people are heavily taxed. Dance is now called pagan, and in many places completely forbidden. The drummer then creates no new music, the singer no new songs, the artist fashions no exciting new masks, no clubs, no urns.

But the spirit which was responsible for the dynamic dance and the exciting art forms of yesterday is merely underground . . . Sometime it will spring forth in a seemingly new form. This time, let us hope, the world will open its arms to welcome it and will place it without reservation where it belongs with the greatest.

SALLY KAMIN

THE POTENTIAL LIBRARY FOR THE DANCER

Crude carvings on the walls of caves and on rocks and later the various dancing figures on pottery were the first visual records of the dance. But in the beginning of the fifteenth century manuscripts began to appear which reflected the searching preoccupation of scholars and dance masters devoted to the art of dance

movement, and who left clear records of this creative art as it
was then practiced.

With the advent of the printing press a vast literature of the
dance appeared, and every phase in the evolution of the art, in
word and picture, was noted between covers. From the scholar,
scientist, abbé, from the historian and the performer, through the
centuries volume after volume came off the presses in all lan-
guages. It would astonish many a dance enthusiast who might
think of accumulating a complete dance library eventually that
there are more than 10,000 dance books in existence.

Although the literature of the dance dating from the fifteenth century to the present is extensive and rich, its accessi-
bility to the dancer, to the research worker and student of the
dance is extremely meager and frequently nonexistent. This is
all the more regrettable if one considers that in spite of this inadequacy the dance has become one of the great artistic expressions of the national cultural idiom. But the interest in the dance
may easily run the risk of vitiating its great potency if it is denied
the means of nurturing, developing and replenishing itself.

In terms of the enthusiasm our nation has exhibited and
in terms of the wealth of the community, it would be fitting that
the great literature of the dance should be made easily available
to our people. There are innumerable books, pamphlets, auto-
graph material, prints, programs and other memorabilia which
are now in a few private libraries that should be made available to
the public. The dance literature, of course, is as many-faceted as
the variations of dance expression. It ranges from a mere pictorial presentation of an arrested movement of an individual
dancer to the philosophical thoughts stimulated by dance performances. There are adequate volumes on the history of the
dance; there are treatises on the critical approach to the art, its
place and function in society. There is the ethnologic dance;
and it is undoubtedly of great importance for the student to be
aware of the prolific literature of the anthropologic, tribal and

sacred dance; for this offers a generous source of information on the mores and the culture of primitive peoples. In the regional and folk dance field there is an enormous collection of important indigenous pamphlet material, for the most part written by historians who developed an incidental interest in the dance.

The great records of the pre-classic dance, of the elaborate spectacles and of balletic literature from the fifteenth century to the present, are invaluable to the contemporary historian. The early series of dictionaries, grammars, technical manuals of the various schools and books on dance notation reflect the painstaking devotion of instructors and scholars, the fruit of whose labor is used in our own effort to continue the knowledge bequeathed to us.

A field of literature of comparatively recent vintage deals with the free, creative and modern dance. It also embraces critical and technical as well as historic material. And those who have made valuable contributions in this field are well known pedagogues, philosophers, historians and critics. Then we find many books directly or indirectly related to the dance: on music, costumes and décor; on mime and pantomime. Also there are available countless souvenir program books as records of the various dance companies which have performed all over the world.

Finally, parallel with the progress of the dance as an art form, from the earliest period to the present, there have been panegyrics against the dance as a destructive and immoral force. The literature on this theme, both by ecclesiasts and laymen, is noted for its naiveté, venom and lack of foresight; but it is a faithful reflection of the long and difficult struggle to establish the dance as part of the cultural pattern of the community.

This historic victory can best be preserved by making the vast dance literature available to dancers and other workers in the field by establishing dance libraries and archives in every great center in our country.

TRUDY GOTH

THE "LABORATORY" METHOD

Nothing can be more dangerous to the development of the dance
—be it the ballet or modern dance—than to live on what the
"great ones" have done and to follow anxiously their footsteps
(in the most literal sense of the word). Any art which is stag-
nant writes its own death sentence. Disciples without initiative,
without the inmost urge to free themselves from the influence
of the past and to find new ways of self-expression do their teachers little honor.

Any cataclysmic event in world history seems to coincide
with, or bring forth in its aftermath, the carriers of new thoughts,
the creators of new movements. They are the incarnate transition from an established way of thinking to something new. After
the first World War it was Mary Wigman in Europe and Graham,
Humphrey and Weidman in America who proved the greatness
of the past by building upon it their own house.

Two decades have since passed. Another holocaust has be-
fallen mankind. Will it show any marked effect on the creative
spirit of the new dance generation? We have no way of knowing. All we can and must do is to make it possible for them to
show their creations. In recent years, the critics of the modern
dance have pointed out the amazing dearth of new experiments
in choreography. It is certainly not sufficient to present new dance
pieces, if the technique of movement lacks any "pioneering" aspect. Today we seem to be in a stage of transition in which the
creativeness of the new and young dancer is still under the influence of the "great ones." And tomorrow—?

There is an increasing awareness that the coming period will
develop new dance forms, that very likely the choreographer and
performer will relate himself more closely to the theater than the
concert hall. Whichever trend the dance may follow—be it a new

form of the theatrical dance, or any other manifestation—it is the young dancer and choreographer who will have to make it come true. And it is he who is caught in a vicious circle of economic and artistic difficulties. To develop artistically, to mold and unfold the inner expression of his personality, he must have the opportunity to experiment. He can only compose and rehearse his ballets or dance dramas in his spare time between working, studying or looking for a job in a show. He must, moreover, exert all his energy to keep aflame the enthusiasm of his unpaid co-workers for his creation. His greatest handicaps are the enormous expenses for whatever he may attempt to do—the costuming, the pianist, the rent of studios for rehearsal time—and, of course, the lack of any appropriate possibility to show his work. If he does not belong to a group, the only outlet he has may be an occasional chance to perform at a college or club.

The need is paramount for organizations to make the performance of the young dancer's choreographic work possible. Undoubtedly, he can only be helped when he helps himself and takes the lead in solving his own organizational and performance problems within a group of other dancers.

But even if he has solved these so necessary facilities for his creative work through an organization, in order to grow in his art he still needs help in the form of constructive criticism and well-meant advice. As the scientist works in a true spirit of collaboration with his co-workers for months and often for years in his laboratory, experimenting and testing the results of his experiments, before offering them to the general public, so should the young choreographer test his experiments, the results of his creative spirit and technical skill, before showing them to an audience.

It has been my experience that it makes little difference whether the Workshop produces one or two ballets a season, or none which are excellent from the viewpoint of content and execution. What really matters is that the Workshop affords an opportunity to the artist—whether choreographer, dancer, musician or designer—which he finds nowhere else.

One of the most important things for all young artists is to find out their possibilities and limitations. But most of them seem to aim too far. They feel compelled to embrace the world and, with it, all its problems when they attempt the gigantic task of squeezing all their feelings and thoughts into one ballet idea. Here they face the artistic advisers of the Workshop who will point out to them the danger that lies in the scope of their endeavor, the flaws in their work and the pitfalls they ought to avoid.

It must be understood that the "advisory board" of such a Workshop can merely *advise*, that its function is to guide and to help, not to restrict or to cripple the artistic impulse of the young choreographer. Neither the genuineness of the young artist's Faustian feelings nor the intensity of his energies is doubted. On the contrary, I am fully aware of the tremendous potentialities stored up in them, and I also realize that the dance can best be served through the release of these potentialities. But I also see the Workshop's task in helping channel the young artist's energies properly and in making him see that the most colossal, all-embracing theme can best be expressed symbolically through simple means and the simplest story. And my experience has taught me that this is the major problem of the young choreographer.

The dance pattern for his ideas is usually satisfactory, in other words, he is technically well prepared. His difficulty lies in characterization, in pointing up the necessary highlights, and most of all in finding the right style. Many of the young choreographers have not yet comprehended that each idea, each piece of music—from the very beginning—makes a different approach necessary.

Their great chance when working through the laboratory method of the Workshop lies not only in the fact that they can show their dance ideas but that, in the process of their work, they come together with other artists, with other and new ideas. And the mutual influence, often unconsciously exerted on their creative attempts, is highly stimulating and salutary for their future endeavors. Therefore, the laboratory method for the creation of new dances provides a true basis for interchange of ideas and for dealing with the fundamental problems of dance composition, both in thematic material and form. Such experiments are of the utmost importance, if young choreographers are to have the guidance they need and the fullest opportunity to develop their talents. Inspiration, ambition and a good technique may tempt them to create new dance compositions, but these ingredients may not always suffice for a truly artistic production. Only a collective artistic effort and the continuous process of creating and eliminating lays the groundwork for any possible achievement of the future choreographer.

CHARLES WEIDMAN

RANDOM REMARKS

I have always believed that the audience and the performer are indivisible. Both artist and audience enter the house—although through different doors—from the same street. They have both seen the same headlines, they have both left the same world of reality behind them. And while the artist puts on his make-up, the audience leaves its everyday disillusionment in the checkroom.

Real art can never be escape from life. In histrionic terms, illusions are not false impressions nor misconceptions of reality. The world of illusion which the audience expects from the artist is, in fact, the world of their real selves, the image of their own world, the translation of their hopes and fears, their joys and sufferings into the magic of the stage.

The artist must not run away from himself, from his "center of being." He is the bearer of a message, and it is his responsibility to tell it—in whatever medium it may be—intelligibly, forcefully and with his utmost artistic ability. He may sometimes fail in the delivery of his message, but he must never fail in his purpose.

It is often said of the modern dance that it is not easily understood, that its silent language of movement is so intricate as to veil its meaning. But since any dance presentation lives only while it is being performed and since it can hardly be preserved for later in files and books, it would utterly fail to accomplish its task or even to justify its existence could it not clearly convey its message. Only poets, musicians, painters or sculptors can dare challenge their contemporaries with their media of art and yield to the judgment of posterity. The dancer can do this as little as can the actor or singer. L'art pour l'art is for him the death sentence expressed by his own feeble attempt to convince his audience.

I have always been impatient with the "art pour l'artist." Clarity and understandability has remained the basis of my dance creations. Their intent, concerned with human values and the experience of our times, must be carried by the fullest emotional impact the artist can muster. Then, with the conception of the idea, the intelligibility of its message and the emotional intensity of presentation, the artist's primordial task is fulfilled and—however his artistic deliverance may be judged—his sincerity cannot be doubted.

Some may say that I am going too far when I desire to make my dance creations as easily understandable as a movie. But this may explain why more and more I have come to believe in the pantomimic dance drama. The word "pantomime" does not mean to me the presentation of a dumb show, as most dictionaries define it, or the mere telling of a story or action without the use of explanatory words. To me it is the transport of an idea into movement, the animation of the feeling behind the idea, an animation in which suddenly all commas and periods, all silent moments of an unwritten play become a reality in movement. Moreover, it may be likened to that emotional sequence of a growing world of images which we may experience when listening to a symphony, full of logical continuity and expressiveness where words might seem feeble and music inadequate.

I may be prejudiced in favor of the pantomimic dance, because I have found that my gift as a dancer is essentially tied up with my dramatic talent as an actor, or—let us better say—as a mime. The modern mime must be a modern dancer, and as such his entire body must be alive. This cannot be acquired by emotional experience, only by hard physical training. It may be best called bodily awareness. In order to test this bodily awareness in one of my dance compositions, I went so far as to exclude the face, i.e., the facial expression, completely from the pantomimic presentation.

Any idea being projected produces its specific movement and gesture pattern which is, in itself, purely abstract. Though, basically, pantomime is not mere storytelling, a story may be, and usually is, achieved by what is done. But to attain such ends, the means must be determined by strict form, since form alone leads to artistry.

In seeking to reach my audience and to convey my message in the easiest understandable manner, I often chose the channels of humor. There are various kinds of humor, but first and foremost it must be said that, whenever a humorous element is required, it can come only from the performer himself and must be projected by him.

In the beginning I employed the most obvious humor, the sadistic type of humor, the effect of which is almost guaranteed with every audience. However, with time, I was continually looking for a broader expression of what I wanted to achieve, and I attempted to abstract the essence of any emotion projected through movement. Here is an example. Instead of being frantic as, let us say, a minstrel would be when a bucket of water is thrown over him, I tried to convey the same idea without impersonating a minstrel and with no bucket of water causing the emotion. This attempt finally crystallized into a dance called *Kinetic Pantomime*. In this composition I so juggled, reversed and distorted cause and effect, impulse and reaction that a kaleidoscopic effect was created without once resorting to any literary representation.

It has been a long and arduous way from this comedy pantomime to Thurber's *Fables*. But my basic approach to subject matter, though it has widened and developed, has never changed. Content and form are equally important to my choreographic pantomimes. I have never believed that artistry can be achieved without adhering to the strictest form, nor that the heart of the public can be reached, if the artist is blind to the life that surrounds him or tries to shut himself off from it by escaping into mere fantasy and romance. Art demands that we be part of life and merge with it. Art and life are as indivisible an entity as the artist and his audience.

HELEN TAMIRIS

PRESENT PROBLEMS AND POSSIBILITIES

Now that the commercial theater has discovered the dance and is enriching itself with the principles that choreographers have arrived at through years of experimentation, the tendency is to think that the dance should give up its life as an independent art form and stay in the theater where it belongs.

That the dancer belongs in the theater goes without saying. One of the signs of the times is the need that some writers have to incorporate the dance as an integral part into their scripts. That audiences have responded to the revitalization of the Broadway musical theater can be attested to by the results at the box office of many Broadway musicals that have utilized creative dance.

However, having won its place in the theater again, where it can reach large masses of the people, the dance can only maintain its vitality there by continuing its experimentations, by develop-

ing its techniques, by giving performers opportunities to develop
their talents. By this I mean enlarging the field of independent
dance, dance on its own terms and not only in its collaborative
role in the theater.

Perhaps it is significant that whenever an artist chooses to
work strictly in his own medium, starting from his own conceptions, such as unasked-for symphonies, easel pictures or choreographic compositions that are not commissioned, he generally
has a hard time finding audiences for these works and consequently an even harder time making ends meet. Because this independent approach is unprofitable, should it be dropped in
favor of collaborative efforts? I say no: because the artist must
be given a chance to develop his unique contribution in whatever
medium he operates. Actually the vitality of creative collaboration
depends upon the artist's development of his own ideology, his
own style and craft. This can only be gained by working on themes
that come from him, seem important to him and are expressed
purely through his own medium. He is then better able to give
of himself in a collaborative effort and in return is enriched by
contact with the other arts. As to the performing artist, he has
a better chance to develop his talent because he can work with
different choreographers in a variety of roles.

At the moment the ballet field is in a more advantageous
position to operate on its own terms. It can find fairly extensive
financial support, enabling it to maintain large and small companies, where choreographers and dancers can devote themselves
primarily to independent dance works. The modern dance, on
the other hand, never has had sufficient patronage to sustain any
large company. The economic backbone of whatever small company emerged was the private resources of the individual choreographer around whom the company was formed. However, it
would be false to assume that the modern dance is by this evidence less popular; it is taught in many schools and colleges of
America.

Beginning with the late twenties, the modern dance found support among students, intellectual groups and trade unions. An essential part of its approach lay in divesting the dance of its outer glamour and trickery, with more reliance on the substance of its thought and movement. Dancing throughout a great part of recent history had been given the role of the good-time girl of the arts. The modern dance, rejecting this degrading position, insisted that movement was capable of expressing mature conceptions.

Partisans of either the modern dance or ballet, when speaking of the future of the dance, inevitably see the flowering of only the form to which they are devoted. The truth of the matter is that at this point in history both are finding large audiences. The current vitality of both mediums, in its acceptance by the theater and in the concert field, is due to the fact that each form, within the last twenty years, has learned from the other. The ballet became aware of a wider range of movement, of the potentialities of handling serious themes and of the fact that America was not an untouchable subject. The modern dance only reached its current wide public by recognizing values it had previously denigrated—such as the use of rich and colorful costumes, the value of spectacle and virtuosity in their proper place—and the technique itself broadened to include vital concepts of movement and line traditionally associated with the ballet. Both have profited from this exchange. Also in the theater field, ballet choreographers cannot avoid the necessity of casting some modern dancers in their shows and modern choreographers, on the other hand, find it necessary to use some ballet dancers in their companies.

The dance as a whole is riding the crest of popularity today. No musical is complete without a substantial portion devoted to dance. However, this is the time to take stock and see how the dance can consolidate itself, broaden its horizons, for nothing is more vicious than Broadway's craze for novelty. What will we do when the novelty wears off? The only answer is that creative, vital art is always new. Consequently, the real problem is how to maintain and develop our creative vitality. This concerns both the ballet and modern fields. If things persist as they are, the dance as a whole will continue to have a chaotic and uncertain future. The ballet in spite of its subsidies has never paid for itself. Someone has always covered its losses. At best its support is a precarious, willful one, dependent upon the whim and surplus cash of "patrons." To "cross our fingers" and "hope for the best" is certainly no way to build a future.

If we want to create a future, making it a time of continuously developing achievement in dance and choreography, we must convince our communities, states and nation that we have something to give them and that they must help us in return. In this way we will be assured of a constantly growing reserve of fresh talent, nourishing the whole country and not Broadway alone. Such a group of dance artists would be capable of meeting new challenges and creating new audiences.

FREDERICK ASHTON: Born September 17, 1906 at Guayaquil, Ecuador. Educated by the Dominican Fathers in Lima, Peru, and Dover College, Dover, Kent. Studied dancing under Massine, Lipinska and Rambert. Chief work with Ballet Rambert and Sadler's Wells Ballet. In U.S. choreographed Virgil Thomson's Opera *Four Saints in Three Acts*; for Monte Carlo Ballet *Devil's Holiday*; for Ballet Theatre *Patineurs*. Principal choreographer and one of the artistic directors of Sadler's Wells Ballet at Royal Opera House, Covent Garden, London. Best known ballets: *Façade, Dante Sonata, Apparitions, Horoscope, Checkmate, Symphonic Variations, The Wanderer, Wedding Bouquet, Cinderella* (1949), *Illuminations* (1950).

GEORGE BALANCHINE: Before leaving Russia in 1924, at the age of twenty, Balanchine choreographed a number of works including a *General March* by Chopin, *Waltzes* by Ravel, *Boeuf sur le Toit* by Milhaud, *Enigma* by Arensky, *Pulcinella* by Stravinsky, *Salome* by Strauss, *La Nuit* by Rubinstein, several of his own musical compositions, pieces by Scriabine and Medtner, dances to recitation of poems, dances for the State Opera production of *Coq d'Or*, and for productions of Toller's *Broken Brow* and Shaw's *Caesar and Cleopatra*. Balanchine has choreographed opera ballets in London and Copenhagen, in Monte Carlo, at the Metropolitan in New York. He is now principal choreographer for the New York City Ballet (Ballet Society). Best known for: *Le Rossignol, Apollon Musagètes, Mozartiana, Serenade, Orpheus, Le Baiser de la Fée, Le Bourgeois Gentilhomme, Circus Polka, Danses Concertantes, Elegie, Symphony in C* (1948), *Divertimento* (1949), *Firebird* (1910, revived 1949), *Jones Beach* (1950), *Mazurka* from a *Life for the Tsar* (1950), *Sylvia: Pas de Deux* (1950), *La Valse* (1951).

EUGÈNE BERMAN: Born 1899 at St. Petersburg, Russia. He is an American citizen since 1945. Studied art in Russia (1914–1918), Paris and Italy (1919–1939). Resident of U.S. since 1937. Designer of décors for ballets: *Icare* (Serge Lifar, 1938), *Devil's Holiday* (Frederick Ashton, 1939), *Concerto Barocco* (George Balanchine, 1941), *Romeo and Juliet* (Anthony Tudor, 1943), *Danses Concertantes, Le Bourgeois Gentilhomme* (Ballet Theatre, 1944), *Giselle* (new décors for Ballet Theatre, 1949). Also designed décors for some ballets not produced and for various plays and operas.

THOMAS BOUCHARD: Came to America from Europe in 1913. Constantly experimenting in photography, he traveled from one state to another, stopping longest in Texas where open country, horses and the spontaneous way of living appealed to him. In 1926 he returned to Europe, worked in France and had the first one-man show of photography ever given in Paris. In 1932 he was back in New York developing a new technique of movement in modern dance still-photography. He is now producing 16mm dance films, the most provocative to date being his *The Shakers* and *The Golden Fleece*. His lifelong interest in painting and close association with the best contemporary artists, both European and American, has led him naturally to the making of a series of 16mm educational films in color of painters and their work, again developing a new technique of motion.

MERCE CUNNINGHAM: Born Centralia, Washington; attended Cornish School, Seattle, Washington. Soloist with Martha Graham, 1940–1946. Solo and group concerts in New York. Made transcontinental tours (solo). Choreographer of *The Seasons* for Ballet Society. Gives professional classes in New York and has been teaching at several universities. Now teaching at American School of Ballet.

RUTH ST. DENIS: Born in Newark, New Jersey, of poor but inquiring parents; and was raised on a farm at Summerville in that same state. Mother was a physician, father an inventor. Left the farm in early youth and moved to Brooklyn, where first real theatrical engagement came her way, with Mrs. Leslie Carter in David Belasco's American version of *Zaza*. At the end of five years in various Belasco companies, she was seized one day with attraction toward the Orient. Solo career as an Oriental dancer extended roughly from 1906 to 1914, when she met Ted Shawn. They combined their talents in the school of Denishawn. Eventually built Denishawn House in the upper reaches of New York City, through whose portals went forth many who now bear distinguished names in the world of the dance: Martha Graham and Doris Humphrey, Charles Weidman and Jack Cole were of this number. In 1940 wrote biography which was published by Harpers under the title of *My Unfinished Life.*—Today she is in Hollywood still dancing. Incorporated the Ruth St. Denis Foundation, a nonprofit American institution devoted to the fulfillment of the spiritualizing of the arts in America.

KITTY DONER: Learned to dance from her parents. Her mother came to America as a ballet dancer in Barnum & Bailey Circus, and later became a ballet mistress of the New York Hippodrome, where Kitty received her early dance training. She was a feature dancer at the Winter Garden Review with Al Jolson for six years; headlined in vaudeville; appeared in music halls in London; made a song and dance film for Warner Brothers, one of the first talking shorts in 1928; appeared in television for CBS; was an assistant producer at the Roxy; choreographed in association with Pauline Koner the first series of ballets for the television program of CBS; also choreographed with Pauline Koner some of the major ice shows and "Skating Vanities" touring America and Europe; was talent scout for Ted Mack's original amateur hour; at present she is completing an autobiographical book in which one of the major movie studios is interested.

ANGNA ENTERS: Mime, dancer, playwright, painter: born New York; privately and self-educated in U.S., Europe, Near East. Creator since March 1926 of some 165 *Episodes* and *Compositions in Dance Form* in "The Theatre of Angna Enters," shown in all large and secondary cities of U.S. and Canada, also most colleges and many art museums of U.S.A., also in London, where she has had eight seasons; Paris; Cuba; Hawaii; and the White House, Washington, D.C. She presented her Greek Mime *Pagan Greece* at the Metropolitan Museum of Art in New York; awarded two Guggenheim Fellowships in 1934 and 1935; exhibited some 1,200 paintings and drawings at Newhouse Galleries, New York, for 14 successive exhibitions since 1933. As Guggenheim Fellow made groups of archaic, primitive, geometric and Hellenistic art forms;

Greco-Roman, Pompeian; Coptic; Egyptian dynastic; Chinese; and Persian art forms. Her 12th New York exhibition marked her debut as a sculptor. Has had solo exhibitions in London, England, and virtually every principal American and Canadian museum of art. Also had solo exhibits of 38 archaic Greek art forms at the Metropolitan Museum of Art; represented in permanent collections of Metropolitan Museum of Art, Honolulu Museum of Art, and many other collections in U.S.A. and Europe. Author of *First Person Plural* self-illustrated, 1937, Stackpole Sons; *Love Possessed Juana*, a play of Inquisition Spain, illustrated with her stage settings and reproducing her music score, published 1939 by Twice A Year Press; *Silly Girl*, the first part of a self-illustrated *Portrait of Personal Remembrance*, published 1944 by Houghton Mifflin Co., bought by Metro-Goldwyn-Mayer; author of two screen plays made into films by Metro-Goldwyn-Mayer: *Lost Angel* and *Tenth Avenue Angel*. Began term contract as contributor of original ideas at Metro-Goldwyn-Mayer Studios in 1945. *Love Possessed Juana* produced in October 1946 by Houston Little Theatre, scheduled for production at the Dramatic Workshop in New York for 1948–49. Also her second play *The Unknown Lover* presented in 1947 at Houston Little Theatre. Contributor of articles to various theater, dance magazines, also general publications such as *Magazine of Art, New Republic*, etc.

JEAN ERDMAN: Born Honolulu, graduated Sarah Lawrence College 1938, prof. training: Martha Graham School, Bennington Summer School of the Dance, Am. School of Ballet, José Fernandez (Spanish dance), Hisamatsu School of Japanese Dance, Mory Kawena Pukui and Huapala (Hawaiian dance). Member and soloist in Martha Graham Company; 1944 organized Jean Erdman Dance Group; individual performances of original compositions in New York, Chicago, etc.; 1947 choreographed *Les Mouches* by Jean-Paul Sartre at Vassar Experimental Theatre; 1948 several recitals in New York and special June course for children and adults at Genevieve Jones Studios, Pittsburgh, Pa. In the spring of 1950, following a successful transcontinental tour, she was invited, with her company, to participate in the Annual Colorado Creative Arts Festival. This was so successful that the company was asked to return in 1951.

TRUDY GOTH: Founder and director of the Choreographers' Workshop has appeared formerly as a concert dancer in Europe and in this country. Hungarian-born, she was educated in Italy and is now an American citizen. Miss Goth studied modern dance with Harold Kreutzberg and the Jooss school, ballet and character dancing with Mme Egorova and Mme Preobrajenska in Paris. In the U.S., she studied with Hanya Holm, Agnes de Mille, Celli and Fornaroli. She was a teacher of wide experience as assistant to the director, civic dancing school in Florence, private schools, colleges in Italy and the staff of Mozarteum Salzburg for festivals. She has given private courses for actors and singers and has been a member of the Dance Department of the New School for Social Research. She has had her own studio since 1943—has her own children's group who dance for benefit performances. Miss Goth was on the staff of the Dunham school for one season. As a dancer: concert tours in Europe and U.S.A. and South America. Appeared on DuMont television. Broadway show: *Yours Is My Heart* with Richard Tauber. In Italy summers 1948–50: assistant stage director to Herbert Graf for open-air opera, production assistant to Venice Modern Music Festival for ballet productions. First experimental television programs directed and choreographed. Taking CW group to Bermuda, first "overseas" tour CW first produced: V. Bettis *As I Lay Dying*, Herbert Ross *Capriccios* and *The Thief Who Loved The Ghost* both acquired by Ballet Theatre. First presented Janet Collins.

MORTON GOULD: Born 1913 in Richmond Hill, N.Y.; at the age of four started to play the piano, at six he had his first composition published; studied composition with Dr. Vincent Jones. At the age of twenty-one engaged by WOR-Mutual Network to conduct and arrange his own program; composed *Pavane*. Gould's works for the most part run a wide gamut from numerous small numbers to compositions in the large forms. However, he has based almost all of his symphonic works on some aspect or part of our American idioms. His best known works: 3 Symphonies, 4 American Symphonettes, the Latin-American Symphonettes, *Foster Gallery*, *Little Symphony*, *Lincoln Legend*, *Cowboy Rhapsody*, Spirituals, *Sonatina for Piano*, etc.; wrote the music for the movies *Delightfully Dangerous* and *Billion Dollar Baby*; wrote the score for *Interplay* (Jerome Robbins) and *Fall River Legend* (Agnes de Mille).

JOSEPH GREGOR: Born 1888, Prof. Dr.; Director of Viennese State Theater; head of the Viennese National Library; author of several books published in Germany, Austria and Switzerland; among them: *Kulturgeschichte des Ballets; Perikles; Shakespeare; Das Spanische Welttheater; Weltgeschichte des Theaters; Richard Strauss; Die Liebe der Danae;* published in London: *The Sisters of Prague.*

HANYA HOLM: Leading American dancer, choreographer and teacher in modern dance. Born in Worms-am-Rhein (Germany); educated in Germany; joined Mary Wigman School, co-director and chief instructor at the Wigman Institute for ten years. In 1931 she came to New York to found the New York Wigman School of the Dance which, since 1936, has been known as the Hanya Holm Studio. *Trend* 1937 New York debut; in 1938 (Bennington Festival) *Dance Sonata* and *Dance of Work and Play.* Then followed: *Metropolitan Daily* (also televised by National Broadcasting Company); *Tragic Exodus; They Too Are Exiles* and *The Golden Fleece.* Productions of Hanya Holm's dance composition at the Colorado Springs Fine Arts Center: 1941 *From This Earth;* 1942 *What So Proudly We Hail, Namesake* and *A Suite of Four Dances;* 1943 *Orestes and the Furies;* 1944 *The Walt Whitman Suite* and *The Gardens of Eden;* 1946 *Windows;* 1947 *And So Ad Infinitum,* an insect comedy by Karel and Josef Capek; *Ozark Set* by Elie Siegmeister and *The Donkey* by Freda Miller; 1947-48 "The Eccentricities of Davy Crockett," one of the three episodes of *Ballet Ballads* by John LaTouche presented by the Experimental Theatre (Music Box Theatre, New York); also choreographed *The Insect Comedy* by Karel and Josef Capek at the City Center, New York. She was one of the founder directors of the New York City Dance Company and her *Ozark Suite* was produced there in 1949. The summer 1950 marked her tenth consecutive year at Colorado College, Colorado Springs. In 1950 she choreographed *Out of This World* (Cole Porter show), in spring 1951 she went to England to do the choreography for *Kiss Me, Kate.*

DORIS HUMPHREY: One of the leading dancers and choreographers of modern dance. Was a featured soloist with the Denishawn dancers. She left this group in 1928 and joined forces with Charles Weidman. Her major works are: *The Shakers, Air on a Ground Base, Descent into a Dangerous Place, La Valse, Decade, Passacaglia;* among her dramatic theater pieces are: *Inquest, Lament for a Bullfighter, Story of Mankind.* Since her retirement as a dancer, she has concentrated on choreography and teaching and has created works for José Limon, Pauline Koner, and others. She received the Guggenheim Fellowship in 1949 for a book on choreography.

MARY JANE HUNGERFORD: Born August 30, 1913, Chicago. M.A. and Ph.D. from Columbia University. Co-founder and Associate Editor of *Educational Dance Magazine* from 1938–1942. Author of: *Creative Tap Dancing* (1938); *A Course in Modern Dance* (1944). Associate Editor of *Dance Magazine,* New York. Teacher of dance in colleges for thirteen years.

ANN HUTCHINSON: Born in New York City of American parentage. Educated in Europe, started her dance training at the Jooss-Leeder School in England. Studied with Martha Graham and other modern dancers and has since been specializing in ballet. Worked in England and America as a dancer and graduated as a dance notator and teacher (Laban dance notation). She is director of the Dance Notation Bureau in New York.

JOAN JUNYER: Born 1904 at Barcelona, Spain. Did scenery and costumes for the ballet *Cuckold's Fair* (Ballet Russe de Monte Carlo 1943), *Minotaur* (Ballet Society 1947) and additional theater works in Spain. He had one-man shows at the Museum of Modern Art in Madrid in 1934 and at the Museum of Modern Art in New York in 1943. He is living in the United States since 1940.

SALLY KAMIN: A graduate of Columbia (Master of Dramatic Arts), started out as an actress with the Wisconsin Players at a time when Angna Enters and Vincenzo Celli were members of the company. She took a few dancing lessons, married a newspaper reporter, studied at the University of Geneva, traveled extensively. Today she is known all over the world where dancers are or bookshops that sell dance books. Her bookshop on the Avenue of the Americas is the center of the dance world in the United States.

IVA KITCHELL (Mrs. Stokely Webster): Born Junction City, Kansas. Studied ballet in New York and Paris. Appeared as soloist Radio City Music Hall, Paramount theaters, and Balaban and Katz theaters in Chicago. Toured Germany in 1938 remaining for two months at the Scala Theatre in Berlin. Made debut in program of dance satire in 1940 at the Barbizon Plaza. Other New York recitals: Carnegie Chamber Music Hall 1943–44, Times Hall 1945, Carnegie Hall 1946, Ziegfeld 1949, Carnegie Hall 1950 and has given 500 performances in the United States, Canada and Hawaii including 7 consecutive seasons at Jacob's Pillow. Has appeared as guest soloist with Carnegie Hall Pops Orchestra, Toronto Promenade Symphony and New Orleans Summer Symphony. Telecasts on NBC and CBS. Repertoire of 40 numbers including *Soul in Search, Ze Ballet, Maisie at the Moovies* and *Something Classic.*

PAULINE KONER: Combines the spirit of modernity with unlimited technique, gained through her early association with the great Fokine. She has appeared in Europe, Egypt and Israel; her many coast-to-coast American tours have included such important appearances as soloist with the New York Philharmonic under the baton of Stokowski at the Metropolitan Opera House, as well as guest appearances at New York's Roxy, Radio City, and Lewisohn Stadium; she choreographed and danced her own program on CBS television. Miss Koner has appeared with her own company in New York and as a guest at the American Dance Festival in New London, Conn., in 1950. In the spring of 1949 she staged a ballet based on *Alice in Wonderland* on the Ford Dealers' Program for television. She has also recently appeared both in Paris and in Mexico and continues as guest artist with José Limon as well as director of her own company. Abner Dean, famous cartoonist, has just completed a ballet script which she is at present choreographing.

RUDOLF LABAN: Born in Bratislava, Czechoslovakia, even in his earliest years found a fascination in observing people's movements. His desire to probe the secrets of physical and mental effort led him on a long course of study, experiment and research. Architecture first attracted him, but did not satisfy. He went to Paris, Berlin, Vienna and other centers of learning to study the arts and sciences essential to the student of movement, among them mathematics, physics, chemistry, physiology and anatomy. He was led from the academic to the practical all over the world in search of indigenous and cultivated activity—to the American Indians, the natives of the Near East, and the Chinese— in order to study at first hand their peculiar habits and the manifestations of their power. Ballet claimed his major attention and in time he became Director of Movement in the Berlin State Opera and one of the best known of choreographers. Reacting against the artificiality of theater, he sought expression of his art and philosophy amongst the common people, and, all over Europe, centers were established in his name for the artisans who came to seek advice on their own working problems, the strains and stresses involved in their various occupations. In these centers they found the bodily awareness, understanding and relief in the courses of movement that were provided especially to meet their needs. The freedom thus bestowed on them found no place amidst the wickedness of Nazidom, and Laban, with some of his pupils, sought sanctuary in England. Today, the Laban Art of Movement Guild, recently incorporated, is the center of the expression in Britain of Laban's growing influence in education. In many schools the children are being trained and selected by Laban methods; also, in art, where, for instance, Laban's emancipation of the ballet from its stylized tradition is evidenced in the work of one of his pupils, Kurt Jooss. The Laban Movement Notation is used all over the world, and in New York there is a special bureau that controls its use in the U.S.A. Among his recent books are: *The Mastery of Movement on the Stage, Modern Educational Dance.* His publishers, MacDonald & Evans, London, are now preparing his *Effort and Recovery.*

JOSÉ LIMON: Born in Mexico, moved to California in his youth where he went to school. Later in New York, he started out as a painter. Joined Humphrey-Weidman group, often seen in Broadway shows,

but concentrated on concert dance. He choreographed *Flying Colors,
Roberta, Keep Off the Grass* and *I'd Rather Be Right*. His most famous
dances are: *Danzas Mexicanas, Song of the West, El Salon Mexico,
Passacaglia, Chorale Preludes,* Bach's *Chaconne in D minor, Lament
for a Bullfighter* (Garcia Lorca). Limon has worked as instructor of
dance at Bennington and Sarah Lawrence College, and has taught at
several universities in the States. Among his recent choreographic works
are *The Moor's Pavane* and *La Malinche*. He is now working for the
Mexican Government several months each year.

CARMELITA MARACCI: This dancer, who has an "exquisite" ballet
technique and refuses to be a ballerina, whose command of the Spanish
style is "superb" and yet declines to be a "Spanish" dancer, was born
in Montevideo, Uruguay. Daughter of an Italian father and a Spanish
mother, she is neither Italian nor Spanish but thoroughly a child of
San Francisco where she grew up, a city compounded of an American
today overlaying a rich Spanish yesterday, with a love of art, music and
dancing which once produced another rebel, Isadora Duncan. She
resides in Hollywood where she perfects her dances of exuberant gaiety,
barbed satire and deep tragedy with her sole interest in her work.
John Martin of *The New York Times* has said of her: "She is a per-
fectionist of the first order. It is rarely that a dancer so succeeds in
compounding exquisiteness with passion in making every moment
possess not only surface finish but inner importance. As it happens,
she is one of the few unmistakably great dancers of our time."

LA MERI: Was born in Louisville, Kentucky, and named after her
father, Russell Meriwether Hughes. As the name indicates, her ancestors were among the first of the Virginia colonists, William Meriwether having been one of the revolutionaries against George III. Most
of La Meri's childhood was spent in San Antonio, Texas, where her
people took up residence. Proximity to the Mexican border is doubtless
responsible for her interest in exotic peoples, although her poetry
shows an early interest in folklore. On her first trip to New York she
took the name Meri Russell Hughes to escape the implied masculinity
of her given name. Broadway agencies promptly shortened this to

Meri Hughes; and an engagement in Mexico City where the Spanish tongue found "Hughes" difficult of pronunciation created the name "La Meri." There were no professional theater people in La Meri's family, although all were music-lovers and excellent amateur performers. It was a restless spirit which started her in her work at the age of seventeen. From that time until today, she has danced her way around the world in a kaleidoscopic career, the sheer chronology of which is a tale in itself. La Meri made her debut as a concert dancer in 1928, in the John Golden Theater, New York. Several weeks later she left her homeland for a concert tour of South America. A tour of Europe followed and it was at Max Reinhardt's theater in Vienna that recognition was first accorded to La Meri's unique talent. Repeated successes in Berlin and later in Scandinavian countries brought La Meri to Paris where she astonished the intellectuals of the Ville Lumière with her mimic genius. Shortly afterward La Meri was invited to become the director of the dance department of the Royal Academy of the Fidenti in Florence, Italy. Rome and Milan soon came to know La Meri as a unique figure in the dance world. Eventually a call came from London which she accepted. Her English debut was so sensational that she was engaged to give 23 recitals there during a period of six weeks. Next, in Australia she presented 121 concerts. Then followed trips to the Far East, Java, India, Malaya, China, Japan, the Philippines and Hawaii. On returning to New York in December 1937 for a dance recital at the Guild Theater she was heralded as one of the most cultured and versatile exponents of the dance. Soon after her New York appearance she left for a second extensive tour of Mexico, Peru, Chile, Argentina, Uruguay, Brazil and Venezuela. Return engagements in Rome, Florence and London followed. Then home again for a tour of 40 concerts in the U.S. In each country she studied extensively the local dance art. Today she is an incomparable figure in the field of the dance. Her success in the countries where the dances she presents originated has no precedent in the history of the dance. She is the author of 7 books of poetry and 4 books on the dance. Many articles on dancing appeared in dance magazines in London and New York as well as in various newspapers in most of the countries toured.

ISAMU NOGUCHI: Contemporary Japanese-American sculptor and designer; designed sets and costumes for *Frontier, Night Journey, Chronicle* (Martha Graham), *The Bells* (Ruth Page-Bentley Stone), *The Seasons* (Merce Cunningham). He did the sets for Martha Graham's *Appalachian Spring, Dark Meadow, Cave of the Heart, Errand into the Maze;* Erick Hawkins' *John Brown* and *Stephen Acrobat,* etc.

RUTH PAGE: Born in Indianapolis, Indiana. Her father, Dr. Lafayette Page, whose forebears emigrated in covered wagons over the Cumberland Mountains from Virginia into Kentucky, was a distinguished surgeon and founder of the James Whitcomb Riley Hospital. Her mother is an accomplished musician. At an early age Ruth learned to love poetry through the daily reading of it with her father. Like most children, she found delight in spontaneous dancing; and at the age of twelve began to study it formally. Soon afterward she attracted the attention of Anna Pavlova and danced with her on her last South American tour. Miss Page continued her studies with Adolph Bolm. He cast her in the role of the Infanta in *The Birthday of the Infanta* which he did for the Chicago Opera Company. The following year he introduced her to London. The next two years Miss Page spent on Broadway and on tour as principal dancer of Irving Berlin's *Music Box Revue.* She continued her studies with Maestro Cecchetti at Monte Carlo and was subsequently engaged by the Diaghileff Ballet Russe. For seven years she was ballet mistress of the Ravinia Opera Company. During the winter seasons of 1926–27 and 1928 Miss Page became the first American guest solo dancer to be engaged by the Metropolitan Opera Company in New York. In 1928 she made her first Oriental tour with a small company, giving 25 performances in the ceremonies attending the enthronement of Emperor Hirohito in Tokyo and continuing her tour in China, Siam and Bali. The Soviet Government in 1930 commissioned her to come to Moscow where she presented a series of "American Dances" before the workers' societies. From 1930 to 1935 she literally danced her way from coast to coast. In the spring of 1931 she created the role of the Princess in the ballet *The Story of the Soldier* by Stravinsky for the International Society of Contemporary Music. In 1932 she first worked with Harold Kreutzberg in Salzburg; they formed a collaboration, for three seasons giving a long series of duo-concerts in America, culminating in a joint tour of Japan and China in 1934. In the same year she became the Ballet Director of the revived Chicago Grand Opera Company, and continued to serve as director and première danseuse in 1935-36-37. After a Scandinavian tour, she founded with Bentley Stone the Page-Stone Ballet Company in 1938. Miss Page worked for the Federal Theatre Project, became Ballet Director of the Chicago Opera Company (1942-45), was choreographer and guest dancer with the Ballet Russe de Monte Carlo (1945-48). She is the choreographer of a great many famous ballets, such as *La Guiablesse, Love Song, Gold Standard, Frankie and Johnny, Iberian Monotone, Americans in Paris, Hear Ye! Hear Ye!, Billy Sunday,* etc. She also choreographed *Music in My Heart* in 1947. She has been in Paris with her company in 1950, with José Limon, Pauline Koner and Talley Beatty as guest artists. She has done choreographic work for the University of Chicago in 1950-51.

PEARL PRIMUS: Born in Trinidad. Contemporary dancer. Appeared in Y.M.H.A. (1943), Café Society Downtown (1943), solo debut Hunter College (1944), on tour 1945-47; featured dancer in the musical *Show Boat* (1946); in the opera *Emperor Jones* (Chicago Opera House, 1946). Specializes in dances on Negro themes. In April 1948 was awarded Julius Rosenwald Fellowship to make a survey of native dances in Africa.

KURT SELIGMANN: Has exhibited his works in almost all the great cities of the world; leading surrealist painter; came to New York from Paris in 1939; regular exhibits in New York, Chicago, Mexico and other places. Seligmann designed the costumes and stage sets for ballets done by Balanchine and Hanya Holm; lectured at the Briarcliff Junior College, Columbia University and High School of Music and Art, New York. He is interested in Black Magic on which subject he wrote a book published by Pantheon.

HELEN TAMIRIS: Dancer and choreographer, studied with Metropolitan Opera Ballet and Fokine, danced with Metropolitan Opera three seasons, toured South America as ballerina. Made concert debut in New York in 1927. Introduced American folk and Negro spirituals

at Salzburg Festival, Austria. Danced in Berlin and Paris. She founded
her own company in 1930, organized Dance Repertory Theater (1930–
31); appeared with own group at Rainbow Room, Radio City
(1942–43). Dance Director, Unity Playhouse Summer Theater, Forest
Park, Pa. (1942–43). Did choreography for many musicals: *It's Up to
You* (1943), *Up in Central Park* (1945), *Show Boat* (1946), *Annie
Get Your Gun* (1946), *Inside U.S.A.* (1948), *Touch and Go* (1949),
Bless You All (1950).

WALDEEN: At the age of six Waldeen started her formal ballet training with Theodore Kosloff in Los Angeles. Breaking with conventional
Russian ballet at the age of fifteen, she began to fuse both modern and
classical dance forms. In 1932, toured Japan with Michio Ito's group,
after numerous solo concerts in this country as well as in Mexico City.
In 1940, the Mexican Ministry of Fine Arts subsidized Waldeen to
create a national school and ballet. In 1944, Waldeen was choreographer
for the Mozart Festival held in Mexico City under the direction of
Sir Thomas Beecham. During 1944 and 1946 she staged the dance
sequences for seven Mexican films, among them *Bugambilia* and *Las
Abandonadas*, starring Dolores del Rio and directed by Emilio Fernandez. She is still in Mexico where she has her own company and
classes.

CHARLES WEIDMAN: Dancer and choreographer, member of Denishawn
for eight years. First professional experience in vaudeville (*Xochitl*
with Martha Graham); established school and concert company with
Doris Humphrey in 1927. His most famous dances are: *Traditions, The
Happy Hypocrite, Quest, Candide, Flickers, Daddy Was a Fireman,
A House Divided, Fables of Our Time*. Among his many well-known
pupils are: José Limon, Sybil Shearer, Eleanor King, William Bales,
Peter Hamilton, Jack Cole, etc.

INDEX

285

INDEX

285